WITHDRAWN
UTSA LIBRARIES

TOWNSEND HARRIS

TOWNSEND HARRIS

FIRST AMERICAN ENVOY IN JAPAN

BY

WILLIAM ELLIOT GRIFFIS

 BOOKS FOR LIBRARIES PRESS
FREEPORT, NEW YORK

First Published 1895
Reprinted 1971

INTERNATIONAL STANDARD BOOK NUMBER:
0-8369-6613-9

LIBRARY OF CONGRESS CATALOG CARD NUMBER:
74-175698

PRINTED IN THE UNITED STATES OF AMERICA
BY
NEW WORLD BOOK MANUFACTURING CO., INC.
HALLANDALE, FLORIDA 33009

Dedicated

TO

MISS BESSIE HARRIS

THE BELOVED NIECE AND EXECUTOR OF THE WILL

OF HIM WHOM THE JAPANESE CALL

"OUR BENEFACTOR"

PREFACE.

JAPAN's re-birth, in this our day, challenges the attention of the historian and philosopher. In the story as told from the outside by foreigners, there is a great blank between Commodore Perry and Lord Elgin. Especially in the works of English writers are there profound ignorance and misapprehension of what Mr. Townsend Harris did. This volume aims to fill a gap in history.

The opening of the long-sealed Empire of Japan to foreign trade and commerce was a decisive event in the history of Eastern Asia and of the world. For such a work, the American envoy was prepared as few men could have been. After fourteen years in a village in the Empire State, thirty-two in the metropolis of the continent, six on the Pacific Ocean and in far-Oriental lands, Townsend Harris, when fifty-two years of age, became, like the great Yoritomo, a lonely dweller in rocky Idzu. There both were exiles, and thence both emerged victorious to re-make Japan. This they did, in each case, by drawing the centre of government from Kiōto to the region of Yedo Bay. Here, however, in the perspective of history, the parallel ends, and dissolves into contrasts. The lord of Kamakura, becoming the first Shōgun, gradually but surely degraded the Emperor. He made his camp the substance, and the throne a shadow. The American envoy, on the contrary, may in a large sense be called the real overthrower of "Tycoonism," the feudal system, and military rule, and the restorer of national unity. He ushered in Dai Nippon's new career. Of the powerful influence of his actions upon the development of the representative institutions now established in Japan, there can be no doubt whatever. In the making of that new kind of Asiatic state and man that have surprised Europe, Townsend Harris was a potency acknowedged by none more than the Japanese themselves. He was the greatest of the foreign diplomatists. He was the recognized teacher of a sensitive people, who call him "the nation's friend."

Besides living for nearly four years either on the spot or in the region of Mr. Harris's labors, I had the honor of knowing him personally, and of enjoying his friendship, from 1874 to 1878. Once, shortly after the time of the German Count Von

Arnhem's severe treatment at the hands of Bismarck, I asked him whether he had kept a record of his experiences in Japan, and would give it to the world. His answer, after reference to the danger of prematurely exposing state secrets, was, "Not while I am living." He told his intimate friends, Judge C. P. Daly and General George W. Cullum, that he should publish nothing during his lifetime, but that he had a journal which he should deposit in either the Geographical or the Historical Society of New York, that might be referred to after his death. Four years ago, this journal, contained in five small volumes, his private letter-books and letters, were placed for editing and publication in the hands of the writer by his niece, Miss Bessie Harris, who also administered upon his estate.

This journal bears all the marks of records made day by day and hour by hour, contemporaneous with the scenes and feelings described, but none whatever of any afterthought. Erasures, alteration, or interlineation in the text are absent. All the more, on this account, has the editor been scrupulously careful to omit or suppress nothing of any political or historical value. Even the italics made by Mr. Harris are reproduced, but the modern standard system of transliterating Japanese names

viii   PREFACE.

and words has been used. What have been omitted are observations on the weather and upon health, purely private and domestic references, repetitions, corrections, guesses at size, measurements, and such minor matters. The main narrative, which culminated in the treaty already made and signed before a man-of-war appeared on the scene, has not been modified.

The biographical sketch and concluding chapters are based on matter furnished in Mr. Harris's letters or by his friends, and upon the carefully sifted data in Japanese and foreign books and documents. I wish to mention with thanks the names of all those who have aided me, — Judge C. P. Daly, president of the American Geographical Society; General George W. Cullum, U. S. A.; Dr. W. A. P. Martin, of Peking, China; Dr. J. C. Hepburn and Rev. S. R. Brown, D. D.; Mr. Tsuda Sen, of Tōkiō; Rev. J. Takasugi; Professor Brander Matthews, of Columbia College, New York; Mrs. James Sherrill and Mr. John Dwyer, of Sandy Hill, N. Y.; and last and most of all, Miss Bessie Harris, the custodian of Mr. Harris's papers.

In the foot-notes, there are several abbreviations. The letters T. A. S. J. signify "Transactions of the Asiatic Society of Japan;" T. J., Professor Chamberlain's "Things Japanese;" M. E., "The Mikado's Empire;" M. C. P. (Life of Commodore) "Matthew Calbraith Perry," etc.

In this year following the revision of our treaty with Japan (expected at the time of its signature by Mr. Harris to take place in 1872), when justice has been meted out to a friendly nation after more than twenty years of wrong done her, the publication of this journal seems appropriate and auspicious.

W. E. G.

ITHACA, N. Y., May 24, 1895.

CONTENTS.

PART I.

PREPARATION FOR WORK IN JAPAN.

CHAPTER		PAGE
I.	Ancestry, Boyhood, and Life in New York	3
II.	Experiences in Oriental Lands and Seas	14

PART II.

MR. HARRIS'S JOURNAL.

III.	Housekeeping in Shimoda	33
IV.	Autumn Experiences in Japan	58
V.	The Visit of the Russians	84
VI.	The First Skirmish of a Long Battle	97
VII.	[The Political Situation.—A Chapter of Explanation]	115
VIII.	Slow but Sure Progress	123
IX.	A Lonely Exile.—The President's Letter	144
X.	Visit of the Portsmouth.—The First Victory	167
XI.	The Triumphal Journey to Yedo	182
XII.	The American Envoy's Audience of the Shōgun	290
XIII.	Preliminaries to the Treaty-Making	237
XIV.	The Hermits instructed in Modern World-Life	253
XV.	The Struggle for the Opening of the Ports	278

PART III.

SUCCESS, REPOSE, AND HONORS.

XVI.	Japan opened to the World	311
XVII.	Home Again.—Social Joys.—Peaceful End.	326
XVIII.	Japan at the End of the Century	334

PART I.
PREPARATION FOR WORK IN JAPAN.

From this window I look on Fuji San,
White with the snows of a thousand years;
To my gates ships will come from the far East
Ten thousand miles.

Stanza attributed to OTA DŌ KUAN, founder of Yedo, †1487.

It was the whale that emancipated fishermen and led them afar. It led them onward and onward still, until they found it, after having almost unconsciously passed from one world to the other.   MICHELET.

The narrow cleft in the sealed door of Japan, into which Perry drove his wedge of diplomacy, was the rescue of American sailors.
                                                    NITOBÉ.

The mission of Perry was that of a pioneer; that of Harris, of a sower. The duty of one was to force a barred door open; that of the other was to keep it so.   NITOBÉ.

In the work of young Ronald McDonald, born at Astoria, Oregon, a seaman from an American whaler, the Plymouth, who in 1848 was set to work by the Japanese at Nagasaki to teach English, " we trace a promise of American educational activity in Japan."   NITOBÉ.

McDonald, before his release, was requested by the Japanese to describe the relative rank of the commander of the Preble, by counting down in the order of succession from the highest chief in the United States. . . . He began with the people.
                                                    HILDRETH.

If the tutorship of the United States in Japan is to be successful, it must be based on deeper and broader principles of philanthropy than have heretofore been practiced in the intercourse of nations — a philanthropy which shall recognize not merely the distinction of strength and power between nations, but the duties of magnanimity, moderation, and humanity.   SEWARD.

CHAPTER I.

ANCESTRY, BOYHOOD, AND LIFE IN NEW YORK.

IN the composite American stock, which has made the United States a new and better Europe, the Welsh element is not the least potent. The ancestors of Townsend Harris were Welshmen who came to America with Roger Williams, and settled in Massachusetts. Later generations emigrated to Ulster County, in the State of New York. Both of the grandfathers of Townsend Harris, Gilbert Harris and John Watson, served as officers in the Continental Army under Gates. John Watson, his mother's father, was in the battle of Saratoga, in which his British cousin, General Fraser, fell.

Gilbert Harris married Thankful Townsend, whose maiden name the future envoy to Japan bore, and who was a woman of strong character. Her home was in a village near Ticonderoga, and here she reared her seven children, in the midst of the alarms and uncertainties of the Revolutionary War. When John Burgoyne, general and dramatist, with a large British, Indian, and Hessian army, made his descent from Canada to expected victory but to actual surrender, he captured Ticonderoga.

In the second war with Great Britain, this same district of our country was ravaged. Some of the British forces, whether red or white is not known, set fire to the Harris home. This act of barbarity was never forgotten or forgiven by Thankful, whose three sons were Fraser, Jonathan, and Townsend.

Jonathan Harris married and settled at Sandy Hill, Washington County, N. Y. He was a hatter, and the magistrate of the village. He introduced the grafting of fruit-trees into his neighborhood. He had six children. Of his five sons, Townsend, the future treaty-maker, was the youngest, and was born October 3, 1804. The house in which he was born, and to which his memory fondly reverted during his lonely days in Japan, was burned down in 1876. Both his parents were persons of intelligence and vigor, and they fostered his early love of books and his taste for reading and study. From infancy to mature life his mother was his chief educator. All the regular schooling which Townsend Harris ever received was at the village primary school and academy. All his life Mr. Harris regretted his lack of a university training. His grandmother Thankful, whose home had been reduced to ashes, taught him " to tell the truth, fear God, and hate the British," and all three things he did all his life. As boy and as man, Townsend Harris would never use a Sheffield knife or wear

English cloth. Fastidiously neat as he always was in his dress, he was careful that his garments were made of French cloth.

When but thirteen years old, in 1817, Townsend was taken by his father to New York, to begin his business career in a dry-goods store. Living in the home of his employer and his father's friend, the bright, quick-witted, and obliging boy soon became a favorite with all the family. A few years later, his father and older brother having come to New York, Townsend joined with them in the business of importing china and earthenware. At this Townsend Harris continued until leaving the United States in 1849. In the great fire of 1835, the crockery store had to be blown up with gunpowder to stop the advance of the flames. In the reorganization of business the new firm was that of John and Townsend Harris.

Trade, however, was not the law of Townsend Harris's life, but its necessity only, and the chosen means to a higher end. Culture was his dominant purpose. He read constantly, critically, and wisely in the best literatures, and observed and studied men and things. He learned the French, Spanish, and Italian languages. He had access to the best libraries, and his memory, naturally retentive, was trained to system. His power of prompt recollection was noteworthy. Living for several years with his mother in one home with his orphaned nieces, he guided their reading and studies and taught them Spanish phrases.

Once, Mr. Harris, "like a Dutch uncle," scolded the young ladies for reading novels, which he unceremoniously seized and threw into the fire. Scarcely, however, were the tears of his sorrowful nieces dried, than their Uncle Townsend presented them with seventy handsome volumes of history, biography, travels, and standard works by well-known women authors, such as Hannah More, Mrs. Opie, Maria Edgeworth, and others.

The mother of Townsend Harris was a stately lady of keen intellect and engaging manners. She was the teacher and inspirer of her youngest son from his cradle days even until her death. The sitting and dining rooms were well furnished with the best books of reference. Conversation at the dinner-table was bright and suggestive, and Townsend Harris made it his pleasurable habit of talking with his mother about the books he had read.

The son delighted to engage the mother in argument, for in her clear views and strong convictions she was of the Federalist or Whig school, while he was an ardent Democrat. She believed in a strong central government, and in wise restraint of popular sentiment, while he emphasized local freedom and the easily expressed will of the people. She looked with no favor but rather with dread upon the theories of democracy. Much of her horror had been caused by the dreadful scenes of the French Revolution, which were an abuse of liberty. Democratic ideas, in her opinion, tended to license. Often did she warn her son of what might be the result should democratic rule gain the ascendancy in our country. She saw into the century ahead. She would often say, "My son, you do not look far enough into the future." Opposed to the idea of a property qualification for voters, Mr. Harris labored to change the laws upon this point. His mother vigorously opposed him, warning him that he might live to see the day when he would regret the freedom given to ignorant emigrants. Holding closely to her convictions, she never allowed her son's witticisms to upset her sober reasonings.

Townsend Harris's love and honor to his mother were dominant passions. He was extremely sensitive to her regard and love. She was his greatest teacher. So strong was this feeling that his brother John could never prevail upon him to take his place and go to England on business. He never left his mother but once, for a trip to Ohio, to make which was in those days considered a great enterprise. She lived to be eighty-three years old. She kept her wonderful memory and reasoning powers undimmed until within three weeks of her death.

Townsend Harris never married. Why he did not was a secret locked in his own breast, which has perished with him. It may be that seeing in his mother so exalted an ideal, and finding in her so noble a reality of womanhood, he felt unable to search long and far enough to find her equal. In chivalry and courtesy to woman the average man was no peer to Mr. Harris. Being a trustee of the Northern Dispensary and serving often on committees, he opposed with vigor and eloquently pleaded against the introduction of clinical lectures. His arguments, whether right or wrong, were based on the ground of the painful publicity to which ladies in poverty but of refined feelings would be thus subject.

Townsend Harris was from the first a public-spirited man. He was keenly interested in human progress both at home and abroad. Having many customers from the West Indies and from South America, he spoke their language, the Spanish, fluently. He took a hearty interest in republicanism, and was a great admirer of Bolivar. Though in politics he was an enthusiastic partisan, he gained all the more influence with his fellow Democrats because he refused to accept office.

He had wonderful patience and powers of persuasion, and often made it a point to win over to good words and works men of vicious ways or turbulent character. His ward was the famous and sometimes infamous "Ninth." In those days, now happily long past, of volunteer fire companies, the fights between rival gangs of rowdies were fearful and often bloody. One of the leading spirits in a leading company, a young Irishman, seemed the incarnation of lawlessness, with apparently no desire to become a decent member of society. Mr. Harris on inquiry found that this promising anarchist was the son of an Irish gentleman who had lost position in life through admiration of the beauty of his father's cook, who drew him away from home. Marrying her and coming to America, he by degrees drifted to the level of his ignorant wife, who added drunkenness to her illiteracy, — a combination which Mr. Harris all his life detested and fought against. The man learned blacksmithing. His children grew up without any moral training. Finally, at his own forge, he was killed by the bursting of a bombshell which, it was said, had been picked up on some old battlefield on Long Island.

Here was Townsend Harris's opportunity. He went to the funeral, and to the astonishment of his friends rode with the boy in a carriage to the grave, and after a kindly talk invited him to come and see him. He kept his word. Kindness captured the ringleader in bloody riots. A lifelong influence was gained, and a complete change of life ensued. Besides pointing out a better way, Mr. Harris lent him books, and studied the bent of his mind. In later years when Mr. Harris was in

Asia, this reformed man represented in Congress the State in which he was then living.

Regretting his own lack of superior educational training, Mr. Harris was from the first eagerly interested in the public school system. Elected a member of the Board of Education of the city of New York, he served during a number of years, and in 1846 and 1847 was its president. Later, he agitated the question of founding the New York Free Academy. In spite of all opposition, by answering objections and using freely his tongue, his pen, and his money, Mr. Harris won the day. The Free Academy became a fixed fact. The idea of the founder was to have a public institution which should continue and carry higher the education of poor boys. In later years when Mr. Harris's purpose was perverted, and the Free Academy became the "College of the City of New York," he grieved sincerely over the change of idea as well as of name.

Strong and fearless in his ideas of unselfish duty, Mr. Harris was, withal, a true devotee of science. When the cholera broke out in 1832, he sent his mother, sister, brother, and four motherless nieces to the Catskill Mountain region for six weeks, while he in company with a physician remained in the city and visited the sick. He nursed his brother's partner when attacked by this disease, and had the satisfaction of seeing his patient recover.

Of national and international affairs Mr. Harris was more than an observer: he was a student. He read regularly some of the leading French and English papers, and kept himself well informed as to the movement in European politics. He was especially interested in the repeal of the corn-laws. During the ministry of Robert Peel he read the parliamentary debates in detail. He also wrote several articles in discussion of the subject in the New York newspapers. On all mercantile subjects and those prominent in congressional discussion he took a hearty interest. In a knowledge of certain phases of political economy this untitled man might well be called a past master.

Personally interested in fire and military companies, this handsome and healthy young man enjoyed with his comrades the excitement of subduing "dear old inflammable New York." He also delighted in the exercise of drill and the parade down Broadway. The great social and public holidays were gold-lettered days in his calendar. On rainy days and in quiet hours chess was his time-beguiling recreation.

In his religious life Mr. Harris had at first been trained in the Presbyterian form of Christianity, and for some time taught a class in the Sunday-school of the Christopher Street Church in New York. Later, he felt a preference for the ritual and communion of the Episcopal fraternity of

Christians, and for a number of years held a pew and worshiped in the Church of the Ascension, then under the charge of Rector and later Bishop Gregory T. Bedell.

Thus passed the life of a typical gentleman of old New York, as it existed chiefly below Fourteenth Street. He was a genuine product of the American Christian home. So dearly did he enjoy his environment, that though often urged by his brother to take the latter's place in England, he steadily refused to leave home and mother. Laughingly he would say that when he did expatriate himself he would go to the Far East which was so shut out from "the world." With books, with his favorite chess, with his mother and nieces, an active and public-spirited citizen, a true American to the very iron in his blood, life seemed overflowing in richness and radiant with promise.

Suddenly night fell upon this home, and a "cloudy and dark day" of grief followed. In November, 1847, his mother died. Six months later the old home was broken up. Added to his personal sorrow came a depression in business which gave Townsend Harris his opportunity. Settling up his commercial affairs, he left New York, resolved to see Golden California and the Mysterious East.

He purchased a half-interest in a vessel bound for California, and sailing around Cape Horn he learned, during the six months' voyage, to know the ocean. He also caught glimpses of life in South America. In San Francisco he purchased the other half of the vessel. He now resolved to do what is no longer possible to do profitably in these days of steamers. He projected a trading voyage to China and the Dutch and English Indies. His plan was to stop at various islands and ports, loading and unloading at each place.

Such an experience, if successful, was admirably calculated to increase his knowledge of Malay, insular, and Oriental human nature, and to give him a wide practical knowledge of the laws of nations and of the conditions of trade and exchange. Above all, it would fit him to take part in the solution of that supreme world-problem of the nineteenth and twentieth centuries, — the harmony of Christendom with Buddhadom and the reconciliation of Occidental and Oriental civilizations.

CHAPTER II.

EXPERIENCES IN ORIENTAL LANDS AND SEAS.

THE materials are not accessible for illustrating in full the life of Mr. Harris during the five years in which he was engaged in commercial voyaging. His "Journal No. 1," begun after a journey through India, and with his face set homeward, is dated at Penang.

In "Journal No. 3," written at Shimoda, Japan, December 25, 1856, he writes: " I will here note where I have been on Christmas Day for the last eight years.

"Christmas, 1849, at sea in the North Pacific Ocean.

"Christmas, 1850, at Manila.
" 1851, at Pulo-Penang.
" 1852, at Singapore.
" 1853, at Hong-Kong.
" 1854, at Calcutta.
" 1855, at Ceylon.
" 1856, in Japan."

From his personal conversations and reminiscences shared with his friends in New York after his return from Japan late in 1862, it is certain that he made extensive trading voyages in the Malayan archipelago, the Dutch East Indies, probably to Australia, and even further afield among the cannibal islands. On one occasion he spent the night with the chief of a man-eating tribe. The smoke-blackened and soot-festooned hut was decorated with a dado of human skulls. The American's host not only expatiated upon the merits of man-meat, but even touched with his fingers Mr. Harris's body at those parts where he declared the choicest bits were to be found.

In his journals, begun after he ceased to be a commercial and became a diplomatic traveler, he occasionally refers to former experiences in Pacific and Indian waters. He remembers especially the flowers, perfumes, stars, and wonders in natural history. His favorite region appears to have been the Golden Chersonese. He visited Penang eight times, and seemed never weary of describing its delights and wonders.

Mr. Harris resided in China during many months, and was for a short time, we believe, acting vice-consul of the United States at Ningpo. On conclusion of the treaty with Japan by Commodore Matthew C. Perry, Mr. Harris wrote to him in terms of warm congratulation. The commodore at Hong-Kong replied January 7, 1854, in terms of hearty gratification.

While in the Middle Kingdom, Mr. Harris's

16 PREPARATION FOR WORK IN JAPAN.

active mind was applied to the extension of American commercial enterprise, and especially to the acquisition by purchase of the island of Formosa. This fair island, misgoverned and only partially settled by the Chinese, and a terror to navigators because of its savage and cannibal inhabitants, equals in area the two States of New Hampshire and Vermont. Mr. Harris made a careful study from many authorities in English, French, Portuguese, and Dutch, writing out his excerpts and impressions. The manuscript, covering one hundred and nineteen pages of a large notebook, shows the reader's critical powers and sound mental digestion. Struck with the capabilities and importance to the United States of Formosa as a coaling-station and depot, and for political and commercial advantages, Mr. Harris from Macao, on the 24th of March, 1854, wrote concerning it to the Secretary of State. The long letter tersely summarizes the whole situation. He proposed the characteristic American method of gaining territory by purchase instead of by conquest.

Throughout these years, the merchant navigator was learning diplomacy at first hand, and studying especially the artifices to which men who are weak in moral courage habitually resort. Oriental and insular human nature relies more on cunning than on frankness. Mr. Harris continually proved the advantage of truth-speaking. He believed that an honest man was more than a match for ten thousand liars. One of the courtliest of men, he hated with ever-deepening hatred both the liar and the politeness that cloaked the deception. He thought that fine manners were a fine art, but that by deceit art was degraded and its beauty turned to ashes.

Townsend Harris and William L. Marcy, President Pierce's able Secretary of State, were personal friends. When these high officers looked about to find the man to develop American relations with Japan, they cast their eyes upon one supremely fitted for the task. It is probable that Marcy wrote to China, summoning Mr. Harris on the plea of personal friendship to assume the responsible task. To get into the Country Behind the Looking-Glass was Townsend Harris's ambition. He quickly left China, and turned his face westward. On his way home, he visited India, made a summer voyage up the sultry Red Sea, looked at Egypt's antiquities, and saw the Pyramids in morning sunlight. Traveling by the new railway from Cairo to Alexandria, he took the steamer Euxine to Gibraltar. There, as he writes, he richly enjoyed the rolling sounds of the majestic Castilian language. He was in London July 7. He had intended to visit Paris, but letters from the United States were so urgent that he took passage on the 16th at Liverpool for home. We quote now from his journal:

"July 27, 1855. At four P. M. we passed the buoy on the bar of New York, which completed my voyage round the world. I expressed a hope to some of the passengers that I should never be required to leave New York for two hundred and fifty miles in any direction."

The summer and early autumn of 1855 form a blank in Mr. Harris's journal, but evidently about the middle of October, he writes: —

"I omit the details of what I did while in the United States, merely noting that on the 4th of August I was appointed Consul-General for Japan. During the same month the President was pleased to intrust me with the making [of] a commercial treaty with the kingdom of Siam, a matter in which Mr. Balestier was unsuccessful in 1851."

Apart from the personal friendship of Secretary Marcy and the esteem of Commodore M. C. Perry, Mr. Harris probably did not himself know the forces which moved President Franklin Pierce to appoint him. To intrust two such difficult tasks as the making of treaties with Siam and Japan to an untried envoy who held rank below that of minister was at least a noteworthy proceeding. On October 21, 1861, Mr. William H. Seward, President Lincoln's Secretary of State, and a Republican, wrote to Townsend Harris, the successful minister of the United States in Japan, and a Democrat: —

"You perhaps are informed now for the first time that your appointment as the first commissioner to Japan was made by President Pierce upon the joint recommendation of Commodore Perry and myself."

The three months on his native soil were spent by Mr. Harris (as his private letter-books, finance accounts, and other data we have read show) in selecting and purchasing presents for the two kings of Siam and the "Tycoon" of Yedo, and in preparing his personal outfit for life in Japan. He was to live at Shimoda, — a pretty place, but for commercial development a cheat and a sham. Apparently promising at its entrance from the sea, it was landlocked. It resembled what the Japanese call a "bukuro machi," or bag street. It had terminal facilities only in one direction, and that the wrong one, — as you went in. The name means Low Field.

Presents for the whole pair of the two-headed government of Siam and for one half of the duarchy of Japan were purchased by Mr. Harris in person. At that time the peculiarities of Siamese royalty were known, but the reality of things in Nippon was not. Then, in Western eyes, the meat in Yedo was more than the life in Kiōto, and the raiment of feudalism more than the national body. Hence, the presents selected were for the "Tycoon," then referred to as "His Majesty the Emperor of Japan."

The tongue of Holland was the only European language which the Japanese knew anything about, it being the basis of their extra-Asiatic culture. Moreover, the kindly offices and recommendation of the Dutch government had been powerful factors in the success of Perry's mission. Mr. Harris's first need, therefore, was an intelligent young Hollander to act as secretary and interpreter. This person, through the aid of the Reverend Thomas De Witt, of the Collegiate Reformed Church of New York, he found in Mr. Henry C. J. Heusken, whose widowed mother lived in Amsterdam. He was brave, capable, enthusiastic, and scholarly. He acted as interpreter to the British and Prussian embassies during the treaty-making epoch following the success of his chief. He also found it necessary to instruct the Japanese, who called themselves interpreters, in modern and genuine Dutch: those tyros having made up their mind that a local mercantile patois, two hundred years old, and steadily flowing in Japanese moulds of thought, was the only proper form of speech. Moreover, as they insisted that every word in the Dutch versions of treaties, etc., should stand in the same order as the equivalent in the Japanese, they had to be taught not only a new language, but a new cycle of ideas. As an indispensable element in Mr. Harris's diplomatic success the name of Henry Heusken deserves permanent remembrance. He was assassinated by cowardly swashbucklers in Yedo January 14, 1861.[1] His tomb, in a Buddhist cemetery in Tōkiō, is but one of many mournful proofs of the great sacrifice of life attending the change of civilization in Japan.

In Mr. Harris's journal we read : —

"It was arranged between the State and Navy departments that the steam frigate San Jacinto would call at Penang, to which place I wished to proceed overland, and then take me to Siam and afterwards to Japan. I soon made the acquaintance of Commodore Armstrong, whose flag is in the San Jacinto, and Captain Bell of the frigate. I put on board of her the presents for the kings of Siam, with my heavy baggage for Japan, with some few stores. I found the commodore and Captain Bell very kind, and I hope we shall prove to be good messmates."

Mr. Heusken embarked on board the United States Steamship San Jacinto, later meeting Mr. Harris at Penang. His active duties as secretary began in Siam.

The San Jacinto was named after the famous battle of April, 1836, by which Texas ceased to be Spanish and Mexican and became American. The man-of-war was built and took her name after

[1] His diary was published in the *Proceedings of the German Asiatic Society of Japan*, June, 1883, and in an English translation in *The Japan Mail* of January, 1884. See Alcock's *Capital of the Tycoon*, vol. ii. pp. 39–55 ; *The Tōkiō Times*, vol. iii. p. 242.

the Lone Star State; which, by joining the constellation of the Union, had added the twenty-eighth light to its azure field. While bearing our new envoy to the lands of the White Elephant and of Fuji-Yama, the San Jacinto's flag bore thirty-one stars. This war steamer was a propeller, but her motion was disagreeable, her speed low, and her machinery uncertain. She was one hundred and forty-nine days out from New York to Penang. The story of her long cruise has been told by the surgeon W. M. Wood, in his interesting book, "Fankwei: The San Jacinto in the Seas of India, China, and Japan." Commodore James Armstrong captured the Barrier Forts at Canton River in 1857. He was commandant of the Pensacola Navy Yard in 1861, and died in the year 1868, when New Japan was born. Captain Henry H. Bell afterwards served as Farragut's fleet captain on the Mississippi. Later, while in command of the East India squadron, he attempted to pass in his barge the rough waves (which even in early ages were called Naniwa) off the bar in Osaka River. Where hundreds of Japanese have lost their lives this gallant officer was drowned April 12, 1867.

Leaving New York October 17, 1855, Consul-General Harris arrived in London on the 29th. He made his financial arrangements with the Baring Brothers, and then called on the American

Minister, James Buchanan. In Paris he saw the great Exposition, the bright and beautiful city, and the treasures of art. He then left by way of Marseilles for Egypt. During his agreeable journey down the Red Sea he became acquainted with Colonel Chester and Miss De Quincey, a daughter of the most subtle master of English prose. Mr. Harris wrote: "She is going out to India to meet her betrothed. She has a sweet voice and sings charmingly. I shall long remember her intelligent face."

In Ceylon at Galle, Mr. Harris studied Buddhist relics and remains, examined Pali manuscripts, and made comparison of his various observations in other countries of the Buddhist world. He dined with Judge Clarke, of whom he writes in his diary: —

"Mr. Clarke is a Teetotaller — of which class the number is increasing in the East. While in France, I drank the delightful mild wine of the South, and, after leaving Marseilles, I came back to my old Asiatic habit — tea and cold water."

Waiting amid the "spicy breezes" from Christmas Eve to January 7, Mr. Harris read Thackeray and studied the story of the foreigners in India. He also made critical survey of Great Britain's policy in India and the administration of her agents. His matured desire and resolve seem to have been *not* to imitate either or have his countrymen do so. His journals are full of keen observations and fascinating detail, some parts of which we shall utilize in annotating his Japan journal.

On January 19, at eight P. M., he reached Penang. This made his seventh visit. He received the heartiest welcome from many men, in several languages. He was kept waiting here in spice-land for the San Jacinto no fewer than seventy-six days. He spent the time in enjoying social hospitalities, in reading, in studying nature and man, both being in rather a mixed and concentrated form. His daily records are those of a close and wide observer, a student of the stars, birds, fish, mammals, reptiles, all forms of vegetable and animal life, as well as of minerals and products for commerce. He seems especially anxious to explode and banish the sensational stories about the comparatively harmless and useful boa-constrictor. Mr. Harris delighted in exposing shams and bullies, in tearing lions' skins from jackasses, in proving that "Tycoons" were frauds. In the boa-constrictor he saw a scavenger rather than a terror, much more dangerous in rhetoric than in fact.

All Fools' Day came, and the San Jacinto, though signaled, was not evident until next day, when her engines, as usual, needed repair. Embarking April 4, the run to Siam was made in nine days. The San Jacinto cast anchor off the Menan bar April 13. Townsend Harris was to follow up the work of Edmund Roberts in 1833, and to make a treaty where Mr. Balestier only six years before had failed. Mr. Parkes, the English consul at Amoy, afterwards Sir Harry Parkes, H. B. M. Minister in Japan and China, was already in Bangkok busy at negotiation. Between the apparent " inability of the Siamese to entertain two ideas at one time " and their natural supposition that the English must necessarily be the basis of the American treaty, Mr. Harris expected to have a severe strain put upon his patience.

He was not disappointed. They who had lived long in this sub-tropical " Land of the Free " had already coined a proverb that " one must come to Siam with three ships ; one loaded with presents, another with patience, and a third ready for things to be carried away." After due formalities, tedious, dramatic, necessary, or exhausting, the treaty was won.

Mr. Harris was convinced afresh that truth does not lie at the basis of the Asiatic civilizations. A series of disagreeable and personal episodes, also, — in the form of " Job's comforters," — neither added to the happiness nor improved the temper of the envoy who at times despaired of success. The instrument, together with that of Edmund Roberts and the later modifications of the Harris treaty, is to be found in the red-book entitled "Treaties and Conventions between the United States and Other Powers, 1776–1887." Eight chapters on Siam and the Siamese in Dr. Wood's "Fankwei" give copious descriptions of the pageants, presents, and outward phases of Mr. Harris's triumph.

Leaving Bangkok May 31, the San Jacinto anchored off Hong-Kong June 12, where the ship suffered from her machinery and Mr. Harris had further discipline in patience until August 12. Here, also, he had the first of many experiences with his rascally Chinese tailor. He learned anew the horrors of that system of slave trade, euphemistically called the "coolie traffic," which Japan, in 1874, improved off the face of the earth. He saw in the harbor the hulk of the old 74-gun ship, Minden, on which Key the prisoner composed "The Star-Spangled Banner" which we still sing to the old English air, "Anacreon in Heaven."

Again Mr. Harris exercised his power of detecting and exposing shams. A Chinaman had brought on board a "wild cat" to sell. It was loaded with ropes and cords for the protection of the sons of Mars and Neptune, some of whom, nevertheless, exhibited signs of nervousness when the civilian envoy proceeded to unwind the living spool. The poor animal, nearly paralyzed with fright and cramped with the tight lacing, was actually unable for some minutes to stand. By noting the absence from the tip of the ear of the tuft of hair always found on the wild species, Mr. Harris recognized at once the harmless "roof-scrambler" of domestic life. A prompt and hearty roar of laughter greeted the most fearful of the epauletted spectators as the artificially spotted puss lapped up her milk and purred with mingled gratitude and satisfaction.

On his greater work of exposing the "Tycoon," the tiger of Yedo, and proving that beneath the painted skin there was only a cat, Mr. Harris proceeded August 12. It was an apt criticism upon the work of a Japanese artist at the World's Columbian Exposition in Chicago, 1893, that he had painted the skin but not the tiger inside the skin; but in 1856 all the world thought the teeth and claws were in Yedo and nothing but the stripes at Kiōto.

On the way up the Formosa Channel he read in Von Siebold of coal in Kiushiu. Several disabled Chinese junks were passed; two were assisted, and the crew of one to save the lives of the waifs was taken on board.

On the 18th of August, the first view of Japanland was caught when Tokura,[1] one of the islands

[1] Since lighthouses have been erected, ships to or from Yokohama and Hong-Kong take the route more than a hundred miles northwardly, running under the extreme southern point of Kiu-

of the Linschoten group, became visible. The Dutchmen who at the end of the sixteenth century were enabled, by means of charts copied at Lisbon by Linschoten from the Portuguese archives, to penetrate the marine mysteries of the Far East, gratefully named their first landfall in Japan after their enterprising countryman. Later in the day, as Mr. Harris looked at Akuishi Island, he thus recorded his impressions: —

"Conflicting emotions caused by the sight of these Japanese possessions. My future brought vividly to mind. Mental and social isolation on the one hand; and on the other one, important public duties, which, if properly discharged, will redound to my credit. A people almost unknown to the world is to be examined and reported on in its social, moral, and political state; the productions of the country, animal, vegetable, and mineral, to be ascertained; the products of the industry of the country found out, and its capacity for commercial intercourse, what are its wants, and what has it to give in exchange. A new and difficult language to be learned, a history which may throw some light on that of China and Korea to be examined, and finally the various religious creeds of Japan are to be looked at. These various matters offer abundant occupation for my mind, and

shiu, having the Sato no Misaki light for a day and night landmark.

will surely prevent anything like *ennui* being felt, if I only give myself heartily to the work, and if that *sine qua non* of all earthly occupation, *health*, be vouchsafed to me by the Great Giver of all good."

The excitement proved too much, and Morpheus was banished that night. Next day he wrote:—

"Rested badly — could not drive Japan and my duties, on which I am so soon to enter, from my mind. Tried every plan to induce sleep, not forgetting Dr. Franklin's air bath, but I did not sleep until after four A. M., and was called at six o'clock, as we breakfast at seven.

"The ship has been going on well during the night, averaging about ten knots per hour. Morning bright and beautiful; wind continues fair, but is not so strong as last night. Saw an albatross, the first I have seen since I last left the coast of California in the month of October, 1850. The bird looked almost like a friend, certainly like an old acquaintance. We are to-day about seventy miles east of the coast of Kiushiu, but the water is like a desert so far as man is concerned; not a ship, junk, boat, or craft of any kind is visible, and this, too, when near the coast of an empire more populous than the United States! What a contrast to the whirl of life on the opposite side of the Pacific! I shall be the first recognized agent from a civilized power to reside in Japan. This forms an epoch in my life, and may be the beginning of a new order of things in Japan. I hope I may so conduct myself that I may have honorable mention in the histories which will be written on Japan and its future destiny."

Mr. Harris had not yet emancipated his pen from the uncouth Dutch spelling, inaccurate European notions, and the provincialism of such cacography as "Siri Jama" for Shiroyama (Hakuzan or white mountain), "Foosi Jama" for Fuji-Yama or San, and "Nippon" for Hondo. The scholars of the British Legation, who were to lay the foundations of critical scholarship, reform transliteration, and prick the bubble of Japan's mythical chronology, Messrs. Satow, Aston, Chamberlain, *et al.*, were still at home. It is not known that Fuji-San had ever been ascended by a white man. Though Siebold Japanese pupils had measured the height of Hakuzan, the writer was the first foreigner who ever reached its top.[1]

Approaching Cape Idzu, many junks were in sight. Towards evening they increased in such numbers that it was difficult to avoid collision. The engines were stopped and the ship lay to during the night, which was one of rain squalls. During this day, August 20, Dr. Wood taught both Mr. Harris and Mr. Heusken the use of a tourniquet in case of accident, and gave hints as to the right use of quinine.

From this point, Mr. Harris tells his own story in his journals.

---

[1] *The Mikado's Empire*, p. 530; Rein's *Japan*, p. 76.

PART II.
MR. HARRIS'S JOURNAL.

If "an ambassador," according to Wotton's definition, "is an honest man sent to lie abroad for his commonwealth," Harris was no diplomat. If, on the contrary, an American Minister to an Oriental Court is a representative of the moral principles of the great Christian Republic, Harris deserves the name in its best sense. NITOBÉ.

The most wholesome influence that can be exerted upon a young individual or nation is to awaken in him or it self-respect and a manly sense of independence. Such it has always been the policy of United States diplomacy to do in Japan. Whatever else changed at each change of the administration, this never changed.
NITOBÉ.

Despite the admiration for military exploits which the Americans have sometimes shown, no country is at bottom more pervaded by a hatred of war, and a sense that national honor stands rooted in national fair dealing. JAMES BRYCE.

However great in number and variety be the nations of the earth, the God who rules over them all (or binds them together) can never be more than one. OKUBO ICHIŌ.

CHAPTER III.

HOUSEKEEPING IN SHIMODA.

THURSDAY, August 21, 1856, six A. M. Find ourselves in sight of land, which proves to be Cape Omaésaki.[1] Large numbers of fishing-boats, near seventy. Like the appearance of the Japanese, clean and well clad. Cheerful looking; pretty fish-boats. At half past seven A. M. under way. Showery. Write letters announcing my arrival to the Governor of Shimoda and Minister of Foreign Affairs, sending to the latter a letter from Mr. Secretary Marcy. Mr. Heusken makes Dutch translations of these various letters. When at the mouth of the harbor, a boat with the American flag at the bow, and Japanese flags, — stripes, white, black, white, horizontal, — came off, bringing a pilot, who soon took us into the petite harbor of Shimoda. It is rather a bight than a harbor, and not more than three vessels like the San Jacinto

[1] In Totomi, the seat of a lighthouse, a few miles southeast of the great naval station of Yokosŭka; near which is the grave of Will Adams, the Englishman, pilot and shipbuilder, who lived in Japan 1600–1620, and where are built the wooden and steel vessels of the Imperial navy, such as won the battle off the Yalu River, September 17, 1894.

can moor at the same time in the inner harbor. The outer harbor is nothing more than an open roadstead. Soon after we anchored, three officials and two Dutch interpreters [1] came off from the Governor with his compliments on my arrival, asking after my health, how long a passage I had, etc., offering to supply water and food to the ship. They also asked when I proposed to land; in reply I said that as the weather was wet I would not land to-day, but if the weather was fair should do so on the morrow, asking what hour it would suit the Governor to receive my visit. In reply to this they said they would ask the Governor and make known his answer to-day. When asked what provisions could be furnished, they said, "The Governor would answer." I asked if a house had been prepared for me. They said again, "The Governor would answer," adding that Shimoda was a very poor place; that it had not yet recovered from the effects of the earthquake of December, 1854, when every house in the place except fourteen were destroyed. These persons soon after left.

Some of the officers went on shore this afternoon, and were much pleased with the appearance of the little place and the people. The houses are all new and fresh looking. They found quite a lot of coal here for us, say some two hundred tons.

At five P. M., the officials again came off, and

---

[1] Native Japanese able to speak Dutch.

said that the letter I had given them for the Governor was then being translated, and that the two for Yedo had been already sent off, and that it would take five days for them to reach Yedo, that the Governor would be ready to receive my visit at one P. M. to-morrow.

The interpreters were in constant trepidation and fear, and large drops of perspiration stood on their foreheads, while every word of question and answer was written down by two of the party. The Commodore is quite unwell this evening.

Friday, August 22, 1856. The officers off again this morning to inquire after the Commodore's health, and finding he was too unwell to go on shore to-day, they said the Governor begged to be excused from seeing me to-day, as he was unwell, etc. I said to-morrow would do as well. They asked if the Commodore would be well enough to go with me to-morrow. I answered I could not say, but that my visit was entirely independent of the Commodore; that when he was well enough he would himself call on the Governor.

I found that it was their plan to delay my visit until the Commodore was well enough, so that they might afterwards deny having received me on my individual account, but solely as one of the Commodore's suite;[1] and this was proved

[1] Those who think that Mr. Harris was too suspicious may remember that Commodore Perry, despite his shrewdness, was sev-

by their saying that when the Governor was well enough to see me, he would send me word. I then said this was a matter concerning the dignity of my government, that the Governor should write to me excusing himself on account of illness, and that I would send that letter to my government, and leave it for its adjustment.

This proposition greatly embarrassed them. The Governor was sick, therefore no letter was required. I insisted. They then offered to write to that effect themselves; this I declined.

I finally closed the discussion by saying that if the Governor wrote his excuse to me before noon of to-morrow, I should be satisfied; but that otherwise, I should come on shore to-morrow at one o'clock to visit him.

The Governor sent off ten Bonito and some small cray-fish as a present to the Commodore. Captain Bell gave them some seeds of a creeper and a large sort of squash, which they at first accepted, but when they were just leaving the ship, they brought them back to the cabin, their courage having failed them. They went ashore, promising to let me know to-day about the visit to the Governor, etc.

Visited the village of Kakizaki,[1] opposite Shi-

eral times deceived, in one instance receiving a "corporal," who pretended to be the "Prince of Idzu." See *Life and Letters of S. Wells Williams*, p. 298.

[1] Oyster Point.

moda. The temple of this place, Yokushen, of the Shintō sect, is set apart for the accommodation of Americans. The rooms are spacious and very neat and clean, and a person might stay here for a few weeks in tolerable comfort. Near this temple is the American cemetery, which contains four neat tombs, prettily fenced in. It is very small, only about fifteen by ten feet.

Kakizaki is a small and poor fishing-village, but the people are clean in person and civil in manner. You see none of the squalor which usually attends poverty in all parts of the world. Their houses are as clean as need be, every inch of ground is cultivated, as the ground is very rolling, rising up in pinnacles of lava or indurated clay ejected from volcanoes, and so steep as not to be arable. It is a pity goats are not introduced here. The pinnacles afford fine grazing for goats, and their habits of climbing would make them at home on them; their milk would be a nutritious food, and cheese might be made from it also, and this would be an object to the Japanese even though they might not eat the flesh.[1]

The views from the ship present a series of serrated hills rising up to fifteen hundred feet high,

---

[1] The first Dutch ships coming to Japan in 1600 were laden with butter and cheese, for which the Japanese cared nothing then and but little now. The Dutchmen soon changed their cargoes to suit the Japanese taste and demand.

most of which are covered with fir, spruce, and cedar trees.

The Temple Rioshen, at Shimoda, is also set apart for the use of Americans. Perhaps I may have to reside in it until a house can be prepared for me.

Late this afternoon, the officers again came off, but I declined to see them, so Mr. Heusken heard what they had to say and reported it to me. The purport was that the Governor was really unable to see me to-morrow, and they offered to bring a doctor's certificate to that effect, and earnestly begged me to postpone my visit until another day. I caused them to be told that I was most anxious to do all I could to oblige the Governor, and that I wished to be on friendly terms with him; I should therefore consent to postpone my visit until Monday; that no visits could be paid on Sunday or any business transacted on that day. They were also told that Commodore Armstrong would not visit the Governor until after I had seen the Governor, and that we should not come together to pay a visit to the Governor. The officers were most urgent to see me, and their anxiety on this point appeared to increase with my refusals, but I persisted, and at last they left quite chap-fallen. It is now understood that I am to visit the Governor on Monday at ten A. M. Some of the officers have been on shore, and report a

HOUSEKEEPING IN SHIMODA. 39

very pretty bazar has been opened, with great display of lacquered ware, etc., etc.

Saturday, August 23, 1856. Go on shore with Captain Bell and Mr. Heusken; visit the Temple Rioshen. It is badly placed for hot weather, being at the foot of a steep hill that shuts out the southwest wind entirely, and is surrounded by stagnant pools and other disagreeables.

We afterwards visited six or seven other temples. They are all built after one pattern, some a little larger and in better order than the others, and having more agreeable situations, but beyond this they are exactly alike. We afterwards walked up the valley some two miles. Saw a large inclosure containing some twenty detached buildings, all new, and in fact some were not yet completed. I learn this is the residence of the Governor. In the afternoon I went again to Kakizaki. I find the temple there has been cleaned out, apparently to prepare it for my reception. I have thought much about my accepting this temple for my residence. The building is as good, if not better than any of the others, but it is isolated, and the approach is through the narrow and crooked alleys of a very poor fishing-village. I should here be unseen and unknown to the *people*, and to go to market my servants, in bad weather, could not cross in a boat, and the road to go and return would be nearly five miles. Again, the treaty says, and my commission says, I am to reside at Shimoda. Now Kakizaki is not Shimoda. I therefore think I shall refuse this temple as my place of residence.

Weather delightful. Barometer 30.10. The air is like that of the United States, full of oxygen.

Sunday, August 24, 1856. Do not leave the ship. In the afternoon the Japanese come off and desire to see me. I decline either to see them or to hear their messages, for the reason that it is Sunday. They urge me at least to hear their message, saying that it is very important, and from the Governor. They also say that when Commodore Perry was here, he made no difference for Sunday,[1] etc., etc. I adhere to my previous determination, telling them through Mr. Heusken, that they can come off to-morrow morning as early as they please, and then state their message.

Monday, August 25, 1856. The officers come off at eight A. M. with a message that the Governor will be ready to receive me at ten o'clock. At that hour go on shore accompanied by Captain Bell and some ten others. I go in the Commodore's boat, having my Secretary with me. The three boats preceded me so that the officers could

---

[1] Compare *Perry's Expedition*, p. 276; *Life and Letters of S. Wells Williams*, pp. 216, 254.

land and form in order before I landed. When my boat had pulled well off from the ship a salute of thirteen guns was fired, waking up the grandest echoes among the hills. On landing I found the streets thronged with persons collected to see us pass. I was conducted to a new building, nearly in the centre of the town.

I was politely received by the Governor and vice-governor. Asked after my health, when I left the United States, etc., etc. They asked in whose honor the salute was fired, and were told that it was in mine, when I perceived that I instantly rose in their estimation. The Governor said he should like to *see* such guns fired, whereupon Captain Bell invited him to visit the ship on Saturday next, as they are now painting on board, and he feared they might soil their clothes. Refreshments were served up in Japanese style. The cooking was excellent and served up with extreme neatness and cleanliness. I am much prepossessed in favor of their cookery. I asked the Governor when I could see him on business. He said I could enter on business then if I pleased. I replied that it would not be good breeding to enter on business on a visit of ceremony. He then said the vice-governor would attend me the next day, at the same hour and place, and that the vice-governor could act as himself, etc., etc.

Our visit lasted nearly two hours, and we were

all much pleased with the appearance and manners of the Japanese. I repeat they are superior to any people east of the Cape of Good Hope.

Tuesday, August 26, 1856. I omitted yesterday to state that a superior interpreter appeared at my interview. He is attached to the office of the Minister for Foreign Affairs; a good interpreter, of most agreeable manners, and a true courtier. *Seven* scribes recorded our sayings and doings yesterday. To-day ashore at ten with Mr. Heusken. Met the vice-governor and the person from Yedo, who evidently has come down since our arrival was reported there, although they say the journey cannot be made under five days from here to Yedo.

My interview was long and far from satisfactory. They did not expect the arrival of a consul. A consul was only to be sent when some difficulty arose, and no such thing had taken place. Shimoda was a poor place, and had been recently desolated by an earthquake. They had no residence prepared for me. I had better go away and return in about a year, when they hoped to have a house ready. The treaty said that a consul was to come if *both* nations wished it,[1] that it was not left to the simple will of the United States

---

[1] "There shall be appointed by the government of the United States, consuls or agents, to reside in Shimoda . . . provided that either of the two governments deem such arrangement necessary." *Perry's Treaty*, art. xi.

HOUSEKEEPING IN SHIMODA. 43

government. Would I land at Kakizaki and take up my residence at the temple there, and leave the question of my official residence to be settled by future negotiations? Yedo was also in a ruinous condition from an earthquake ten months since,[1] therefore they could not offer me a house there while building one here.

The foregoing is the substance of their remarks and propositions, made and renewed and changed in every possible form and manner during three mortal hours. I need hardly write that I courteously but firmly negatived all their propositions. They earnestly protested against the idea that they refused to receive me, or that they meant in any way to break the treaty. They at last begged to adjourn the business until to-morrow at the same hour, to give them time to consult.

The sales in the bazaar cannot be much under two thousand dollars; the prices are most exorbitant. They appear to raise them at each new arrival of a ship here. Ordered spars to make my flag-staff, one of 50 feet, 12 inches by 8, and the other, 30 feet long, 7 inches by 4 inches, and four small pieces.

[1] This great earthquake is graphically described in a well-illustrated book, entitled *The Tribulations of Ansei* (year period, 1854–1859). Most of the dead, alleged to number 104,000, were buried in or cremated near the one enlarged temple-yard of E' Ko In, where also the alleged 166,000 victims of the seismic disturbances of 1656 had been interred or inurned.

Wednesday, August 27, 1856. On shore at ten A. M. by appointment to meet the Governor or vice-governor, but neither of them made his appearance. Ten persons were present, including the Yedo official. They said the Governor was very ill the previous night with a violent headache, so they were unable to consult with him. They then said that the treaty provided for a consul, but not a consul-general; that the additional articles had not been sent out as ratified; that they expected the government of the United States would send out an ambassador with the ratified articles, and then enter on negotiations about sending a consul.

I told them I was surprised the vice-governor should not appear after making an appointment with me; that I considered it as want of respect, and that I must decline entering into any conversation about my affairs with any one but the Governor or vice-governor; that I would go on board the steamer and consult with Commodore Armstrong, and then he would determine whether he would take me up to Yedo, and there get satisfaction.

The officer from Yedo said he was of higher rank than the Governor, and asked why I should object to negotiate with him. I replied that I could only know the official authorities of the place, and with them only have any official intercourse; that for himself I had a high esteem,

HOUSEKEEPING IN SHIMODA.

based on what I had seen of him, but that personal feeling could not give him that status which my official business required. They urged me to proceed in the matter, but to some questions they put I said I had no answer to give them. They constantly renewed and urgently the request that I would proceed with them. I as constantly declined. They then said they would report on what had occurred to the Governor, and requested me to meet them to-morrow at the same hour to meet the vice-governor. I told them that, as the vice-governor had broken his appointment with me, I could not consent to make another appointment until I had some explanation or apology for his absence of this morning; that I wished the Governor or vice-governor to write me a letter and send it to me on board the steamer, stating whether they would receive me in Shimoda or not, and whether they would assign me a house to reside in; that I desired this letter to be sent to me either to-day or to-morrow morning.

They were anxious to know whether I was resolved to go to Yedo, if not received here. I said that would be settled after consultation with the Commodore. They were greatly agitated when I mentioned the going up to Yedo.

Thursday, August 28, 1856. The vice-governor, the high person from Yedo, and a large suite came off this morning. The vice-governor explained his absence yesterday by saying the individual from Yedo was of higher rank than himself, and had full powers from the government to act in my matters. He then said that he was ready to receive me with all the honors due to my high place, and to assign me the only place that was habitable for my residence, the Temple of Yokushen at Kakizaki; that Kakizaki was in point of fact a part of Shimoda, subject to the same governor, magistrates, police, etc., etc.; that the name was only local to distinguish it as a part of Shimoda, as the suburbs of Western cities receive distinctive local names; that the Go-yosho was as its name indicated an "Imperial seat" built solely for the reception of strangers of distinction who came to Shimoda; that the Governor had no power to use it for himself or to authorize its use by others; that I must see how deplorably the place had been injured by the earthquake; that as to the temples in Shimoda they were all actually occupied as places of worship and for cemeteries; that it would be an outrage on the feelings of the people who worshiped there, or who frequently went there to offer prayers at the graves of their ancestors, to find the place used for secular purposes; that the temple at Kakizaki was not of this character; that its purpose was the accommodation of parties who went out to make a religious holiday; that its occupation by me would be inconven-

HOUSEKEEPING IN SHIMODA. 47

ient, but would not be a desecration;[1] that the government at Yedo could not give me any other answer, even if I went up there in the steamer; that my residence was to be considered as only temporary and until they could erect a proper building for me, and that they would adapt the building as much as they could to my wants; finally, that they had offered me the best they had, and if I did not accept it, I could not say they had refused to receive me, or to furnish me with quarters. I told them I would send my answer on shore in two hours by my secretary.

Accordingly I instructed Mr. Heusken to say to the Governor that I was most anxious to avoid any difficulties, and although I feared my government might blame me for accepting a residence at Kakizaki, instead of Shimoda, I would accept it with the full understanding that a suitable house was to be prepared for me as soon as possible, and that I must have a boat and men constantly at my command for my use while there.

I also gave notice that I should want two large boats on Saturday to take my things on shore, and men to take them from the landing to the house, with proper persons to watch them until I came on shore, etc., etc.

---

[1] The Japanese were then right, and in being so, in 1856, showed the utter occultation of the ancient Shintō faith (until 1870) by Buddhism. See *The Religions of Japan*, chapter vii.

Friday, August 29, 1856. Mr. Heusken goes on shore with the carpenter to aid him in selecting a spar, etc., and afterwards to go over to Kakizaki to indicate what alterations, etc., are required in the temple to fit it for my residence, etc.

The Governor informs me that three rooms in my house will be required for Japanese officers who are to be with me night and day "to await my pleasure." I return a message that I require *all* the rooms, and that under no circumstances would I permit any Japanese, except servants, to be in my house, or even to enter it without my permission.

The carpenter comes off at three P. M. saying he cannot find a stick that will answer for my flagstaff. Mr. Heusken at six P. M. informs me that the Japanese say they have cut three trees that will answer, but they cannot be got to the ship before Monday morning. The authorities have agreed to give me all my rooms, and to withdraw their threatened police force.

Dr. Wood, fleet surgeon, tells me a story which strongly illustrates the determination of the authorities to prevent the people from having any intercourse with us, except what is unavoidable.

While in the bazaar a man came to him for medical advice for a cutaneous affection; after examination, the doctor wrote a prescription and gave it to the man telling him (through the interpreter) to take the paper on board the San Jacinto, where medicine would be given to him which would cure him. The man, with many thanks, took the paper and went away. An hour afterwards he returned, looking much alarmed. He came to the doctor, and gave him a paper, which he found to be the prescription. The doctor made signs that he should take the paper to the ship. The man shook his head and again forced the paper into the doctor's hands, making significant motions with his finger that his head would be cut off if he took the paper to the ship!!!

Saturday, August 30, 1856. Busy writing letters until one P. M. After dinner the Yedo officer came off with five others. The Governor sent his compliments to me and requested me to visit him at the Go-yosho at ten A. M. of Monday. I accepted. They then asked if the Commodore would come off with me. I said I presumed he would if well enough, and, as he was better to-day, I had no doubt he would come. They then asked when the Governor could visit the ship, and Tuesday was suggested. I discovered that the invitation to me was a ruse to get the Commodore to visit the Governor *first*, and then the Governor could visit the ship. I told them frankly that, by the rule of our country and all Western etiquette, the Commodore of a ship or squadron makes the first visit, and the reason the Commodore had not already visited the Governor was the illness of the Commodore in the first place, and then afterwards the illness of the Governor; this gave them great satisfaction. The Commodore came in afterwards, and he accepted the invitation for Monday, and at the same time told them that he should have gone with me at my first visit. This startled and pleased them, for they evidently had not forgotten that he had told some of them that *he would not visit the Governor until after I had been received.* Then it was settled that the Governor would visit the ship on Tuesday at eleven A. M.

I was requested not to land until as late a day as possible, in order to give them the utmost time to prepare the temple for my reception. Wednesday morning was named, and they then told me that they would be there to receive me in due form.

I am compelled to pay seventy-eight dollars for a spar to make my flag-staff — an enormous price!

Learn that some great personage has arrived at the residence of the Governor, as a long procession was seen by some of our officers, preceded by heralds bearing the coat of arms, then a number of norimono, one very large,[1] a led horse, servants bearing luggage, etc., etc.

[1] According to the etiquette and carefully graduated honors and paraphernalia of feudalism. The large norimono or palanquin of officers of rank had the needlessly large and heavy bearer's beam *curved* on top.

Sunday, August 31, 1856. A lovely day. Write many letters. Japanese come off to see me. I refuse to see any one on Sunday. I am resolved to set an example of a proper observance of the Sabbath by abstaining from all business or pleasures on that day. I do not mean I should not take a quiet walk, or any such amusement. I do not mean to set an example of Puritanism, but I will try to make it what I believe it was intended to be, a day of rest.

Monday, September 1, 1856. At ten A. M. go on shore with Commodore Armstrong and a suite of officers. At the Go-yosho meet the new Governor, vice-governor, and the other Governor. It appears there are two Governors and two vice-governors for this place; they pass six months in Shimoda, then six in Yedo. The new one arrives in pursuance of this rule. The conversation began with complimentary inquiries about health, etc., etc.; then I was asked what was the secret object of my government in sending me to Japan. I answered that I knew nothing beyond the fact of my appointment and our treaty rights. I was asked if I should go to Hakodaté? I replied, that would depend on circumstances. If I was wanted there I should go.

They then ran over all the old objections, and civilly asked me to go away; and on my declining to do so, they asked the Commodore if he had no power to take me away. That was answered by saying that he was a military man. His orders were to bring the consul - general to Shimoda and land him there, and then his part was done. They asked would he take a letter from the Japanese government to the American government explaining their embarrassed position, and asking for my removal. The Commodore answered that all communications for his government from the Japanese would of necessity come through the consul-general. Next, would the Commodore write to his government explaining the reasons why the Japanese refused to receive the consul-general. This question, covering as it did a positive intention to refuse me, excited much surprise, and received a positive negative. I was then asked would I forward a letter from the Japanese government to the American government. I answered I would if it was written by the Minister of Foreign Affairs. Would not the Governor of Shimoda do as well? He had full powers to treat with me, therefore it was the same thing. I replied that it might be the same thing to them, but it was not in our eyes. Would I write to my government asking for my own removal? This was declined.

It was now twelve o'clock, two mortal hours having been frittered away in renewing and twisting the foregoing into all possible forms. Refreshments were served. The Governors retired for a short time, and after their return, and the tiffin being over, the Commodore and his suite, except Fleet Surgeon Wood, retired, leaving me with the doctor and my interpreter.

They now took another turn, apologized for delaying and wasting so much time in trivial questions, but their excuse was their want of knowledge of such matters — that it was a new thing, etc., etc. They asked me if I had any new negotiations to propose. I answered none at that time. Did I intend to make new regulations about sailors who were shipwrecked, or should I change the place of the consulate without giving notice to them? I answered no.

They inquired what were my powers and privileges as a consul. To which I gave a short synopsis of both. They then begged me again to write my government the strong objections they had to receiving a consul at this time, stating that they had opened Shimoda to the Dutch and Russians, and that they would send a consul here as soon as they knew I was received here. (This was news.) I replied that I could not write any formal letter; that if I did, it would not be attended to on such a point; that I should, as a matter of course, give my government an account of all that had occurred here, but they might be sure it would not elicit any reply; that if they wanted to communicate with the government of the United States, let their

Minister of Foreign Affairs write a letter, and he might depend on receiving a speedy answer.

They said their laws forbade it. Here, for the third or fourth time, they begged me not to be offended with them. They were acting under orders. The matter was new to them, and from their ignorance it appeared the more alarming. It being now near two, I prepared to leave them. I should remark that at tiffin-time I was told the boats were ready to go to the frigate to bring off my baggage, and asked if they should go. I answered in the affirmative. Now this fact took place during a discussion in which they had, in fact, declared they would not receive me, and it convinced me they were acting a part in which they did not even hope to succeed.

The people are of a genial disposition, and are evidently inclined towards intercourse with foreigners, but the despotic rule of the country, and the terror they have of their so-called *inflexible* laws, forbid them to express their wishes.

I do not like the look of the new Governor. He has a dark, sullen look, and I fear I shall have trouble with him; I much regret the change. Got on board near three P. M., and commenced at once sending off my traps; all of the supplies, furniture, and some heavy luggage were sent off, and all in pretty good order, except a hat in a leather box, which was destroyed.

Tuesday, September 2, 1856. The new Governor and the old and vice-governor, our Yedo friend, and a large suite came on board at ten A. M. Men were exercised at the guns, and went through all the manœuvres of an action, marines were put through the manual and marching, etc., and a salute was fired. Then to table, and their performances in the way of eating and drinking were noteworthy. What was not eaten was carried away.[1] Ham, tongue, salt beef, and such preserved food as is found on board a ship, seemed, all of it, to suit their appetites. The new Governor was cold and rude; not even the raw brandy, which he and others drank, seemed to warm his heart, or thaw him towards us.

They asked when I should land, and were told to-morrow at five P. M. I was informed that two officers of rank would be sent to escort me to my new residence. The spar for my lower flag-staff only reached the ship at one P. M. The carpenter says it shall be done to-morrow.

Wednesday, September 3, 1856. Go on shore and select spot for flag-staff to stand. Return and write letter to Secretary of State, — twelve foolscap pages.

Four P. M. Instead of the flag-staff's being

[1] This was in good form. "Leavings are lucky" is a Japanese proverb, and the capacious sleeve of the old-fashioned haori served the polite purpose well.

ready at noon, it is not yet completed, and there is a fair chance it will not be sent ashore to-night. Mr. Heusken was taken ashore to interpret about the bills, etc., with a positive promise he should be brought back at half past twelve. At half past two P. M. he procured a shore boat and came off. So much for promises. I decide to land to-day, so I send off all my remaining traps, and attended by two officials leave the ship at five P. M., having taken a kind leave of all.

As I left the ship the men manned the rigging and gave me three hearty cheers. The men in my boat responded, and a counter-cheer of two more came from the ship. Through surf, and then the band on the quarter-deck struck up " Hail Columbia." I was both flattered and touched by this mark of attention. It showed at least that I had so conducted myself while on board the San Jacinto (off and on, five months) that I had secured the good will of all on board, and so I came on shore for my final landing in Japan. On reaching my temple, I found the vice-governor and a suite of officials awaiting my arrival to welcome me, which they did in very good terms, at the same time showing me a present of fowls, eggs, and lobsters from the Governor.

Two things I must note which caused me some regret in the San Jacinto: the first, that Commodore Armstrong was again quite unwell, with considerable fever, and the other that he and Captain Bell refused to permit me to pay anything for my mess while I was on board, saying I had not cost the mess one cent extra; that I never drank any wine, nor had called for any different cookery; that I had not given any trouble, nor added to their expenses. They therefore declined receiving anything from me. This was contrary to agreement, as before I left New York I agreed with the Commodore and Captain Bell that I should be allowed to pay my share of the mess.

We were up till after midnight getting copies made of my dispatches. The spar came ashore just at dusk, too late to put up my staff.

CHAPTER IV.

AUTUMN EXPERIENCES IN JAPAN.

THURSDAY, September 4, 1856. Slept very little, from excitement and mosquitoes;[1] the latter are *enormous* in size. Men on shore to put up my flag-staff. Heavy lot. Slow work. Spar falls, breaks cross-trees; fortunately no one hurt. At last get a reinforcement from the ship; flag-staff erected. Men form a ring round it, and at half past two P. M. of this day I hoist the "First Consular Flag" ever seen in this empire. Grave reflections. Ominous of change. Undoubted beginning of the end. Query, — if for the real good of Japan?

The San Jacinto left at five o'clock, saluting me by dipping her flag, which was answered by me, and then she left me "alone in my glory," not feeling very sad, for, in fact, I was too busy in opening boxes, searching out eatables and mosquito-nets, to think of being down-hearted. Go to bed at eight P. M., and sleep well.

[1] One of the pests of Japan. The native Ka-cho (mosquito-house or net) is made of cubical shape and fills the whole room, being hung at the corners by rings and hooks in the supporting timbers of the dwelling. On the other hand, house-flies are few,

Friday, September 5, 1856. Busy all day in opening packages, arranging contents, ordering various articles from the Japanese. Got an old belfry made into a nice pigeon-house, in which I installed my four pairs of pigeons. Clear all day.

Saturday, September 6, 1856. Same employment as yesterday. Am getting things to look a little comfortable. Find that the Ichi-bu is equal to sixteen hundred sen or " cash." This takes two thirds off the price of everything I buy, as the Japanese have only allowed us sixteen hundred sen for the dollar, although the dollar weighs three times as much as the Ichi-bu, consequently is worth forty-eight hundred sen.[1]

Moriyama, the Yedo official, visited me to-day on a mere visit of friendship, as he said. Gave him cakes and champagne.

Hear a curious insect of the cricket tribe to-night; sound was precisely like a miniature locomotive at great speed. Bats in rooms. See enormous *tête du mort* spider, the legs extended five and a half inches as the insect stood. Unpleasant

and ants are not numerous. Fleas, or nomi (devourers), are abundant, but the bedbug is unknown.

[1] Ichi-bu, one bu or part. Zeni, or sen, was the general name for the copper or iron " cash," or *cast* coin with a square hole in the centre for stringing. The modern unit of Japanese money is the sen or cent and the yen or dollar, both struck in a die, one hundred of the former making one of the latter.

discovery of large rats in numbers running about the house. Light showers in the night.

Sunday, September 7, 1856. No work to-day. Hoist my flag, which is to be flown on Sundays, holidays, Japanese ditto, and when foreign ships are here. The Japanese were much pleased when I told them I should hoist my flag in honor of their holidays, and gave me list for six months.

Monday, September 8, 1856. Weather same as yesterday. Get on very slowly in fitting up the house with shelves, closets, tables, etc., etc. Every carpenter that comes to do anything is attended by an officer. It may be to keep him from stealing, but more likely to prevent any communication between us.

I have required my poultry to be all hens or pullets. They inform me that in Japan fowls are always hatched in pairs, one cock and one hen, therefore they must give them to me in the same manner. Send to each of the first Governors five pints of champagne, one quart brandy, two quarts whiskey, one anizette. This afternoon we discover a Russian cemetery, with three tombs of the same patterns as the Americans. They are of persons who belonged to the Russian frigate Diana,[1] and died in 1854 and 1855. One tomb is evidently

[1] Which had been caught and destroyed in the great tidal wave and earthquake of December 22, 1855, by which Shimoda was nearly ruined and depopulated.

that of an officer, but I cannot read the letters to make out his name or rank.

This tomb is decorated with *two crosses* deeply cut in the stone; one is four inches, the other about sixteen inches long. The presence of these crosses serves to prove that the Japanese of the present day have not that excessive hatred of the cross [1] that was said to animate them formerly. On Saturday last I showed Moriyama my "Mitchell's Atlas," the frontispiece of which contains a colored engraving of the " Landing of Columbus," in which a large cross is prominently engraved. Moriyama paid no attention to it, or rather said nothing. Spaulding [2] says that he asked a Japanese for his autograph, which he was about to write in his (Spaulding's) prayer-book, but, discovering a cross in the frontispiece, he with great trepidation refused to write.

Tuesday, September 9, 1856. I applied on Friday last (5th) for two boys as house-servants. Am told to-day that they must write to Yedo about them. Got measures of distance from Japanese. I am anxious to get my house arranged, so that I may begin to wander about the country and see how it looks. Moriyama and suite visited me this afternoon. He said he came from the

[1] A feeling which was locally intense, and resulted in violent manifestations almost wholly in Kiushiu and southwestern Hondo.
[2] J. W. Spaulding's *The Japan Expedition*, p. 225. N. Y. 1855.

Governor to inquire if I was frightened by the thunder of last night — a Japanese ruse.

He quietly changed to the subject of Japanese servants, which I had asked for last week. He said there were none at Shimoda, must write to other places; that they had to reflect on every new proposition a long time; that they could not decide as quickly as the men of the West, etc., etc. I replied that I believed that servants could at once be procured for me in Shimoda; that it was treating me improperly to leave me to wait on myself. I showed him my blistered hands which had *so become* by my being compelled to do work in fault of proper servants. He then begged me to give them some more time to procure them (*i. e.*, to invent lies to deny them, if they should think best to do so). I said I did not wish to appear impatient, and would wait for the remainder of the week. I complained of the very great delay there was in executing my orders. I had for many days been expecting a number of slight things to be done, naming some of them, and although time enough to do them four times over had elapsed, yet none of them had been done; that I felt that I was neglected, and expected it would be remedied.

He at once began blowing up the officers who were with him, and gave me some of their excuses — a greater tissue of lies was never heard. The matter was closed by an assurance on his part that I should have the matters attended to in the morning. After this he got quite jolly on champagne.

Thursday, September 11, 1856. Men are here working on various matters for my house. Had a flare-up with the officials, who told me some egregious lies, in answer to some requests I made. I told them plainly I knew they lied; that if they wished me to have any confidence in them, they must always speak the truth; that if I asked anything they were not authorized to grant, or about which they wished to consult, let them simply say they were not prepared to answer me; but that to tell lies to me was treating me like a child, and that I should consider myself as insulted thereby; that in my country a man who lied was disgraced, and that to call a man a liar was the grossest insult could be given him; that I hoped they would for the future — if they told me anything — simply tell me the truth, and that I should then respect them, which I could not do when they told me falsehoods. Send Moriyama an atlas as a present.

Friday, September 12, 1856. The vice-governor and Moriyama with the usual suite. The object of the visit was my demand for two boys as house-servants. It was a rare scene of Japanese deceit, falsehood, flattery, and politeness. I at last got them cornered, and they were compelled to promise me to supply my wants by the 16th.

They fought hard to have the boys leave at sunset and return at daylight, but I was firm, and carried my point.

I may here remark that at all these visits they readily drink all I offer them, wine, cordials, brandy, whiskey, etc., etc., and many of them drink more than enough. Spirits of all kinds they drink raw.

Saturday, September 13, 1856. To-day is the anniversary of the patron saint of Shimoda,[1] and is one of their greatest holidays; but as my house is not in order, I remain at home arranging books, etc., and trying to eradicate the cockroaches, which I have brought from the San Jacinto by thousands. They are a pest of the most disagreeable kind.

Mr. Heusken went out to see what was doing, and says he saw a large procession bearing a metal mirror, and pieces of white paper (emblem of the Shintō religion). A large drum, borne by three men, was beaten by one. The fashion of the drum was like the Chinese, *i. e.*, a cylinder with one parchment head. He did not see any change of dress.

A number of persons were throwing themselves into extravagant attitudes, and shouting or screaming loudly. The procession went to a temple, where a large quantity of holy water was showered on them by the attending priest. After their devotions they visited another temple, after which he

---

[1] Ushijiwa no Jinja.

left. He did not see any of the theatricals referred to by Kaempfer, Fischer, and Herr Doeff.

Sunday, September 14, 1856. Some of my Chinese servants went out to walk. They were followed by three policemen. They offered to purchase some fruit, but were refused, and finally, on asking for a drink of water from a man who was by a well, he refused and ran away with the drinking-vessel.

Monday, September 15, 1856. I expect the Governor to visit me to-day, as I wrote him on Saturday asking him to order the proper officer to receive from Mr. Heusken $500 in silver coin, and to give him the *same weight* of Japanese silver money. I am sure he will refuse, as they have heretofore refused, to take the dollar for more than their Ichi-bu, or quarter of a tael of silver. The value of the tael is about $1.36. The Ichi-bu is therefore worth thirty-four cents. We have heretofore paid nearly two hundred per cent. over price, from their only allowing us thirty-four cents for our dollar. But this must have an end, and I am fully instructed by my government to insist on our money being taken at its proper value.

In the afternoon, Moriyama and the third Governor and suite visited me, bringing two boys of the ages of fifteen and sixteen years. Their names are Sukézo and Takézo; the latter I take for my servant, and the other for Mr. Heusken.

On showing Kaempfer's work on Japan to the Governor, he at once pointed out the place of his and Moriyama's houses in Yedo, showing the general correctness of the plan of that city. I tried in various ways to get at the population of Yedo from them, but without any success. They said it was a large place, that there was such a large number of persons going and coming daily that it was out of their power to state the population, etc., etc. Complained to the Governor that my servants on Sunday last had been followed by policemen, that they had been refused fruit which they offered to buy, and even denied a drink of water. I remonstrated sharply against such conduct as disgraceful, inhospitable, etc., etc., and they promised that the matter should be inquired into.

Got some fine ripe grapes and persimmons to-day, and am promised a regular supply so long as they are in season. They have constantly denied to me having any such fruits here, and it was only after my cook had seen them in the streets on Sunday, and I charged them with falsehood about fruit, that they would bring them to me.

Tuesday, September 16, 1856. At eleven o'clock go out for a walk. The paths lead over towards Yedo Bay. The views were enchanting, sky clear, water blue, white caps cresting the waves, highlands on the opposite side of Yedo Bay (N. E. side) dimly seen, Japanese junks with their large square sails scudding merrily before the wind. Ground here is cultivated *wherever water can be procured to irrigate it.* It appears to be equally rich on the steep hillsides as on the little plains. A streamlet of water is found running down the gorge between two hills, the ground is cut into terraces, then the water is led from the highest parts right and left from the stream to the upper terraces, thence it trickles down to the next, and the next, until all the terraces have been watered down to the foot of the hill. I never saw such fine crops of rice, or rice of so good a quality, as here. Rice is the chief produce. Some maize, millet, a little wheat, barley, and buckwheat are also grown. A great variety of pulse and lentils is also grown. I see that many oleaginous seeds, of whose names I am ignorant, are also cultivated. A bulbous root, the Taro of the South Seas, is also grown here. We pursued our pleasant walk until we reached the highest hill in this vicinity, and from that we could just see the top of the celebrated Fuji-Yama, the highest mountain in Japan, and not many miles from Yedo.

Tuesday, September 23, 1856. Yesterday at four P. M. the wind began to blow fresh from E. S. E. with rain. The wind continued to freshen until at eight P. M. it became a heavy typhoon,[1]

[1] Chinese Tai-fun (great wind). See *T. A. S. J.* for scientific analysis and description of these cyclones. The circularity of

which continued up to midnight, when it moderated. The wind at four P. M. was S. S. E., and continued to haul to S. S. W., at which point the gale was heaviest. After midnight the wind stood W. N. W.

I was under much apprehension that my house would be blown down, as it shook in every post and beam, and swayed to and fro as the heavy gusts struck it. My kitchen was partly unroofed, and flag-staff blown over so as to stand at an angle of 65°. In the harbor every junk was cast ashore, and many lives lost and much property destroyed. In Kakizaki, full one half the houses were blown down and some persons killed. The landing-jetty and breakwater are totally destroyed.

At Shimoda the bazaar part of the Go-yosho is totally destroyed, and a large amount of beautiful lacquer and inlaid ware lost. One hundred houses blown down and twenty lives lost. The Japanese say it was the severest storm ever known at this place.

Wednesday, October 1, 1856. The Dutch steam frigate Medusa,[1] Captain Fabius, arrived here

these storms, whose motion in a periphery is contrary to that made by the hands of a watch, is indicated in Mr. Harris's notes on the wind.

[1] For eight years this man-of-war was active in the waters of Japan. On the 11th of July, 1863, having been fired on by the clansmen of Chōshiu while in the Straits of Shimonoséki, Captain Casembroot shelled the Japanese batteries. The next year, as

to-day from Hakodaté en route to Nagasaki. I went on board, and was kindly received by Captain Fabius, who gave me a salute of eleven guns on leaving.

Captain Fabius informs me that a mine of superior coals has been discovered at Hakodaté, which will greatly reduce the price of that article at that place, besides giving a superior quality.

Captain Fabius also says that two steam vessels are now being constructed in Holland for the Japanese,[1] which are to be paid for as follows: say one-fifth part in each of the following articles, copper, lacquer-ware, etc., wax, camphor, and money or bullion for the remaining twenty per cent.

Dutch mechanics of every branch connected with ship-building have been brought out for the Japanese, and they are now giving instruction to the Japanese in all the various branches above referred to at Nagasaki.

It appears that for some years the Dutch have received a part of the returns of their annual cargo in money or bullion.

one of the four Dutch ships in the combined squadrons of England, France, the Netherlands, and the United States, assisted in the bombardment and destruction of the batteries. See *Century Magazine*, April, 1892, and *De Medusa in de Wateren van Japan*, door Jhr. F. de Casembroot. The Hague, 1865.

[1] The beginning of the modern marine of Japan. See the "Evolution of the Japanese Navy," *Harper's Weekly*, pp. 1023–26, 1894.

The King of Holland has, as it is said, written a letter to the Emperor of Japan strongly urging him to open his kingdom [1] to the commerce of *all nations*.

Friday, October 3, 1856. The Medusa sailed to-day for Nagasaki.

Saturday, October 4, 1856. I am fifty-two years old to-day. God grant that the short remainder of my life may be more usefully and honorably spent than the preceding and larger portion of it.

Sunday, October 5, 1856. The American schooner General Pierce arrived here from Hakodaté. She left no American vessels there, as it is too early for them. She comes here to complete her trading. Both the Medusa and General Pierce were in the typhoon of the 22d ult.

Thursday, October 9, 1856. The General Pierce left to-day. Wrote by her to the Secretary of State, and others.

Wednesday, October 22, 1856. I have not been well since the 17th of September. I am suffering from a bad wound in my left foot caused by treading on a large nail, and also from a total loss of appetite, want of sleep, and depression of spirits. I attribute all but the wound to two causes: first, inability to take exercise in the open air, and second, from smoking too much; the latter I must

---

[1] See Matthew Calbraith Perry, p. 277.

break off. As I am now much better, I shall begin to go out for exercise and hope to be in robust health again. The climate here is delightful.

The Japanese have three times sent me the flesh of what they call a wild hog.[1] The flesh is peculiar; it is very tender, juicy, and of an excellent flavor; the taste is something between delicate veal and the tenderloins of pork. I am promised a full supply during the cold weather, which will be a great relief to my housekeeping. The typhoon destroyed all the grapes, but I have been well supplied with a great variety of the persimmon, some as large as a pippin, and all of good quality. Chestnuts have also been sent to me.

To-day a horse was brought to me to examine the saddle, bridle, etc. They are queer affairs, but I have ordered a horse and trappings to be sent to me from Yedo, not only for actual use, but to give me increased importance in the eye of the natives. For the same reason I have ordered a norimono.

The Japanese officials are daily becoming more and more friendly and more open in their communications with me. I hope this will grow and lead to good results by and by.

[1] Shishi, or *Sus leucomystax*, the wild boar so numerous in Japan, and found also in Formosa, is said by Swinhoe to be the wild stock of the Chinese pig. It casts a large shadow in the native mythology and caricature.

My poor pigeons have all been killed in one night by my cat. I have sent up to Yedo for more. The Itachi, a species of large weasel,[1] is a sad enemy to my hen-coops.

Thursday, October 23, 1856. A lovely day. The weather is as balmy and mild as in New York in October, but we have no smoke or haze in the air, and at night the thermometer does not fall below 60°.

Took a walk of some five miles; the country is very beautiful, is broken up in steep volcanic cones, but every possible spot is terraced and cultivated like a garden. The labor expended in cutting down the rock to form some of these terraces is something wonderful. My walk led me first to Vandalia Point, the most southeastern part of the land; from this I had a view of the vast Pacific, and it was a curious thought, that looking due south there was no land between me and Australia. Some five thousand miles! Turning more to the eastward, I saw the island of Oshima,[2] with its volcano smoking on its summit. The day is almost calm, so the smoke arose like a mighty pil-

---

[1] The weasel family is well represented in Japan. The itachi, "the din of whose rat-chasing is so common a clamor in the houses of European residents," has a busy representative also in mythology. For a scientific description, see *T. A. S. J.*, vol. viii. p. 416.

[2] For an account of Vries Island or Oshima, see *T. A. S. J.*, vol. v. p. 64, and vol. xi. p. 162. It was the place of exile of the famous archer Tamétomo.

lar for thousands of feet; it then spread out forming a vast white cloud.

This volcano has been in action for some centuries, and occasionally treats us here to an earthquake, as it did in December, 1853,[1] when a mighty wave rolled in on Shimoda, encountering, as it entered, a flourishing town of some eight or ten thousand souls. When the wave receded, it left only fourteen houses standing, all the rest, temples, bazaars, and a large number of the inhabitants, were swept into the bay by the reflux of this mighty wave, which was said to have been thirty feet high; four times it returned; but the deed of destruction was perfected by the first one.

I passed through the village of Satora on the Yedo Bay, thence, through another village back of Kakizaki whose name I do not know, home. I saw to-day, cherry, peach, pear, and persimmon trees, grapevines, ivy, althea, the last just putting out new leaves, blue privet, very pretty, many ferns, pine-trees in variety, cedar, spruce, fir, and camphor trees. Camellia japonica forms the jungle here, and is cut for fuel. I saw a few bushes of the common rose, but no flowers were on them. Among flowers whose names I know I found bluebell, Canterbury, and Scotch thistle, the first I ever saw in the East, heart's-ease, yellow shamrock,

[1] In 1892 the smoke ceased and a great earthquake followed. The volcanic cone is 2600 feet high.

daisy, and others whose forms are familiar but whose names I do not know, and then many that were strange to me. How much I wish I was a botanist!

The fine, clear, bracing air, the high cultivation you see everywhere, combined with views which are of the most picturesque kind, and which are constantly changing, make a walk here a thing to be desired and long remembered.

Friday, October 24, 1856. Walked to the top of the hill that overlooks the harbor. A wooden cannon, about twelve pound bore, is strongly bound with bamboo hoops from end to end; the hoops are close together.[1] Here also are two old iron guns, nine-pounders, bearing the shield of the Dutch East India Company. These guns are only for signals. A lookout-house is erected here, and a guard is always here from daylight to dark. It commands a vast range of vision, and a ship could in clear weather be seen some twenty miles off.

On my return I met a mountain priest,[2] one of a class whose vow binds him to ascend all mountains he can meet with. He bears a staff sur-

[1] These wooden mortars set upright are used to fire off " day fireworks " for signals or for amusement. *M. E.* p. 521. These " fire-flowers," which bloom in daylight, have been introduced at Coney Island and other summer pleasure places in America.

[2] Yamabushi. The sect was founded in the ninth century. Their history is given in Satow and Hawes' *Hand Book for Japan*, pp. 408, 412.

mounted with a circle of iron; within is a trident like that of Siva. Four loose rings are attached to the circle, two on each side; these make a jingling noise when the priest shakes his staff. I get forty-eight hundred of the small copper coin of Japanese for one dollar; ten of these given to the priest produced a long prayer and a great jingling of his rings. The priest was of a good pleasant countenance and very robust in appearance.

Saturday, October 25, 1856. The vice-governor visited me to-day. He borrowed the "Treaties of the United States with Foreign Nations" for the purpose of having it translated. It will be a heavy work for them, as they will have to do it by means of a dictionary in English and Dutch. The two Kamis,[1] who are Governors here, are to visit me on Thursday next.

I have visited the prison of Shimoda. It corresponds generally with Golownin's description of the prisons at Hakodaté and Matsmai, but what he calls cages are simply cells made of squared joists of timber placed some three inches apart. I am sure they are larger and not so solitary as the stone cells in the prisons of the United States. Imprisonment as a punishment for the Japanese is unknown: the punishments are either death or whipping, and the accused is only in prison until he can be tried. The Japanese code is somewhat

[1] Kami means superior or lord.

sanguinary. Death is inflicted for murder, arson, burglary, grand larceny, and for violent deportment towards a father. The parent cannot put his children to death, but on complaint of disobedience of his children the government will punish the child with whipping, or death, according to the nature of the offense. The Japanese declare that infanticide of legitimate children is unknown in Japan.[1] In cases where the parents are too poor to bear the incumbrance of an additional child the government makes an allowance to them for the purpose. Paupers are placed with their relatives and an allowance made for their support, but if the pauper goes out begging, the allowance ceases. There is no law to prohibit begging, and, in fact, it would be difficult to frame one in a country where all the priesthood, beside a large number of monks, hermits, and nuns, live solely on charity. There were three prisoners in the jail awaiting trial, two for gambling and one for a small larceny; they were to be tried to-day, and will either go home acquitted or else well whipped to-night. Whipping is inflicted with a small bamboo or rattan over the shoulders or back. The Japanese cannot understand our imprisonment for punishment.[2]

---

[1] See the actual facts, so different from this statement, in Professor Garret Dropper's paper on "The Population of Japan during the Tokugawa Era" in *T. A. S. J.* vol. xxiii.

[2] There are many more and larger prisons in Japan of the

They say for a man to be in a good house and have enough of food and clothing cannot be a punishment to a large portion of men, who only care for their animal wants and have no self-respect, and as they never walk for pleasure they cannot think it hard to be deprived of wandering about.

Monday, October 27, 1856. Took a walk over the hills and up the valley of Shimoda, making a circuit of some ten miles, part of it on the road to Yedo. This is simply a foot or bridle-path of some six to eight feet wide, and is only practicable on foot or on horseback. Every new walk I take shows me more and more of the patient industry of the Japanese, and creates new admiration of their agriculture, while the landscape from the top of the hills, overlooking the terraces rising one above another like the steps of a giant staircase, and running over the rich fields of the valley, and terminating with a glimpse of the blue water of the sea, forms a series of charming views which are well worthy the pencils of able artists. So far as buildings or monuments are concerned, there is nothing to mark the age of the country.

There are no venerable ivy-grown ruins; — no

Méiji era (1868–1895) as compared with the times when arrest, trial, decapitation, and burial often occurred on the same day, and when the death penalty was attached to over two hundred offenses. Prison reform is based on the best Western models, and penology is carefully studied.

temples bearing the marks of the tooth of time on their stones. The temples and houses are from necessity built from wood or bamboo wattles plastered with clay, as a stone edifice would be very dangerous in a country so frequently visited with violent earthquakes.[1]

In my rambles over the hills I have met with some proofs that Shimoda has been settled for many centuries, — I mean in the stone quarries.[2] The stone is a soft and light-colored sandstone which is easily wrought. In many places you see the face of the quarry in a smooth perpendicular wall, cut down in quarrying the stones. The great number of these quarries, their vast size, and the fact that the débris in many places is covered with trees of the largest size, all go to prove the antiquity of the place. This stone is used for foundations, for flagging, for ovens and cooking-places, for tombstones, for altars, for images, and, in fact, for all the purposes, except houses, to which stone can be applied. I see that some of it is shipped away to other places.

The cotton here is a second crop which springs up just before the first is taken from the ground;

---

[1] Though in recent years stone buildings have been numerously erected in Japanese cities, yet the injury done to them in earthquakes is greater than to wooden houses.

[2] Most of the new government buildings in Tōkiō have been built of Shimoda stone, which, at present, is the chief product of the port.

the stool and bolls are small, and the latter few in number, but the staple is long, strong, and fine. The hemp of Japan is probably the best in the world. It is water-rotted, and for this purpose a small rivulet is dammed up to give sufficient depth to immerse the hemp, which is neatly put up in cylindrical bales.

There is quite a number of water-mills on the principal stream of Shimoda. They are driven by undershot wheels, and are used for grinding rice, buckwheat, etc. Rice, being the staple food of the country, is of course the chief occupation of the mills. The water is sadly mismanaged, and a small increase of labor would convert many of the mills to an overshot power, but they appear to be either ignorant of the difference of power, or indifferent as to its application.

There are deer, wolves, hares, and wild monkeys among the hills of this place.

I was much moved to-day on finding in the woods a bachelor's-button. This humble flower, with its sweet perfume, brought up so many home associations that I was inclined to be homesick and miserable for the space of an hour.

I am now trying to learn Japanese. I have begun with some words to my servants, and can give them all the orders necessary for my attendance.

Wednesday, October 29, 1856. The Japanese

are much surprised to see me bathing in cold water,[1] and particularly when the thermometer stands at 50°, as it does this morning.

The Japanese are a clean people; every one bathes every day. The mechanic, day-laborers, — all, male and female, old and young, — bathe every day after their labor is completed. There are many public bath-houses in Shimoda. The charge is six sen, or the eighth part of one cent. The wealthy people have their baths in their own houses, but the working classes, all, of both sexes, old and young, enter the same bath-room, and there perform their ablutions in a state of perfect nudity.

Thursday, October 30, 1856. This will be remembered hereafter as an important day in the history of Japan.

The laws forbidding the Imperial Governor of a city to visit any foreigner at his residence is to-day to be broken, and I am to receive the two Governors with the vice-governor in a friendly and informal way.

They arrived about noon with a large suite, but

---

[1] "The charm of the Japanese system of hot bathing is proved by the fact that almost all the foreigners resident in the country abandon their cold tubs in its favor. There seems, too, to be something in the climate which renders hot baths healthier than cold. By persisting in the use of cold water one man gets rheumatism, a second gets fever, a third a never-ending continuance of colds and coughs. So nearly all end by coming round to the Japanese plan." *T. J.* p. 54.

only four came into my private apartments with the two Governors and vice-governor. The Governors were very anxious on the subject of coast surveys, and inquired where Lieutenant Rodgers [1] was, whether he would return here to survey, whether the American government had given orders for any new expedition to survey the coasts, etc., and if I knew what the English intended doing in the matter of surveys, etc., etc.

I told them that Lieutenant Rodgers had returned to the United States, that I did not know of any intended expedition here for a similar purpose, and that the English had no such squadron out here at present.

They wished me to promise to order off any vessels that might come here for such a purpose, but I told them that would be out of my power. I then informed them that the United States government and all the other governments of the world expended large sums in surveying their coasts and harbors, and that those surveys were published

[1] "Fighting John Rodgers," U. S. N., was born in Maryland in 1812, served in the Seminole and Mexican wars, and as commander of the Vincennes was from 1853 to 1856 in charge of the United States Surveying and Exploring Expedition to the North Pacific, China Sea, etc., which penetrated into the Arctic seas. See Habersheim's *The North Pacific Exploring Expedition*, Philadelphia, 1857. In the Civil War he commanded the Galena and monitor Weehawken in the battle with the ironclad Atlanta. He was made Rear-Admiral in 1869, and in 1871 commanded the Korean expedition. See *Korea, the Hermit Nation*, chapter xlvi.

with charts so that any nation in the world could have them; that the whole world was surveyed except Japan; that these surveys made many books, and that all shipmasters purchased these books, for they were sold freely to all, before they went on any voyage to a part of the world that was new to them; that all this was done for the security of ships, it being the great object of all civilized nations to encourage commerce, which, next to agriculture, was the great spring of prosperity of nations; that for the same reasons both America and England, as well as other nations, had hundreds of lighthouses on their coasts, and the channels leading into their harbors were carefully marked out with buoys, etc. All of this astonished them much, and appeared to remove some of their anxiety, although at the beginning they told me that it was a matter of life and death to them, as they must perform the hara-kiri or "happy dispatch"[1] (suicide) if the surveys went on.[2] Moriyama has

[1] The word hara-kiri, which means belly-cut, is rarely used by Japanese gentlemen, who prefer the term seppuku (opening of the abdomen) for the same reason that in our polite society we prefer the trisyllable of uncertain Latin to the homely Anglo-Saxon word. The custom, introduced possibly from the Malays, in vogue in the Middle Ages, developed into a privilege about the fifteenth century. It is now nearly but not wholly obsolete, cases being known even in 1894.

[2] Japan has now one of the best lighthouse systems in the world, with nearly one hundred and fifty lighthouses or lightships, and the Bureau of Hydrography ranks very high. Charts are cheap and excellent.

been fasting for some fifty days on this account, but he was so much consoled by what I said that he ate flesh meat most heartily. He thanked me warmly for my friendly deportment towards them, and got down on his knees and prayed fervently for my welfare. My company partook of my refreshments (which were prepared in our manner) without any hesitation, and by their eating showed their approval. They drank punch, brandy, whiskey, cherry bounce, champagne, and cordials, but the punch and champagne were their favorite drinks.

The last Governor warmed entirely, and showed himself, like the other Japanese, of a most genial temper. They did not eat or drink to excess in any respect, and their conduct during the whole visit was that of well-bred persons. I made the second Governor a present of a Colt's pistol of five discharges, with which he was much pleased. After staying about four hours, they took their leave with abundant thanks for my hospitality. This P. M. they brought me a leg of real venison; it is excellent, tender, juicy, and well flavored.

CHAPTER V.

THE VISIT OF THE RUSSIANS.

SATURDAY, November 8,[1] 1856. The Russian corvette Olivoutsa, Commodore Possiet [2] and Commander Korsanoff. She brought with her a schooner built by the Russians at the river Amoor, for the Japanese, and is a present, as I understand. The schooner is built on the same lines as the one before seen by me, and makes an aggregate of *five* schooners (all on the same model) now owned by the Japanese.

Commodore Possiet is the bearer of the ratified treaty made with Japan, and will probably remain here some weeks. I went on board the corvette soon after she anchored, and was much pleased with the officers. The corvette is a poor affair, old in age and older in model. She is armed with old-fashioned carronades, and looks to me like one of the old ships of the Russian American Company, although she now wears the Imperial flag. I was not saluted by the corvette. I also went on board the schooner; she has a pretty cabin, very hand-

---

[1] 9th by mistake, in the journal.
[2] After whom the Russian seaport near the Korean frontier, and the possible terminal of the trans-Siberian railway, is named.

THE VISIT OF THE RUSSIANS. 85

somely furnished; has oilcloth on the floor, tables of fine woods, and the hangings are of mazarine blue velvet. She is commanded by Lieutenant Kolaxaltsoff. I presume she is intended as a present on the exchange of ratifications.

Commodore Possiet promised me a copy of the Russian treaty with Japan, and in return I am to give him the American and Dutch treaties with Japan, and the treaty with Siam, which I made when at Bangkok.

Tuesday, November 11, 1856. Captains Possiet and Corasacoff, the lieutenant commanding the schooner, and three young officers dined with me to-day. Previous to this I had a visit from two of the young officers; they spoke French very well. I never passed a more agreeable evening. The Russians behaved like polished men of the world, and at my table they did not merit the charge so often brought against them of being hard drinkers. They ate with good appetites (and my dinner was both good and abundant) and took their wine in moderation. I do think the same number of American or English officers would have drunk twice the quantity of wine the Russians did. Captain Possiet informed me that the vice-governor told him that he wished him not to pay any money at present, for that the American consul-general had made a demand on the government to have a just value put on the dollar, and that they expected a favorable answer in a few days.

Captain Possiet brought me a copy of the Russian treaty with Japan, which I have had translated from the Dutch. He gave me a Dutch translation, and I shall send it to the Secretary of State.

Thursday, November 13, 1856. The Russians came on shore this morning early to arrange my flag-staff. The Captain Possiet paid me a visit quite alone. He desires that our visits should be without ceremony, and as between friends; that I should make myself at home with him, and he will do the same with me; all this I was quite willing to accede to. We had much conversation about the harbor of Shimoda, its insecurity, its small size, the incapacity of Shimoda to furnish supplies even to one ship of war, and the total absence of a commercial population. We agreed on the absolute necessity of an exchange of Shimoda for another port.

Captain Possiet gave me a copy of a letter he wrote, by order of Admiral Pontaitine, after the wreck of the Diana frigate, on the subject of the harbor of Shimoda, to the Japanese authorities.

Captain Possiet informs me that had the Diana not met with her misfortune, she would have examined a number of harbors on the east coast of Japan, and he is of opinion that an exchange would have been made of Shimoda for some more eligible place.

The Russian sailors finished work on my flag-staff about four P. M., when they left. I gave them a dinner, with plenty of brandy and tea, and I gave one dollar to each of the five men who were employed in the work.

Friday, November 14, 1856. I dined with Mr. Heusken on board the corvette Volutsa. Captain Possiet gave me a salute of thirteen guns, although by the rules of the Russian service a consul-general is saluted with eleven guns. Captain Possiet told me that he gave me thirteen guns so that I should not receive less than he gave the Japanese Governor of Shimoda. I passed a very agreeable evening. The more I see of the Russian officers the more I am pleased with them. They are polished in manner and are exceedingly well informed. There is scarcely one of them that does not speak two or more languages.

They speak in high terms of French generals and soldiers. They say the first have skill equal to any in the world, and the last are unsurpassed in military courage and enthusiasm. The English, on the contrary, they put directly opposite, — generals without skill, and men without one of the first requisites of a soldier, except mere bulldog courage; that to deprive an English army of its full supply of food and comfortable quarters is to demoralize it; that an English soldier dreads an attack on his belly more than a blow aimed at his head. A current remark at Sebastopol during the siege was, that A or B had been out on so many occasions of sorties. The question was instantly asked, Against which force? If against the English, the querist would shrug his shoulders and say, "That was nothing;" but if against the French he would say, "Ah! then you had something to do."

Constant conversations are held by Captain Possiet with the Japanese on the subject of finally and fully opening Japan to the commerce of the world. All agree that it is only a question of time, and Moriyama Yénoské goes so far as to place it less than three years distant.

All these things will help to prepare the way for me in my attempt to make a treaty which shall at once open Japan (at different dates for different ports) to our commerce.

Sunday, November 16, 1856. I regularly read the service of the "Protestant Episcopal Church of the United States" every Sunday. I am probably the first resident of Japan who ever used that service. How long will it be before that same service will be used in Japan in consecrated churches?

It is to me one of the pregnant facts that grow up daily under my observation, and which are the natural result of my residence here in a protected capacity.

Tuesday, November 18, 1856. I wrote to the Governor yesterday, urging a reply to my letters on the subject of the currency. To-day the vice-governor, a high official, and my old friend Moriyama Yénoské came to visit me. They apologize for their long absence, saying the arrival of the Russians had kept them much occupied, etc., etc. They brought me a cage containing six pretty tame pigeons, a present from the Governor, and they told me that he had written to Yedo expressly for them, as they are scarce in Japan.

I knew the visit of ceremony and the present were all a pretense, and that something else was behind, and a short time brought it out. They (as if casually) said my letter of yesterday to the Governor had been at once forwarded to Yedo by a "special post," and that as soon as an answer was received the Governor would let me know it. I told them I was happy to see them at all times, but I could not consent to receive verbal answers to or notices of my written communications. I told them that I knew that the Shōgun had written at least two letters to the King of Holland; that the high officers of Japan had written more than thirty letters to the Russians within the last two years; and that numerous letters had been written also to Captain Fabius of the Dutch steam frigate Medusa, when he was here; that I could not consent to be treated with less formality than they had shown to the Russians and Dutch, and therefore I must insist on written answers to my letters.

Saturday, November 22, 1856. The Russians have presented to the Japanese all the guns that were on board the frigate Diana. They consist of 18 short 24-pounders, 30 long 24-pounders, 4 Paixhan 68-pounders, shell guns.

The Russians are assisting the Japanese in getting up all the fittings necessary for mounting the guns properly, such as screws, quoins, etc., etc., etc., all of which were lost when the Diana sunk.

Monday, November 24, 1856. The Go-yosho people came to inform me that my Chinese cook and tailor went to the apothecary's shops in Shimoda yesterday and asked for opium,[1] and were told they had none; but the Chinese characters being on the drawers, they discovered it, and demanded it in my name, and with a show of violence. They took the whole they found in two shops, which was all the opium there was in Shimoda. They said to me that opium was only used as a medicine, and that it was unjust that two men should have the whole of it, particularly as it was not wanted for medical purposes; they respectfully asked that I would order the Chinese to

---

[1] Opium-smoking has been forbidden under very severe penalties by the Japanese government, and the importation of the drug except for medicinal purposes is not allowed. Laudanum is sold under the Japanized Dutch name of Rauda there being no "l" in Japanese.

THE VISIT OF THE RUSSIANS. 91

restore the greater part of it. I gave orders that the whole should be taken from them. Mr. Heusken got a lump of some six ounces from the tailor, but the cook had dissolved his in water to refine it, in the Chinese way, so as to make it fit for smoking, and refused to give it up. I went to him myself. He was very surly, and after some time brought me a dish containing a small quantity of sediment and water. I demanded the filtered liquid, and it was not until I had given him his choice between a prison and the surrender of the drug that he gave it up. The lump was restored to the Japanese, but they said they could do nothing with the solution, so that was thrown away. I directed the officers to tell the shopkeepers that my people were not to be supplied with opium, saké,[1] or any kind of intoxicating beverage.

Tuesday, November 25, 1856. Evacuation Day in New York. What recollection of my "soldier life" this day brings up, my marching up and down Broadway, Bowery, Hudson Street, Greenwich Street to the Battery, to the Park, and there firing off "real guns," as Mr. Mantalini said.

Wednesday, November 26, 1856. Moriyama Yénoské came to see me, as he said, with a message from the Governor. Three horses have been offered, but none suit the Japanese; one is too old

---

[1] Rice-beer. By distillation, liquors of high alcoholic strength may be obtained.

and clumsy, one too young and vicious, the third is too ill-looking for me.

The Governor is a good judge of a horse, and has promised to select one that will suit. He says he is responsible for my personal safety to both the American and Japanese governments, and if I should be killed by a vicious horse, he would have to perform the hara-kiri. I told Yénoské that I should be satisfied with any horse the Governor might select, etc. Commodore Possiet and Mr. Heusken took a walk southwest from Shimoda, and were followed by a Gobangoshi.[1] The Commodore in a decided and stern manner ordered him to go about his business and not to follow him, and the man left them. But soon afterwards he reappeared, and pertinaciously kept with them. The Commodore then seized the man, and gave him a thorough shaking, and when he was released the Gobangoshi started off running like a deer, and no more appeared.

Monday, December 1, 1856. Visit the corvette, but am soon interrupted by a lot of Japanese officials who came to see the Commodore on the subject of boat landings. Commodore Perry's additional articles provided that certain landing-places should be provided at Shimoda and Hakodaté, and

---

[1] Goshi were independent farmers who owned their own land, but in time of war or public danger aided the feudal lord of the country with personal service.

the Japanese now wish to confine us to landing at these places alone. I resist the proposition, as does the Commodore.

In order to have a clear understanding about the orders I give, I have procured a book in which I write every order, and there are columns left in which to enter the name of the interpreter to whom the order was given, with the date of it, and another column for the date at which it was executed. By this means I shall know whether my orders have been given by Mr. Heusken or forgotten by him, and also whether the interpreter neglects them after he has received them. So far it works to a charm, and I have had more done in the last two days than in the previous fortnight.

Friday, December 5, 1856. The Commodore sends me word that the ratified treaties are to be exchanged on Sunday next, and invites me to "assist" on the occasion.

I must regret that I cannot attend. I am suffering from a very severe cold and great hoarseness; but the most important reason is, that I cannot consistently "assist" in any such matter on a Sunday. From the time of my arrival I have refused to attend to any kind of business on that day; and after a short time the Japanese ceased to ask it of me. Should I now join the Russians, I shall contradict all my previous acts on this account, and lose my character for *consistency*, a point that cannot be too carefully watched in dealing with people like the Japanese. They delight to convict a man of inconsistency.

Sunday, December 7, 1856. The corvette fired a salute as the Commodore landed about eleven A. M., and at one fired a salute of twenty-one guns in honor of the exchange of ratifications. The Russian, American, and Japanese flags were hoisted from the three masts from noon until sunset. After the exchange was completed, the Commodore and the Japanese commissioners proceeded to the place where the guns of the frigate Diana were placed.

The guns had been neatly furbished up, and a double guard of honor composed of Russians and Japanese was mounted over them. The guns were then formally presented to the Japanese; the commissioners then attended the Commodore to the corvette, where they received a salute and a dinner, and thus completed the ceremonies of the day.

Monday, December 8, 1856. The third Governor, Moriyama, and some others visited me to-day. After kind messages and inquiries on behalf of the Governors, they said they had been ordered to inform me of the exchange of ratifications, etc. Moriyama was quite communicative and oracular; said that a great change was impending in Japanese affairs, as it relates to foreign intercourse, and that it would surprise all when it took place, from its suddenness, etc., etc.

The Governor and Moriyama told me that the largest Japanese vessels were about two hundred tons burden, and that, enumerating all vessels of sixty tons up to two hundred tons, the aggregate number was about one hundred thousand!!! [1] This aggregate was so astounding that I made them repeat it in different forms, so that I might be sure there was no misunderstanding as to their meaning; but they all adhered to it, remarking that if they had counted all their craft of fifty tons down to fishing-boats the number would be enormous.

They said they had seen seven hundred junks, all over sixty tons, in Shimoda harbor at one time! If their figures be correct, the tonnage of Japan exceeds that of any nation in the world.

Tuesday, December 9, 1856. Up at seven A. M. to go on board the corvette to see the Commodore before he meets the Japanese to-day on the subject

[1] The official statistics from 1873 to 1879 show the number of Japanese junks with a capacity of over 500 koku (roughly, about 2500 bushels) to have been 21,156, 21,147, 19,208, 18,420, 17,387, 17,614, 17,755, respectively. Those of over 500 koku capacity show annually decreasing figures, from 1536 in 1873 to 1369 in 1879. From 1885 the building of junks of less than 600 koku capacity has been forbidden. In 1892 besides 643 steamers and 778 sailing-vessels in European form, there were 18,193 junks and 585,456 fishing-smacks, sail, scull, and row boats of all descriptions. It is not probable that Japan ever possessed over half the tonnage reported to Mr. Harris.

of the currency. I got him to agree that he would refuse to pay except on the basis I had named, viz., one dollar to pass for three bus, that he would pay that amount to them, and, if they were dissatisfied, he would place the difference in my hands, until the arrival of a Russian consul, to await the final settlement of the question. I am much pleased with this, as it will greatly strengthen my demands for the adjustment of the question. Am told the corvette will leave on Friday next, and am invited to dine with them for the last time on Thursday next.

Thursday, December 11, 1856. Send my tailor on board the Russian corvette. He had the impudence to ask me to give him a good character! Who can ever hope to fathom the want of moral principle in a Chinese?

The weather is the most lovely ever seen at this season of the year in a similar latitude; the sky is as blue as a sapphire.

My black pet hen commenced to incubate on the 9th instant, therefore I shall look for some chicks from her about New Year's Day.

Sunday, December 14, 1856. The corvette went to sea early this morning. The Commodore paid one third of the Japanese bill for pilotage and boat hire, and sent the other two thirds to me to await the final settlement of their accounts.

CHAPTER VI.

THE FIRST SKIRMISH OF A LONG BATTLE.

THURSDAY, December 18, 1856. To-day the vice-governor called, and being anxious to settle the question of the guards I admitted him. I demanded the immediate removal of the people who have been in my Compound from the day of my arrival. The vice-governor said he would report it to the Governor. I complained that the shopkeepers of Shimoda would not sell anything to my people, or even give the prices. I added that I had before complained of this, and had been promised redress, but things went on just as they did before. I also demanded ten silver bus to make presents to my Japanese servants on Christmas Day, according to the custom of my country. The vice-governor said that orders to the shopkeepers should again be given; as to the bus, he must report that to the Governors.

Saturday, December 20, 1856. At last my horse has arrived. It is not a high-mettled racer, but will answer my purpose. The price is nineteen kobangs, about twenty-six dollars. The saddle and bridle are real curiosities, and cost thirty kobangs, about forty-two dollars, or about sixty per cent. more than the horse! The groom to attend the horse costs me seven bus per month, about one dollar and seventy-five cents. The horse is shod with *straw sandals*, which last about an hour on the road.

Monday, December 22, 1856. I am refused the bus. I am told I must give orders on the Go-yosho and the money will be paid to the bearer of the order. I reply that such a proposition is offensive, and must not be renewed, and I do not get the money. I renew my complaint about the guards, and demand their immediate removal. I am told it must be referred to Yedo for settlement.

Tuesday, December 23, 1856. Mr. Heusken walked out to-day alone and unarmed. On the road he met a Japanese wearing a coat of arms on his sleeve.[1] As soon as he saw Mr. Heusken he flourished a long stick he had in a threatening manner, and then drew his sword, which was also flourished. Mr. Heusken at first halted, and then, being unarmed, turned back. I directed him never to go out unarmed again.

Thursday, December 25, 1856. Merry Christmas! how happy are those who live in lands where these joyous greetings can be exchanged! As for me, I am sick and solitary, living, as one may say,

[1] The samurai or two-sworded gentry wore their clan or family crest on the back, breasts, and sleeves of their haori or coat.

in a prison; a large one it is true, but still a prison.

Friday, December 26, 1856. Moriyama Yénoské has gone to Yedo to see about the currency question, and to try to hurry a decision. I have given notice that I will not allow any spies to come into my presence, or even on my premises; that when they wish to see me I will only receive the principals and interpreters, excluding spies and secretaries. The Japanese term for spy is "*a looker across.*" [1]

Wednesday, December 31, 1856. The last day of the year! How many events of great importance to me have occurred during this year! I am very low-spirited from ill-health, and from the very slow progress I am making with the Japanese. However, I must keep up my spirits and hope for the best. My pet hen has presented me with five chicks, the merest mites of chickens ever seen.

January 1, 1857. Happy New Year! What a busy day in dear old New York. What universal joy appears on the faces that throng the streets, each hurrying along to get through "his list of calls." [2]

[1] Ométsŭké from *o* honorific, *mé* the eye, *tsŭké*, apply or fix; hence the odd translations "cross-eyed men," or "eye-appliers." They were the censors, spies, "doubles" required by the abnormal system of government under the Shōguns. *M. E.* p. 295.

[2] It is highly probable that the custom of calling on friends at New Year's Day was introduced into New Netherland by the

It is a good custom, and one that I hope will never be given up. How many friendships are then renewed which, without the occurrence of this day of "oblivion of neglect," would otherwise die a natural death. I pass the day in calling, in imagination, on my friends; but as to Japan, not a soul has darkened my door. I could only exchange greetings with Mr. Heusken, and present my Chinese servants with the expected *cumshaw*.[1] All my New Years since Christmas, 1849, were passed in the same places as my Christmases, except New Year's Day of 1855, which was at Benares, in Northwestern India. The preceding Christmas was at Calcutta.

Saturday, January 3, 1857. Assam, my [Chinese] butler, goes to Shimoda — is refused a few cakes he wished to buy for refreshment.

Monday, January 5, 1857. Vice-governor calls to say that orders have been given to all shopkeepers to give prices, or sell anything my people may ask for. I asked when those orders were given. He said they have been frequently given, but were specially renewed eight days ago. I then told him what had occurred on Saturday, and added

Dutch from Japan, where the renewal of friendships and hospitality is an age-old institution. Until 1872 the Japanese used the Chinese or lunar calendar, which in 1857 made the end of the year fall on January 25, and New Year's Day on January 26.

[1] The Chinese or pidgin (business)-English pronunciation of "commission."

that I did not believe one word they said; that it was an infraction of the treaty, etc., etc. I also told him that I demanded the instant removal of the guards, that their presence made me in reality a prisoner, and was a gross outrage and open violation of the treaty.

The poor vice-governor shook in every joint, and the perspiration streamed from his forehead and that of the interpreter. I also complained of the insult to Mr. Heusken, and demanded the arrest and punishment of the offender. The vice-governor begged me to believe that everything should be done to give me satisfaction that lay in their power, that they wished to keep the treaty faithfully, and that he would hurry over to the Governor at once, etc., etc.

Tuesday, January 6, 1857. Invited to meet the Governors at the Go-yosho to-morrow. Although quite ill, I consented.

Wednesday, January 7, 1857. Went to the Go-yosho at noon, and there met the two Kami, — the two Governors of Shimoda; the two vice-governors were present also, but *no secretaries.*

The business commenced by the Governors informing me that they had been directed to give an answer to my letter of October 25 to the Minister of Foreign Affairs. I inquired if it was a written answer? They said it was not. I told them I must decline any verbal answer delivered by a third person to a written letter from me. They asked if I objected to their rank. I told them no. They told me that the laws of Japan forbade the writing of letters to foreigners. I told them I knew better; that letters had been written by the highest officials, and even by the Emperor himself to Commodore Perry, to the Russians, and to the Dutch; that to assert such palpable falsehoods was to treat me like a child, and that if they repeated it I should feel myself insulted. They did not open any other matter. I then repeated what I had told the vice-governor on the 5th about the guards and the shops, and enlarged upon it, telling them that it was not only a breach of the treaty, but a violation of the laws of nations, and that my government would never submit to such treatment.

The Governors were in great trouble; they gave me their private word of honor that the complaints about the shopkeepers should be instantly attended to, and begged me to wait until they could write to Yedo about the officers which are stationed at my house; that I mistook their nature; that they were there simply to protect me against intrusion from the Japanese; that the Shimoda people were very rude, and would be sure to give me cause of offense, if the officers were not there to keep them away; and closed by saying they had no power to remove the officers, but must refer to Yedo.

FIRST SKIRMISH OF A LONG BATTLE. 103

In reply, I told them they could not disguise the fact of my being under guard by a mere change of name; that I had no fears of the Shimoda people, who I knew were friendly when not under the eyes of their officials; that I would not consent to the delay of one day longer as to the guards; that more than three months had elapsed since I had requested their removal; and, finally, so long as they remained, I declared I should consider myself a prisoner and would not leave the Compound, and that I would write to my government the manner in which they had treated me.

The trouble of the Governors increased. Finally, they told me the officers should be removed. "When?" said I. "Very soon," was the reply. "How many days?" They hesitated. I repeated firmly, that now I had so strongly brought the matter up, and that they had consented to the removal of the guards, that every day they remained was a new outrage, and they must abide the consequences. They then said that the officers should be removed to-morrow. Knowing their duplicity, I told them the removal must be real and not nominal; they must not post them near or even in sight of my house; that if they made any such attempt I should consider it an aggravation of the wrong already done me. They assented to the justice of my remarks, and said the officers should be brought back to the Go-yosho.

They then said they hoped I would not, at what had passed, interrupt the good feelings heretofore existing between us; that they were most anxious to give me every proof of their friendship, etc., etc.

I told them they had a queer way of showing friendship and hospitality; that I had been in the country four months and a half, and had never yet been invited to enter the house of a Japanese, and that they had even refused to dine with me on my New Year's Day, making a flimsy excuse; that in my country New Year's Day was kept as it is in Japan, by friendly visits, etc., etc., but not a single Japanese came near me on that day, and closed by saying that in America such conduct would be called inhospitable.

I then asked if the man that threatened Mr. Heusken had been arrested. They said they did not know who it was, therefore they could not arrest him. I told them the person was one of a small class; that he had a crest on his clothes, and wore a sword, and that if they did not arrest him I should have a right to think the person was acting either under direct orders from them, or according to their secret wishes, adding that hereafter we should go out armed, and any insult would be promptly punished by us, since they were either unable or unwilling to punish such persons.

I then remarked, that with such a system of

espionage as they had, I well knew that everything that occurred to us in our walk was reported to them.

I then inquired about the currency question, and received the old reply, " waiting for decision from Yedo." I told them that it had the appearance of a determination on their part to postpone the question indefinitely; they eagerly assured me that it was their wish to close the matter as speedily as possible. So, after four hours of stormy debate, I went home, where I was agreeably surprised to find the officers and guard packing up to leave, and in effect they did leave in the evening. So much for showing them a bold face.

Thursday, January 8, 1857. Quite ill. Write a letter to Minister of Foreign Affairs about the verbal answer offered to me. One of the Governors goes to Yedo to-day; I suppose in consequence of the flare-up of yesterday. I am determined to take firm ground with the Japanese. I will cordially meet any real offers of amity, but words will not do. *They are the greatest liars on earth.*[1]

[1] Mr. Harris, in his later journals, in his public and private letters, and in his conversations with his friends and with the editor, showed that he never included the Japanese people under such a sweeping generalization. On the contrary, he praised highly the common folks for their honesty and the government for keeping its plighted word when given in treaty form.

Thursday, January 15. Ill, ill, ill. I am constantly wasting away in flesh. I am most careful in my diet, but all is of no avail. What it is that ails me I cannot say. I left Penang on the 2d of April last, and am now forty pounds lighter than I then was. We are well supplied with wild boar's hams, some venison, plenty of fine golden pheasants, and large and good hares.

Sunday, January 18, 1857. First snow seen on the hilltops. I cannot sleep, nor can I study. I have laid aside the Japanese entirely. My reading is unsatisfactory; I have a craving for something I cannot define.

Thursday, Friday, and Saturday, January 26, 27, 28. Festival of the Japanese New Year; every one released from labor; all in their best clothes; faces shining with saké, and everybody paying visits of ceremony to everybody. Persons of rank put on their kami-shimo,[1] or dress of ceremony, on these occasions. I went on Thursday to see the decorations of the houses. Evergreens, rice in the straw, oranges, and radishes, were festooned about the front of every house; before each house was a piece of cypress branch planted in the ground to represent a tree, while at the base of the tree a quantity of firewood, some fourteen inches

---

[1] Literally, "High-low," a dress in old Japan corresponding to our "evening dress," worn alike by high officers, multi-millionaires, and by waiters and barbers.

long, was set on end, forming a bulk of some seven feet in circumference. The fuel was kept in its place by straw ropes. At some houses, wheat straw was neatly twisted into the form of a cornucopia ; in others, the universal shoe of Japan, *i. e.*, a straw sandal, was hung up. Every one appeared under the influence of saké, while but few were intoxicated and none quarrelsome.

Saturday, January 31, 1857. To-day closes the first month of the year. I wish I could say that my health and spirits were as good as the weather is fine.

Saturday, February 21. One of the Governors of Shimoda calls on me on his return from Yedo. After the usual compliments, he presented me with two pieces of Japanese crape, a really good article, and a Japanese sword! It was in a common white wood scabbard, and had a handle to slip on of the same, in fact, was simply a packing-case. He told me the blade was one he had worn for some years ; that it was by the first sword-maker of Japan. [He said] that, having procured another blade, he had shifted the scabbard and mountings to it, and therefore presented me with the blade ; that no foreigner had ever before obtained such a blade.

To all this I made the required replies. The blade is really a superb one, and has the "shark-teeth mark" the whole length of it. This, I am told, is not a mere surface mark, but extends through the metal, like the pamoin in some Malay krisses.¹

The Governor invited me to visit him and his colleague at their private residence, — which I accepted. He then asked me if I would have European or Japanese cookery. I selected the latter. So I am at last to see the inside of their residence.

Tuesday, February 24,² 1857. Norimonos were sent at nine this morning, but I did not leave until eleven, when I proceeded with quite a train of attendants. The norimono is a horrible affair. The only position you can assume is to sit on your heels,³ Japanese fashion, or else cross-legged. It is only four feet long, and about three and a half feet high. I was received with all formality by the two Governors in an anteroom; I was then conducted to an inner apartment furnished with seats [and] brasiers. After drinking a cup of tea, and

---

[1] An examination of the historical, chemical, and metallurgical relations between the Japanese and Malay iron and steel weapons, as well as a comparative study of suicide (hara-kiri), should be made.

[2] For February 23, see further on.

[3] Japanese surgeons think that this habit of sitting in a way that prevents proper circulation of the blood in the lower limbs, continued during ages, and in individuals often for hours at a time, is the chief cause of the short-leggedness of the Japanese. While their bodies are of normal dimensions, they are from a half inch to two inches short in the parts below the *symphisis pubis*.

FIRST SKIRMISH OF A LONG BATTLE. 109

smoking three whiffs of tobacco, I was then conducted to the room of my entertainment. This room, out of compliment to me, was furnished with seats and tables. On the table before me were pipes, tobacco, [and] a brasier. My seat was on the left of the Governor and close to the toko [1] or sacred place, and consequently the seat of honor.

The meal consisted of fish cooked in every possible Japanese way, and fish raw, the latter cut from a large fish which was brought to me to see. It was in a large dish, decorated with a mast and sail, the colors of the latter indicating welcome. A *paté* made of lobster was very nice. Sweet potatoes and radishes served up in various forms were the vegetables. Contrary to my expectations, neither rice nor bread was served with the dishes. Some ten courses were served, all brought to me in wooden cups brightly lacquered. On a table placed across the foot of the room was a dwarfed cedar-tree, decorated with storks cut out of radish, and neatly colored; these were fastened to the tree

---

[1] The toko-no-ma, literally, bedroom, or place of the couch, is an alcove which is believed to have been anciently either the raised sleeping-bench along the wall as still seen in the Aino hut, or the kang over the warmed flues seen in a Chinese or Korean house. In modern times the toko-no-ma is the alcove in which the sword-rack rests, ornamental shelves are set, pictures hung, and works of art kept. It is usually raised a few inches above the floor. See Morse's *Japanese Homes*.

by springs of twisted wire, which continued in motion for a long time. Flowers also, both real and artificial, were used to decorate the dishes of cakes, bonbons, etc., etc., which were also placed on this table. I was told the storks were a wish for my longevity, and that the various flowers had a complimentary meaning in them. After all the fish dishes were done, rice was served, without salt or any other condiment. Saké was the beverage, but I plead ill-health, and only drank tea.

When the heavy part of the meal was over, the Governor had brought to him the prettiest toy tea-making apparatus I ever saw. It was in a neat plain wooden case, which, when opened, displayed a tiny furnace for boiling water, teapot and cups, a jar of tea, mats for the teapot and cups, a scoop for the tea, and a curious machine for heating the tea over the fire before it is put in the water. My host then proceeded to boil the water, measure and heat the tea, place it in pot, pour on the boiling water, and then pour out a cup and hand it to me with his own hands, whereat all the Japanese fell into immense admiration. Then the matter was expounded to me, that the making of tea by the Governor, and serving it with his own hands, was a proof of friendship only given to those of exalted character and position, and I was requested to view it in that light, whereupon I agreed so to regard it. Then the Governor requested my acceptance of the whole concern, as a proof of his great regard, and this was also agreed to.[1]

The conversation now took the usual Japanese turn. The lubricity of these people passes belief; the moment business is over, the one and only subject on which they dare converse comes up. I was asked a hundred different questions about American females; I will not soil my paper with the greater part of them.

I was asked if their people could receive some instruction in beating the drum when the next man-of-war came. I replied I had no doubt the commander would be willing to gratify them on that point; they said they had brass drums copied from the Dutch; they asked me about the various signals given by beat of drum, which I answered as well as I could; then — oh, shame! . . . I gladly took my leave at three P. M., and reached home quite jaded out.

Monday, February 23, 1857. I applied to the Japanese to fire a salute for me on Washington's Birthday; but, as it fell on Sunday, I wished the salute to be on Monday. This was agreed to, and this morning they sent over two handsome brass howitzers exactly copied in every respect from one Commodore Perry gave them. Every appointment about the gun, down to the smallest particular, was

---

[1] The ceremony of cha no yu, here described, has a voluminous native literature for its illustration.

exactly copied, percussion locks, drag-ropes, powder or cartridge holder, and all. The cartridges were made of paper, and for wads they used wood. The firing was good, quite as good as I have seen among civilized persons. Judging from the report, their powder is much better than that of the Chinese or Siamese. The Japanese say they have made one thousand howitzers like those used at the salute!

Wednesday, February 25, 1857. Met the Governors at the Go-yosho at noon to-day. They brought in, with great ceremony, a box, which was reverentially placed before me. Then a vice-governor opened the box, which I found contained five pieces of a very poor satin damask, which I was told was from five members of the Regency at Yedo, one piece from each person. This over, another box was brought, which, as I was told, contained an answer to my two letters to Yedo, and at last they mustered courage to open it and unfold a sheet of paper about five feet long by eighteen inches wide, written quite full, and bearing the seals and signatures of the following princes, who are members of the Regency, with a Dutch translation of the same, which they placed in Mr. Heusken's hands: —

Hotta, Bitchiu no Kami.　Abé, Isé no Kami.
Makino, Bizen no Kami.　Kuzé, Yamato no Kami.
Naito, Kii no Kami.

I directed Mr. Heusken to put the letter and translation in the box and close it. The Governors wished me to have it translated into English at once. This I declined, saying I should prefer having it done at leisure, and that in the mean time I should like to hear their answer on the currency question.

Now ensued a scene, quite Japanese, which occupied full two hours. The substance of it was that they admitted the justice of my demand in part, but said my offer (five per cent.) to pay for recoining was not sufficient; that they should lose by it, and they therefore begged me to reconsider it, and make them an increased offer. I asked them what was the cost of coining money in Japan. They gravely replied twenty-five per cent. Twenty-five per cent.! I told them it was simply impossible; that the cost in Europe and America for such labor was not one per cent.; that I would bring competent moneyers from the United States, who would do the whole work for five per cent., and even less. They said the laws of Japan forbade the employment of foreigners about their coinage.

I endeavored to elicit a direct offer from them, but without success. Among other statements made by them was this, — that gold and silver, before coinage, had no value; that it was the mint stamp that gave it its value, etc. I told them their government had an undoubted right to deal with the precious metals produced in Japan as they pleased, but they had no such right over a foreigner, and that to attempt to exercise such a right over him would, in effect, be a confiscation of his property; that they might stamp pieces of paper or leather, and compel their own subjects to take them in lieu of gold and silver, but they could not expect the foreigner to take them in exchange for his merchandise, or to have his coins measured by the intrinsic value of such worthless tokens.

This ground was traveled over and over again, the Japanese always reasoning in a circle, and trying to gain their point by simple pertinacity. I passed four weary hours, and left at four P. M., appointing the next day to meet again.

On reaching home, Mr. Heusken translated the Dutch copy of the letter, and I found it to be a simple announcement that all business was to be transacted with the Governors of Shimoda or Hakodaté, and not one word in reference to the President's letter to the Emperor of Japan, of which I told them I was the bearer.[1]

[1] Here end the records in "Journal No. 3," commencing July 7, 1856, ending February 25, 1857.

CHAPTER VII.

THE POLITICAL SITUATION. — A CHAPTER OF EXPLANATION.

To save further explanations and to make Mr. Harris's records more intelligible, let us here note the forces and the lines of battle. It is no disgrace to Japanese men of to-day that he so often calls attention to the blackness of moral darkness that overshadowed nearly all government dealings in the Japan of the Anséi Era. Nevertheless, it is even yet true that the two things most noticed and condemned by Mr. Harris, lying and licentiousness, are still the national sins. Both for politeness's sake and for trivial reasons, much intellect is wasted in calling white black and black white, while official statistics show one divorce to every three marriages as still the rule. In Mr. Harris's day, the very government itself, being a fraud, built on lies, and liable at any moment to totter to its fall, needed a buttressing of falsehood to hold it up and stave off the crash. Hence the originality, ingenuity, and energy shown in prevarication painfully impressed the American envoy. His record of their lies is appalling. It seemed to him a dissipation of a mental power much better put to use in other directions, while the mass and toughness of the fabrications resembled masonry.

Compelled by the force of circumstances to make the Perry treaty, the Yedo government had relapsed into slumber, only to be rudely awakened in pettish ill-humor by the promptness of the Americans. Besides, the more wily ones had expected, after making the treaty, to be able to nullify it by their choice of distant or worthless ports. It was not at first that Mr. Harris discovered, what all along the Yedo officers knew, that Shimoda was nearly useless for foreign commerce. Open to the sea, it was shut in by ranges of high hills, and lay near the end of a barren promontory, remote from trade, highways, and markets. Its chief use now is as a stone-quarry for the public buildings in Tōkiō.

In glancing at the historical situation, the dwarf of to-day can see further than could the giant of a generation ago. The more Japanese history is studied the more is it seen to be but slightly bizarre, peculiar, or anomalous, and the more is it analogous to that of Europe. Sprung, in all probability, from two distinct stocks, the Malay islanders and the immigrants from the Asiatic highlands, the primitive men of Nippon brought with them the rude feudalism which was common to both Korea and Malaysia. The clan of Yamato, becoming paramount over the other inhabitants of Hondo, or the main island, exalted their chief to the rank of the gods. They quelled the Ainos and their aboriginal neighbors with bolts and blades of dogma as well as of iron. It was superior theology as well as improved weapons that won the day in central Japan.[1] In the seventh century the introduction from China of the centralized system of imperialism, with standing armies, codes of law, boards of government at the capital, and civil governors sent out to the provinces to rule conjointly with the military magistrates, brought the remotest ends of Hondo, Yezo, Shikoku, and Kiushiu under the sway of the Awful Gate, or Mikado. These centuries, from the seventh to the twelfth, of the undivided rule of the Emperor — despite the fact that in later generations the Fujiwara, Taira, and other noble families practically barred access to the Mikado, monopolized power and office, and dictated nominations to the throne — are looked upon as the golden age of Japan. Even in this year of grace 1895, or, in the purely mythical chronology of the Japanese empire, the twenty-five hundred and fifty-fourth, and of actual history possibly the sixteen hundredth, a native philosopher, in an elaborate treatise on ethics, makes the central principle of all morals Loyalty to the Throne.

[1] See *The Religions of Japan.* New York, 1895.

In Roman history the development of the Pretorium, which made and deposed emperors and dictated the policy of the empire, has a striking parallel in the Bakufu, or Shōgunate, by which Japan was, with a few brief intervals, governed from A. D. 1184 to 1868. The word pretorium meant, first of all, a general's tent; and so did the word bakufu, from baku, a curtain, such as was used to mark off the general's headquarters, and fu, authority or government. In time, this tent inclosed and overshadowed all Japan. The typical product of Japanese architecture, the yashiki; or clan-caravansary, of which Yedo was full, was but a wooden tent. Kamakura first, and then Yedo, was the camp city of the Japanese pretorian guard. The Shōgun's central castle, girt with moats and masonry, was surrounded by the wooden tents of his vassals. The Camp and the Throne, Yedo and Kiōto, Shōgun and Emperor, divided the political and moral assets of the nation; the former holding the purse and sword, the latter monopolizing divinity and honors.

In theory, all the land belonged to the Mikado, but parallel with the development of duarchy was that of feudalism. After the civil magistracies of the Middle Ages had been swallowed up in the military offices (created by Yoritomo soon after his own appointment as Shōgun, 1192 A. D.), the next step was to turn districts into

THE POLITICAL SITUATION. 119

fiefs, and the next to make the feudal allotments hereditary in the families of the Shōgun's nominees. The force of feudalism could no further go when these fiefs were parceled out by the Shōgun without reference to the Mikado's will, and this Iyéyasŭ did in 1604 and later. He further so distributed the lands of his kinsmen and most loyal vassals that the eighteen jealous princes of ancient fame and continuing power, and the other daimiōs who held land and rule before Iyéyasŭ's time, could never combine to overthrow the Shōgunate, or Yedo Pretorium.

On the chessboard of Japan, the master-move, or "king's hand," has always been to get possession of the Mikado and issue edicts in the name of the Son of Heaven. For two hundred and fifty years, because of the iron hand of Iyéyasŭ and his successors, none had been able to make that move. Further, the country had been so long at peace, under the system which seemed fixed forever, that most people forgot that things had ever been different. Not only was feudalism, with its two foci at Yedo and Kiōto coextensive with the whole empire, but in intensiveness its influence permeated every department of life, even morals and religion.[1] The Mikado, whom none except a few august nobles of the court had ever seen, whose

[1] See this assertion abundantly justified in Dr. G. W. Knox's papers in *T. A. S. J.* vol. xx., and in *The Religions of Japan.*

feet never touched the ground, whose palace was a miya, or temple, and his capital and capitol a miya-ko, whose countenance was a "dragon's," who was a son of the gods, all men loved. The Shōgun, whose iron hand every man, woman, and child felt and feared, was the one to be reverently obeyed. This was Japanese politics and religion for centuries.

With foreigners and all the world excluded by edict, with "the evil sect called Christian" extirpated, with the millions of Japan included and made *adscripti glebæ* by feudal law and by the reduction to ashes of all seaworthy ships, by a ban laid on travel to other lands, and by death pronounced upon both passenger abroad and Christian within, Japan was isolated from the shock of change.

The apparition of Perry's fleet had indeed been a nightmare; yet even with two ports open to the "ugly" and "hairy" foreigners, was it not possible to keep things as they were? Could not the aliens' eyes be blinked, the veil be kept over Kiōto, and the Mikado still float on "purple clouds" as the "spiritual" emperor only, and the mystery-play be continued? This, on the Japanese side, and from the Yedo point of view, was the problem and set scheme laboriously contrived and vigilantly maintained.

This pretorian purpose might have succeeded

had there been no students or thinkers in Japan. Unfortunately for the Pretorium at Yedo, men studied history, pondered and wrote, and the pen proved mightier than the sword. In reality, even while Townsend Harris was at Shimoda, could he have had the statistics of men imprisoned, tortured, banished, beheaded, or compelled to commit hara-kiri for uttering the truth; could he have seen the list of books purged by the censors, or confiscated and suppressed by the Yedo government; could he have seen the eager students furtively copying with wearisome labor English and Dutch books at peril of reputation and life, while even those who would study philosophy, introduce new arts, sciences, or weapons of war, jeoparded their lives, — his eyes would have been opened as were the lad's at Dothan. He would have seen that even the later assassinations and incendiarisms were wrought by men loyal to the Mikado, who hoped, by embroiling the Bakufu with foreign nations, to hasten its fall.

Mr. Harris was the bearer of a letter from the President of the United States addressed to "the Emperor" in Yedo. To the American envoy, the idea of there being two Emperors, one "spiritual" and the other "temporal," a figment of the government interpreters, was not perplexing. Such an arrangement was implied in the Perry Treaty, and had apparently a close analogy in Siam. A critical student might wonder at two suns in the same system, yet, considering that both sun and moon furnished light, ask which was the fire and which the reflector, Kiōto or Yedo? Later (November 20, 1857) Mr. Harris wrote: "Among the mysteries of this mysterious land, none is more puzzling to me than this Mikado. The Japanese negotiators spoke of him in almost contemptuous terms during the course of our discussions, and yet he appears to have a greater influence over the refractory nobles of this land than the Tycoon and Council of State."

Even a decade of life spent by the American envoy in the morally fetid atmospheres of the East had scarcely blunted the edge of his surprise at the mystery surrounding political affairs in Japan, and especially at the subterfuges daily resorted to, daily exposed, and daily repeated. He was, however, so far forearmed that he resolved on no pretext whatever should the President's letter leave his hands until deposited by him in person before the Tycoon in Yedo. He knew that the consuming curiosity of the Japanese would be his strongest ally.

CHAPTER VIII.

SLOW BUT SURE PROGRESS.

THURSDAY, February 26, 1857.[1] On reaching the Go-yosho to-day, the Governors asked me if I had perused the letter from the Regency, etc., etc., and said they had something to add, which was that they had full powers to receive from me any propositions I had to make, and to treat on all the matters referred to in my two letters to the Minister of Foreign Affairs, and then began to question me as to certain matters contained therein.

I told them I was not yet ready to answer, but rather to ask questions, and that I wished to know the nature of their powers. Could they give me answers at once on all matters I might propose without waiting to hear from Yedo? They assured me in the most solemn manner that they could. I then asked could they make a new treaty without such reference?

Their answer soon proved what I before suspected, that in any minor matter they could decide,

[1] Here begins "Journal No. 4," commencing February 26, 1857, ending December 7, 1857.

but on any important one they could only hear and report. I then said, "I have some matters under the treaty which properly come under your jurisdiction, and will now proceed to open them." They wished to renew the discussion of the currency, but I told them unless they had some new matter, or a distinct proposition to make, I should prefer leaving that for the present.

I then stated that the port of Nagasaki had been opened to the Russians as a place where their ships could obtain necessary supplies and coals for steamers, and I demanded the same rights for the Americans. This was finally agreed to. My next was, that in the case of American ships in want of supplies and not having money, goods should be taken in payment. They said this was already granted by our treaty. I told them if that was the case, of course they could have no objection to reaffirming it, and this was agreed to. My next was, that Americans committing offenses in Japan should be tried by the consul and punished, if guilty, according to Japanese laws. To my great and agreeable surprise this was agreed to without demur.[1]

[1] This clause, so heartily agreed to by the Japanese, was later the intolerable burden under which the governments of both Yedo and Tōkiō groaned for a generation, the rock on which several cabinets were wrecked, and on account of which civil war was more than once on the point of breaking out. In the treaties made with England and the United States in 1894, the abolition of consular courts is provided for.

SLOW BUT SURE PROGRESS. 125

I next told them that I demanded the right for Americans to lease ground, buy, build, repair, or alter such buildings at their pleasure, and that they should be supplied with materials and laborers for such purposes whenever they might require them. I told them I founded this claim on the 12th and 13th Articles made with the Dutch at Nagasaki, on the 9th of November, 1855, by which all the ground at Déshima was leased to the Dutch, and the buildings sold to them, and that they also had the right to build, alter, or repair, etc., etc.; that I claimed those same privileges under the 9th Article of the Treaty of Kanagawa.

The Governors were amazed; they never heard of any such convention; it did not, it could not exist; when, where, and by whom was it made? I told them. It was not known to the government at Yedo; had never been ratified, and therefore had never gone into effect. I then read the 29th Article, which declared the convention should go into full effect on the 1st of January, 1856, and extended the time of exchange of the ratifications to the 9th of November, 1857; but the ratifications had been exchanged, and that I had with my own eyes seen the ratified Japanese copy. They then asked where the ratifications were exchanged, and where it was that I saw it? I told them that Captain Fabius of the Dutch Navy brought the Dutch ratification to Nagasaki, in August or September last, and that when he came here in the frigate Medusa he had the ratified convention on board, and that what I held in my hand was an authenticated translation of it.

Now, will it be believed that during all this time (more than one hour) the Governors had an authentic copy of that very convention lying before them in a dispatch box? It was so; and all this barefaced falsehood was a fair specimen of Japanese diplomacy.

They then took new ground; the Dutch had been in Japan more than two hundred years; that these were old matters, and had no relation to the present state of affairs. I replied that I claimed none of the rights the Dutch had before the Treaty of Kanagawa was signed; that I only claimed the same new right as had been granted to the Dutch; that under the old regulations the Dutch lived in Déshima simply on sufferance, had no written rights, and were liable to be ordered away at any moment; but the convention of November 9, 1855, placed them on new and secure ground; they had acquired fixed and indefeasible rights, and among others that of permanent residence in Japan.

Again the ground was shifted. The privileges granted to the Dutch were, in effect, to the Dutch government represented by a factory, and not to the Dutch at large; as I had told them the government of the United States never engaged in trade, of course it could not have a factory; and, as a natural consequence, the claim on my part was ill-founded. I replied that it was a privilege of trade and residence granted to Dutchmen, no matter whom they represented; that the effect was the same, whether they traded for themselves or for the Dutch government. Four o'clock having arrived, I left them to meet again to-morrow at the same hour.

Friday, February 27, 1857. At the Go-yosho at noon. The Governors opened the business by traveling over the same ground as yesterday (on my last proposition) for nearly two hours, not one new idea or argument being stated. At last, when they questioned the correctness of my translation, I suddenly asked them to give me a copy of the 12th and 13th Articles according to their version, which they promised to do, apparently for the moment forgetting their denial of any knowledge of such a convention only yesterday.

I next claimed the right to have purchases made for me by any person I might employ, and that payment should be made directly to the seller without the interference of any Japanese official. I also claimed that the limits of seven ri[1] and five ri at Shimoda and Hakodaté did not apply to me as Consul-General, but that the whole Empire of Japan was included in my consulate.

[1] Ri = two and a half English miles.

There was less falsehood in their replies to this point than there was to the preceding one, but this arose from the want of opportunity rather than the want of inclination. Two hours were thus consumed, and I left at four P. M., they promising to send me their version of the 12th and 13th Articles of the Dutch convention.

Monday, March 2, 1857. Moriyama Yenoské comes here to-day with their version of the 12th and 13th Articles of the Dutch convention. They agree in every essential with my version.

He introduced the "currency question" by saying how very anxious he was to have it settled, and tried to persuade me to open the question with him. He assured me that he knew of his own knowledge it did cost twenty-five per cent. on all their coinage; and, on being pressed, he admitted that a whole army of officers was quartered on the mint; that some of them had very large salaries. I inferred from what he said that the mint is a sort of pension establishment for the Empire.

Tuesday, March 3, 1857. Met the Governors. The currency question was introduced, and they at last made a distinct offer. They said that heretofore the dollar had been taken by them for sixteen hundred sen (or cash); that this was not right; they proposed to weigh coins brought here by the Americans, gold coin with Japanese gold coin, and silver coin against Japanese silver coin, weight for weight, and from the amount of Japanese coin to deduct fifteen per cent. to pay for the loss of melting and coining. I told them the demand was unreasonable, and that I could not agree to it. They then asked me to give them a counter-proposition; I accordingly made three distinct offers: —

(1) The dollar in silver to pass by tale for three bus, or forty-eight hundred sen.

(2) Weighing the coin as proposed by them and deducting five per cent.

(3) That inasmuch as they said their coin was composed of pure silver, or pure gold without alloy, that if that statement was correct, I would allow them ten per cent. discount, and that any alloy found in their coin should be deducted from that allowance, and that any increase of alloy in the coin brought by Americans, over the present standard, should go to swell the discount.

The third proposition was instantly rejected, with such manifest trepidation that I am convinced that their coin contains a large amount of alloy. They also said that to weigh the coin would be more just than to have it pass by tale, as from wear or other causes old coins were never as heavy as new ones. We then went over the ground again on my two last propositions.

At last I told them I had something of great importance to communicate confidentially and to them alone. To my great surprise the room was at once cleared of all but the two Governors and Moriyama.

I then read to them an extract from a letter to me from the Secretary of State, which was to the effect that, if the Japanese sought to evade the treaty, the President would not hesitate to ask Congress to give him power to use such arguments as they could not resist.

The fluttering was fearful, the effect strong. They thanked me for the confidence I had placed in them, by reading that part of the Secretary's letter, and asked if they might communicate the same to their government. I told them they could do so. They then asked me to give them a written translation of the paragraph, so that they might make a correct translation. This I declined, but told them I would have it translated, and that Moriyama might use that paper in my presence to translate it to them, but that the paper must be returned to me. This ended our proceedings for the day at half-past four P. M.

Wednesday, March 4, 1857. Met the Governors at noon. The room was cleared, and I then handed them the Dutch translation referred to yesterday, and it was carefully translated into Japanese by Moriyama, and then the paper was returned to me.

Traveled over the debates of yesterday like a

horse in a mill. I finally demanded a categorical answer to the three points open, viz., currency, residence of Americans, and the consular rights. They requested me to place all my propositions in writing; this I declined, telling them, that once I had placed my name to a paper it could not be modified, and that I wished to leave a door open by which we might arrive at a solution of the questions. It was finally agreed, that Mr. Heusken, as from himself, should give them an unsigned paper containing the substance of my demands, the paper to be sent to the Governor's residence in the morning of to-morrow; and that we should meet again for the dispatch of business on Friday.

Friday, March 6, 1857. Met the Governors at the usual place, i. e. the Go-yosho.

I asked them if they were prepared to give me answers to the points remaining unsettled, and soon found they were anything but ready. They said these were important matters and must be calmly considered; that the Japanese took a great while to consider every question; that in this respect they differed from the Americans who decided promptly on all questions.

The currency question again came up, and was again gone over for the twentieth time. At last I told them my mind was made up, and that I would not allow more than five per cent. for recoinage; that their demands were exorbitant; that

their plea that it cost twenty-five per cent. I had
fully met by offering to have it done for five per
cent., and that it appeared as though the government
wished to squeeze the Americans who come
here.

This elicited a direct offer on their part of taking
our coins at six per cent. discount. To show
how great a step this was in our favor, it should
be remembered that heretofore the dollar passed
for sixteen hundred sen, but the last offer of the
Japanese would give four thousand six hundred
and seventy for the dollar, or nearly two hundred
per cent. more than they formerly allowed.

I refused to advance from the five per cent.
The Prince of Shinano rose from his seat and
came to me; and, while standing, begged me as a
personal favor to him to yield the one per cent. of
difference; that they were most anxious to have
the matter settled, but that it was impossible for
them to go further than they had done, and (mark
this) that, if they took the coin of the Americans
at less than six per cent., the government would
lose by the operation of recoinage. Contrast this
with their solemn assurance that it cost twenty-
five per cent. to coin the money of Japan![1] The

[1] Regular mints were first established in Japan in 1601. The
seigniorage was charged at an extravagant rate. See " The Currency
Question" (1854-1869), in Inazo Nitobé's *United States and
Japan*, pp. 71-74.

SLOW BUT SURE PROGRESS.   133

mendacity of these men passes all human belief. We finally adjourned to some day next week.

I am really ill, yet I am forced day after day to listen to useless debates, on points that have been exhausted and are only varied by some new phase of falsehood.

Saturday, March 7, 1857. On looking over my journal for February 25, I find I have omitted two important matters.

On the 4th of October, 1855, the Secretary of State wrote me that the Navy Department had received dispatches from Lieutenant Rodgers to the effect that Reed and Dougherty, two Americans who had gone to Japan to establish themselves there, had been ordered away from Shimoda and refused permission to land at Hakodaté. Lieutenant Rodgers also wrote[1] that the Japanese version of the 7th Article of Commodore Perry's treaty contained the words, " such as may be necessary for them," in connection with the agreement to permit Americans to make purchases of goods in Japan. I was informed by the Department that these words were not contained in the English, Dutch, or Chinese versions of the treaty, and I was directed to inquire into the matter, and see if they were actually inserted in the Japanese version.

[1] See pp. 453-457 of *Perry's Narrative* for the note of Commander John Rodgers, with other documents and information on this matter of Messrs. Reed and Dougherty.

I asked the Governors if they had an authentic copy of the Treaty of Kanagawa, and, on their answering in the affirmative, I requested them to turn to the 7th Article of the treaty, and then asked them if the words above noted were contained in it. They at once said they were not in the article. I then told them Lieutenant Rodgers was here, that the Governor had assured him that these words were contained in the Japanese version of the treaty.

With unmoved faces they assured me they never heard of any such statement; that the Governor could not have said so, and that there must be some mistake about it. I then complained of the ordering away of Messrs. Reed and Dougherty from Shimoda and refusing them permission to land in Hakodaté. They answered that that was wrong; that they ought not to have ordered them away from Shimoda, nor have refused them permission to land at Hakodaté.

Sunday, March 8, 1857. A cannon from the signal hill announced a foreign ship at noon to-day, and caused emotions of sincere pleasure.

On ascending a height near the consulate I saw the blessed stars and stripes flying from a barque which was standing towards the inner harbor, having a signal for a pilot flying. The pilot was seen pulling off to her, but as the pilot neared her she filled away, stood off until she was fairly in

Yedo Bay, and then stood southward. What does it mean? It was like the Flying Dutchman.

Monday, March 9, 1857. At nine this morning the barque again made her appearance and anchored in the outer harbor. Mr. Heusken went on board, and when he returned he brought with him Captain Horner of the barque Messenger Bird from Boston via the Sandwich Islands. Mr. Edward F. Hall, the super-cargo, presented a letter of introduction written by Hon. David L. Gregg, U. S. Commissioner to the Sandwich Islands. Captain Horner has his wife and two children on board, one an infant born at sea off the Caroline Islands.

Mr. Hall having come via San Francisco, I got newspapers up to the 8th of November, or six months later than my last dates. So Mr. Buchanan is President. When I last saw him in London, on the 31st of October last, I told him that I had no doubt he would be the next President. I am glad to hear it, and trust that under his administration peace and quiet will settle on the land. As the newspapers were only from the 20th of October to the 8th of November, there is a large hiatus in details, and Mr. Hall being only eighteen years of age could not give me many particulars. Mr. Hall informs me that he has an assorted cargo, and wishes to trade here, and that he shall then proceed to Hakodaté, and thence to the Amoor River, at which last place he is to establish himself in business as a ship-chandler. I told him that I was still negotiating with the Japanese about the currency, and told him he could depend on not losing over six per cent. on the money he should expend here, and which gave him great satisfaction.

Sent word to the Governors that I wished to see them to-morrow.

Tuesday, March 10, 1857. Met the Governors. Told them the arrival of a ship required a settlement of the currency question. They stuck at the six, and I at the five per cent. I proposed that this ship should settle at the six per cent., but that it should not be used as a precedent. They said they required ten days to settle the currency question, as they must send to Yedo.

They then opened on ground that even astonished me, used as I am to Japanese falsehood. They roundly declared the Dutch convention did not exist; that it was a false report. I told them, with some sternness, that I had seen it with my own eyes, on board the Dutch frigate (Medusa), in October last. They then said it had not been ratified. This I also stopped by saying that it did bear the ratification of the Japanese government. This point was asserted and reasserted by them time and again, and as often met by a plain statement of the truth by me.

Now came a new turn; they said the 12th and 13th Articles had been stricken out of the Japanese copy.

In reply, I asked, if that was so, how was it that they gave me a correct version of the 12th and 13th Articles from their copy? The Governor said he got a copy made for himself when at Yedo, before it was acted on by the government. I asked to see his copy, when, lo, it was a printed and not a manuscript copy. I called their attention to the fact, but they made no reply.

I then said that the evidence of the authenticity of my version was quite satisfactory to me, and that it would be so to my government, who would act on it as authentic. They then repeated that those two articles never went into operation, etc., etc. I told them that Captain Fabius of the Dutch Navy had informed me that the buildings at Déshima had been sold to the Dutch, and the ground leased to them. They vehemently denied the truth of that statement. I told them that negative proof was nothing against credible, positive testimony. It was now past four, and I closed a very stormy interview, with an appointment for the next day.

Wednesday, March 11, 1857. I went yesterday on board the Messenger Bird and saw Mrs. Horner, a nice person indeed, with a bouncing baby in her arms. This *home* sight almost made me *homesick*.

At the Go-yosho at half past eleven. The Governors again wished to open the currency question. I told them if they would give me satisfaction on the other unsettled points, I would satisfy them in the matter of the currency. After a great deal of debate, in which, however, they did not repeat the barefaced assertions of yesterday, they requested me to put the two claims of residence of Americans and consular rights on paper, and give them time to consider about it, as it was a matter of much gravity, etc., etc. I assented to this, and so closed our business for the present. Again visited the barque, and after chatting for an hour went home.

Captain and Mrs. Horner and Mr. Hall are to breakfast with me on Friday noon.

Friday, March 13, 1857. Breakfast party as above. Walk to a place where can see Oshima. Day fine and pass it most agreeably. Company leave at five P. M.

In the evening write a letter to the Governors, on the two points, which I support with a few of the strongest arguments.

Saturday, March 14, 1857. Mr. Heusken has translated Mr. Hall's lists of merchandise, and goes with him to assist as his interpreter.

Sunday, March 15, 1857. I have never been so ill for seven years as I am to-day.

Saturday, March 28. Moriyama calls, and

wished to discuss the two points, which I decline. In answer to my questions, as to the state of public opinion at Yedo, regarding intercourse with foreigners, he says that, taking ten persons in authority, three would be in favor of opening the country at once; two would be in favor, but with delay; three would refuse so long as force is not used, but would yield to such a demonstration without fighting; and two would fight to the last. Moriyama says the Governor wishes to call on me to-morrow. I request the Prince to excuse me on Sunday, but that I shall be very happy to see him on any other day of the week.

Sunday, March 29, 1857. The barque Messenger Bird went to sea early this morning, bound to Hakodaté, and the river Amoor.

Monday, March 30, 1857. The Governor visited me to-day. He was attended by a very large train, but only a vice-governor and the interpreter were admitted to my private rooms. I have completely broken up the system of having a cloud of secretaries and spies crowding into my private rooms. All are delighted, except the writers and spies. Gave the Prince a Colt's revolver, one of three that were put in the case of arms I purchased for the King of Siam, in lieu of discount.

Wednesday, April 1, 1857. Dispatch letter, dated March 28, to Council of State in reply to their letter received February 25. I have delayed writing this letter so long, in the hope of bringing things to a quiet close here.

Friday, 3d April. Governors wish to see me. Go to Go-yosho at two P. M. They wish to know the contents of my letter to Council of State. Sorry, but it would be improper in me to disclose it. They ask the meaning of certain words in 12th Article of the Treaty. I ask for a piece of ground for a garden, which is promised.

Monday, April 6, 1857. Moriyama calls about garden spot. Have given me the piece asked for, about one eighth of an acre. Rent six bus per annum.

Tuesday, April 7, 1857. Moriyama again; brings me a gardener, the occupant of the land I have hired. Have a chat with Moriyama, as he is quite alone, and therefore more communicative. He says that I shall soon have an answer to the two points, and that it will be satisfactory to me; that I must not hurry them too much; that but a short time need elapse before a commercial treaty can be negotiated, etc., etc. He says the letter to me was signed by the whole of the High Council of Regents, the power next the Shōgun; that there is another council of five to seven persons who are under the Regents. The Regents are not hereditary officers; they are appointed by the Shōgun, and hold office during his pleasure alone. That the story of an appeal lying to the Princes of the

Empire, when there is a difference of opinion between the Shōgun and his Regents, when the defeated party, if a Regent, performs the hara-kiri, if the Shōgun, resigns, is not true. No appeal from the Shōgun exists;[1] his veto is final. If a Regent proposes a measure which is negatived by the Shōgun, no harm arises, but if he renews the recommendation, and it is again rejected, then the Regent does perform the hara-kiri.

No reports of the Treasury, War, Marine, or Commerce. The results are only known to the Shōgun and Regents and the heads of each department. Moriyama says, "It would be considered impolite for a person to make any inquiries concerning a department with which he is not connected." The English of it is that he dare not make such inquiries. I put down the information I get from time to time from the Japanese. I know there is much falsehood, but I cannot at the time separate the true from the false.

Shimonoséki, one of the interpreters, told Mr. Heusken that all the buildings at Déshima had been sold to the Dutch.

Easter Sunday, April 12, 1857. I have kept a very good account of the festivals of the Church since my arrival here. It has served to bring up

[1] No doubt the average Japanese in 1857 believed this to be true.

many pleasant recollections and associations of ideas in my mind. The day is a lovely one; the fields around me are green with the waving wheat, or finely decorated with flowers. An abundance of violets grow about here.

Monday, April 13. A strong wind and driving rain from the southwest serves to inaugurate Easter Monday at Shimoda.

Moriyama calls on me, nominally to see me, but in reality to settle the wages of my two Japanese boys, which is at last settled at six bus per month, or about two dollars. The vice-governor last December wanted me to pay them sixteen dollars per month.

Moriyama tells me, as a most profound State secret, that the Prince of Satsuma is father-in-law to the Shōgun. I knew this last October. M. says that although the Shōgun has the supreme power to appoint or displace the members of the High Council, yet he is influenced by a council of six persons or families, to wit, three princes of the blood and the powerful nobles; among the latter is the Prince of Satsuma. In other words, that an oligarchy governs Japan. Moriyama says that Japan will be opened to foreigners within the year. He admits that the Japanese are now negotiating a commercial treaty with the Dutch, but I should greatly distrust the provisions of a treaty so made. The Dutch are altogether too fond of monopolies to make a treaty suited to the present wants of the commercial world.

Moriyama informs me that the guns presented to the Japanese (fifty-two in number) have been taken to Yedo; that eight or nine of them are to be mounted on a corvette they have built on the Western model. The corvette is one hundred and twenty feet keel.

Tuesday, April 14, 1857. The chief of the Go-yosho came to see me to-day. At last they have brought me my account for seven months; the total looks alarming, as it is two million eighty-seven thousand and nine of their coins, but luckily that is fully liquidated with the sum of four hundred and forty-seven dollars. My servants (*i. e.* the Chinese) are the heaviest item of my expenses here, as their wages amount to more than seven hundred dollars per annum; that is, for four men, and I also give them their food and lodging; while for five Japanese, I pay one hundred and thirty-two dollars per annum, and they board themselves.

The Go-yosho man also brought me a Japanese Dictionary, and promises in a few days to bring me some school-books, works of fiction and history.

I think that two thousand dollars per annum will cover my expenses. But had I not brought them to terms about the currency, I should have found my salary insufficient for my support.

CHAPTER IX.

A LONELY EXILE.—THE PRESIDENT'S LETTER.

WEDNESDAY, April 15, 1857. Moriyama visited the consulate to-day. I had proposed to the Governors that, when the next American man-of-war came here, salutes should be exchanged after our fashion.

Moriyama says the Governor would be much pleased by such a mark of friendship as would be indicated by a salute to the flag of Japan, but proposed to return it in the Japanese manner, *i. e.*, after the salute to send a high officer dressed in his kami-shimo, or robes of ceremony, to return thanks for the salute. I told him that would hardly be satisfactory; that our custom was to give gun for gun,[1] the ship, being a visitor, to salute first, and then to have it returned from the land.

[1] There is no record, so far as we know after an examination of the archives of the United States Navy Department, of an American warship firing a salute to the flag of a European power on other than equal terms, except in the one instance of *the first* salute ever fired by a foreign magistrate or government to the American flag, by the Dutch Governor Johannes de Graeff, at St. Eustatius, West Indies, November 17, 1776. See the *New England Magazine*, July, 1893. When in 1820 the Portuguese governor of Teneriffe declined to return the salute of the U. S. S.

I told him that I was anxious that the Japanese should take their place among the civilized nations of the world, and that all these small things were so many steps in that direction. I then entered at large into the system of salutes, and explained the manner in which they were given and returned.

The Governors having expressed a wish for books of all branches of military and naval science, as taught at West Point and at the Naval School, I sent them word that if they would address a letter on the subject I should at once forward it to the Secretary of State, and that I had no doubt the books would be at once sent.

Moriyama then said that he wished to ask me a question, and that he wanted me to consider it as a dream, *i. e.* to forget it. The query was, "Suppose the Governors of Shimoda should wish to make a commercial treaty with you, what would you do?" I replied that I should first ask to see their full powers, and, if those were satisfactory, that I would then show them mine; and after that we would go to work at a treaty at once. He said if that was so that they had misunderstood me; that they supposed that I would only negotiate at

Cyane, Lieutenant M. C. Perry commanding, except with one gun less, — "as it was not customary for Portugal to return an equal number of guns to republican governments, but only to those of acknowledged sovereigns," — he got no salute, and the Cyane burned no powder in compliment to Portugal or the governor. *M. C. P.*, pp. 54, 55.

Yedo, and with the High Council. I told them that they had confounded two things; that what I had to say confidentially, as from my government, could only be said at Yedo; so also the President's letter could only be delivered by me at Yedo, and in the Imperial presence, etc. That negotiations were a different thing; that I was ready to negotiate with any person of proper rank who could show me the requisite full powers.

He declared that they were not negotiating with the Dutch a commercial treaty; that as soon as they were ready to negotiate on that point, they would negotiate with me.

Moriyama says that almost all the books of Japan are simple reprints of Chinese classics, such as Confucius, Mencius, etc., but that I shall have copies of such purely Japanese works as they have.[1]

Saturday, April 18, 1857. My servants consist of a butler, cook and his mate, washman, two houseboys, one water-carrier, one sweeper, one gardener, one groom — in all ten persons, and not one that I can do without.

I am much concerned at the non-arrival of the San Jacinto. Commodore Armstrong promised to

[1] The first real survey of Japanese literature given in a foreign language is that of Mr. Ernest Satow, Secretary of the British Legation in Japan, and now H. B. M. Minister to Morocco, in the *American Cyclopedia*. The Japanese have a very voluminous literature. See *Japan: in History, Folk-lore, and Art*, Boston, 2d edition, 1895.

be here in March, and now more than one half of April has slipped away. My last letters from the United States were dated March 17, 1856, more than thirteen months ago. How much may have happened in that time! My health is not good.

I wish the frigate would arrive, that I could have some medical advice.

Monday, April 20, 1857. A miserable wet day. Send word to the Governors that I wish to meet them at the Go-yosho to-morrow at noon. I wish to engross the articles already settled with them, and have them make their translation, as the last is always a work of much time, and thus I shall be able to expedite the whole matter the more promptly when I get a decision on the "two points."

Tuesday, April 21, 1857. Met the Governors at noon at the Go-yosho. Agreed to settle the wording of the points already agreed on. Told them I should write them a formal letter requesting them to give me their version of the 7th Article of the Treaty of Kanagawa, as when Lieutenant Rodgers was here (May, 1855) they had interpolated the words " such as may be necessary for them " after the words agreeing to trade. I told them I should also ask them for an explanation of the sending away of Reed and Dougherty from Shimoda, and refusing them permission to land at Hakodaté, in 1855. I inquired when I was to receive an answer on the "two points." They could only repeat that they were anxiously looking for it to arrive here from Yedo.

I found the matter of salutes, mentioned to Moriyama on the 15th, is a perplexing matter to them, so I let it rest where it is for the present.

I requested the Governors to order the Go-yosho officers to answer certain questions which I had received from my government concerning cotton, its production in Japan, etc., which they promised should be done. I called their attention to the breakwater of the jetty now erecting at Kakizaki, that it is so short that at low water of spring tides it will not give any protection to boats. I left at two P. M. After my return home wrote the letter to the Governors, referred to in the beginning of this entry, and settled the wording of the articles.

Saturday, April 25, 1857. I have given some lessons in English to the Imperial surgeon who attends the Governors here; I did this at their request. I found him very apt. He has been absent for some weeks to visit his sick father at Yedo, and to-day came to renew his lessons. I did not give him anything but a letter to the Governors, in which I told them that I should be very happy to give instruction in English after I had been permitted the full exercise of my rights as consul, but so long as I was denied any of those rights I must decline the lessons.

I cannot see what it is that keeps away Commodore Armstrong; if I had a vessel-of-war here I should have speedy answers to my demands on the two points, but I feel sure they will not be settled so long as no ship-of-war comes here. The Commodore promised to be here in March, yet April has nearly passed away, and no ship has come. My last letters from the Department of State were dated in October, 1855, more than eighteen months ago. It is too long a period to leave me here alone, and some order should be given to insure more frequent communication with me.

Monday, April 27, 1857. The Rhododendron Althea is now in beautiful flower, — colors chiefly pink. I have planted some of them in the cemetery where the four Americans are buried.[1]

Flowers of the Peony — China poppy, flowered peony, and " tree-peony " brought me to-day.

Monday, April 27, continued. Moriyama calls for verbal explanations about the wording of the articles already agreed on. Find it is a cunning attempt to interpolate words of different meaning. Moriyama says very coolly that " it is a very different thing to say a thing, or to write it ; " in other

---

[1] Decoration Day, which Mr. Harris thus inaugurated in Japan, is now regularly observed with formal ceremonies by the American residents and officers and sailors from the men-of-war in port. In 1894, Rev. W. F. Dierst of Tōkiō cleaned and reset the gravestones and renovated the cemetery.

words, they are always at liberty to deny anything they have said or promised, so long as it is not in writing.

Tuesday, April 28. Busy to-day in making indexes of the correspondence and documents of the consulate. Have got all my papers in perfect order, and only await the arrival of a ship to dispatch a large amount of correspondence. I feel sure that what I have accomplished will give satisfaction. I have settled the currency, so that one dollar goes as far almost as three did when Commodore Perry left the question.

I have opened the port of Nagasaki to American ships wanting supplies.

Americans are only to be amenable to American authority for offenses committed in Japan.

American ships in distress that have no money can pay for all necessary supplies by barter.

The great point of residence of Americans is still pending, and although it may not *now* be admitted, yet I have placed it on a footing which must ultimately secure it.

The consular rights and franchises stand on the same ground as the rights of residence.

I have fought the battles, and although I may not receive the victory, yet victory will come, and will be owing to my labors.

Wednesday, April 29, 1857. Moriyama visits me and brings the Dutch version of the articles agreed on. I find it correct at last. One would think the translation of a paper to be a simple process, but it is not so with the Japanese, for, beside their duplicity and constant effort to vary the substance, they are so absurd as to wish to have every word placed in the Dutch version exactly in the order it stands in the Japanese; it is very difficult to explain to them the idioms of language, or the grammatical structure of it; or to get them to see that although the placing of the words does not correspond with theirs, yet the meaning is the same. Their knowledge of Dutch is imperfect; they have learned the language as spoken by traders and sailors, and the Dutch they use is not only that of two hundred and fifty years ago, but it is limited to the subjects above referred to.[1] Hence we have great difficulty in conveying an abstract idea to them, and it is almost impossible to speak figuratively[2] to them.

As a specimen of the cool mendacity of the Japanese even about things that are tangible to the sight, I note the following. The island of Oshima

[1] "Interpreter's Dutch" was quite different from that of the scholars in Yedo, who read the Dutch books which, for over a century previous to 1853, were leavening the Japanese mind and preparing it for the transformation of to-day. Laurence Oliphant, in his book, *Lord Elgin's Mission*, makes the same complaint of the word for word translators of English.

[2] On the peculiarities of the Japanese language, its matter of fact character, see Aston's and Chamberlain's Grammars.

is in plain sight of Shimoda, and some twelve or fifteen miles distant from us, so that it comes within the limits of seven ri, or sixteen and five-eighths miles, as settled for the Americans. Yet the Governors coolly tell me that Oshima is twenty-five ri, or fifty-nine and three-eighths miles distant from Shimoda!

Tuesday, May 5, 1857. It is now eight months and three days since the San Jacinto left here. Commodore Armstrong promised me he would be here again in six months.[1] I am a prey to unceasing anxiety; I have not heard a word from Washington since I left the United States, say October, 1855.

What can be the cause of this prolonged absence of an American man-of-war? Where are the English? Where are the French? Above all, where is the Russian Consul? He should have been here before this. I am only nine days distant from Hong-Kong, yet I am more isolated than any American official in any part of the world.

I have important intelligence to send to my government; intelligence that will give an immediate spur to our trade with Japan, yet here it remains,

---

[1] What Commodore Armstrong and the English and French were doing, and the reasons for the delay of the San Jacinto, are told in Dr. Wood's book *Fankwei*. The Opium War in China had begun. See the latest account of it in the *Life of Sir Harry Parkes*, who was afterwards British Minister in Japan.

month after month, without my being able to communicate it to my government, or enabling my countrymen to benefit by it. The absence of a man-of-war also tends to weaken my influence with the Japanese. They have yielded nothing except from fear, and any future ameliorations of our intercourse will only take place after a demonstration of force on our part.

I will not suppose that this apparent neglect arises from indifference or idleness on the part of our naval commanders out here; I therefore am left a prey to all sorts of imaginations as to the detaining causes.

Saturday, May 9, 1857. I have called on the Governors of Shimoda to redeem the promise they made me, before I landed, that "all my supplies should be furnished at the same rates as were charged to the Japanese." I am satisfied that I have been constantly and systematically overcharged, and I sent to the Governors a list of prices at which I am charged, and against them I placed the prices that I have obtained from time to time, from Japanese who are not connected with the government. The difference is very great.

Monday, May 11, 1857. Went over to the Goyosho. I was not pleased with the articles offered to me. I think we have overrated the habit of the Japanese in making elaborately fine articles of any kind. The genius of their government seems to forbid any exercise of ingenuity in producing articles for the gratification of wealth and luxury.

Sumptuary laws rigidly enforce the forms, color, material, and time of changing the dress of all. As to luxury of furniture, the thing is unknown in Japan. I do not hesitate to say that the house of a Prince of the Empire does not contain half the value of furniture that you will find in the house of a sober, steady mechanic in America.

Simplicity and frugality is the great maxim of this country, and it is enforced in a most surprising manner. It would be an endless task to attempt to put down all the acts of a Japanese that are regulated by authority. This is no country for modistes, tailors, jewelers, and the whole army that fatten on the imaginary wants of the West.

Wednesday, May 13, 1857. For the purpose of ascertaining whether gold is really as cheap in Japan as the Japanese pretend, I ordered two mustard-spoons to be made of pure, unalloyed gold. They wished me to give them coin to make the spoons from. This I declined, as it would defeat the object I had in view.

After some days a formal message was sent to me by the Governors, stating that by the laws of Japan gold could only be used to ornament their swords, and that its use by the people in any other form was absolutely prohibited.[1] A greater falsehood was never uttered. It is true that the Japanese own but few ornaments, or, indeed, articles of luxury of any kind, but gold is used in weaving brocades, in decorating saddles, in making a small chain which secures a small basket, which contains a cloth with which they wipe perspiration from their faces, and for women's ornaments.

I told the messenger to say to the Governors that I knew that gold was used for many purposes besides swords; but even if that was not the case, it was nothing to me, as I was not a Japanese, nor bound by Japanese law.

Moriyama comes to say that the Governor has received orders to go to Yedo, and that he is to leave early to-morrow morning; that he is unable to call in person to take leave of me, and begs me to excuse his apparent neglect. I send him messages wishing him a pleasant journey to Yedo, and a favorable reception on his arrival.

Thursday, May 14, 1857. I have received a circular from the United States Patent-office, asking for a great variety of information about cotton,[2]

---

[1] Extract from the *Kindai Geppio* (which contains brief notes on Japanese history from 1844 to 1863, published in Tōkiō, 1873): "11th month, 7th day (1855). The use of gold or silver in making utensils of all kinds was prohibited." This is one of several instances in which Mr. Harris was too severe in his generalizations. In after-years his earlier and hastier judgments were corrected.

[2] In 1895, Japan, with nearly fifty large steam-power cotton-

the whole being put in the form of twenty-seven questions. These I had translated and gave them to the Japanese, requesting them to give me the desired information.

To-day I have their return. It is a beautiful specimen of Japanese craft, cunning, and falsehood. Their great object appears to be, to permit as little to be learned about their country as possible, and to that end all fraud, deceit, falsehood, and even violence are justifiable in their eyes. It is true that this is the most difficult country in the world to get information; no statistics exist; no publications are made on any subject connected with industry. No man makes experiments to improve his implements, or to increase the product of his lands by new modes of culture; as his father sowed and reaped, so does he; and if the crop is large, it is his good fortune; if it be poor, it is his misfortune; as in everything else in Japan, the motto is *Quieta non movere*.

The cultivator never measures his produce to see how it compares with that of his neighbor, or with his own on previous years; he is entirely ignorant of the mode of culture, or crops produced, at places not twenty miles distant from him. The great mass of the people are literally tied to the spot on

mills, with the best improved modern machinery, is competing for the trade with India, having already gained much of the trade in cotton stuffs with China and Korea.

which they were born. Of course government officials, priests, pilgrims, etc., are exceptions. It may be that some few of the traders may go from place to place in pursuit of their calling, but such men in Japan have no eyes for anything but their traffic.

Saturday, May 16, 1857. I ordered a small Belvedere to be erected on the top of a hill near the consulate, so that I might enjoy the cool air during the hot season, and also have a view over the whole of the harbor. To-day they brought me some plans and elevations very neatly done, with estimate of the cost of the work. It seems to be a most important matter to them, as they have been a number of days about it, and many persons are engaged on it. I was satisfied with their plans, and accepted them. The price is fifteen dollars.

I am collecting specimens of natural history, but they are meagre, as the Japanese will not bring me one, on the national principle of concealing everything.

Thursday, May 21, 1857. Nine months to-day since I arrived in Japan, and I am still without any communication with home. Where is Commodore Armstrong?

The Japanese brought a horse for Mr. Heusken to-day. It is dearer than mine, although not so good-looking; but this is Japanese custom — always advance the price, but never lower it.

Tuesday, May 26, 1857. To-day I have a reply from the Governors about the prices charged me by the Go-yosho people.

It is plainly and unequivocally a full support of the Go-yosho rascality in all of its ramifications. They do not regard the promise they gave me last August as worth the breath cost them to utter it. However, to lie is, for a Japanese, simply to speak.

Tuesday, June 2. Moriyama brings me Mr. Portman's [1] Dutch version of the Treaty of Kanagawa, as well as their Dutch version made from the Japanese. I wish to have a copy, to save the trouble of constant reference by means of letters asking for copies of parts of Articles. . . . Burgo no Kami is in disgrace. . . . Took a walk to the southwest of Shimoda, towards Cape Idzu. It is of the same character as the other parts seen; every possible spot is cultivated, and as many inhabitants as can be supported. I find that what I considered as jungle on the steep hillsides is actually all planted — trees, bamboos, rushes, etc.; all are renewed as they are cut off for use. No spot is neglected; I have never seen a person that had the appearance of want marked on his countenance. The children all have faces like "full moons," and the men and women are quite fleshy enough. No

---

[1] The Dutch interpreter for Commodore Perry, and afterwards of the United States Legation in Yedo and Tōkiō, who perished in the steamer Ville du Harve.

one can for a moment suppose, after seeing the people, that they are not well fed.

Wednesday, June 3. Walked up the valley of Shimoda towards Matsusaki, and visited a new hot spring. It is arranged as a bath-house, like those before described, but the water is much warmer, and more strongly impregnated with sulphur. I found a woman in the bath with her child; she was not in the least discomposed, but gave me the usual " ohio "[1] (good morning) with a smiling face. Her skin was very fair, nearly as white as a Circassian's. On my return homewards I called on the Governor, and passed a very agreeable hour with him.

Monday, June 8, 1857. I omitted to enter the arrival here of the new Governor, who comes in place of Shinano no Kami. His name is Nakamura, Déwa no Kami. I have at least carried every point triumphantly with the Japanese, and have got everything conceded that I have been negotiating for since last September. Among my papers will be found a copy of the Convention,[2] which contains the following provisions: —

1. Opens the Port of Nagasaki to American ships.

2. Gives the right of permanent residence to

---

[1] " O " honorific, and " hayō " early.

[2] See the text of this document in *Treaties and Conventions between the United States and Other Powers*, 1776–1887.

Americans at Shimoda and Hakodaté, and the right to appoint a vice-consul at the latter port.

3. Settles the currency, so that where we paid one hundred, we now pay only thirty-four dollars and a half.

4. Americans to be exclusively under the control of their consuls, and to be tried by American law.

5. Concedes the right of the Consul-General to go where he pleases in Japan, and to be furnished with Japanese money to enable him in person, or by his servants, to make his purchases, without the intervention of any Japanese official. This is even more than I was instructed to ask for by my special instructions dated October 4, 1855. No classes of Americans are named in the second article, so that missionaries may actually come and reside in Japan.

Am I elated by this success? Not a whit; I know my dear countrymen but too well to expect any praise for what I have done, and I shall esteem myself lucky if I am not removed from office; not for what I have done, but because I have not made a commercial treaty that would open Japan as freely as England is open to us. Besides, it is so easy to criticise, and so agreeable to condemn; it is much more pleasant to write "imbecile," "ass," or "fool," than to say "able," "discreet," and "competent."

Wednesday, June 17, 1857. To-day we signed the Convention, having been some nine days in settling the wording of the articles, which, by the way, is a work of much difficulty, as the Dutch of the Japanese interpreters is that of the ship captains and traders, used some two hundred and fifty years ago. They have not been taught a single new word in the interim, so they are quite ignorant of all the terms used in treaties, conventions, etc., etc. This, joined to their excessive jealousy and fear of being cheated, makes it excessively difficult to manage such a matter as the present one. They even wanted the words in the Dutch version to stand in the exact order they stood in the Japanese! Owing to the difference of grammatical structure, this would have rendered it perfect gibberish.

Monday, June 22, 1857. I have been in correspondence with the "Council of State" since October 25, 1856, concerning a letter from the President of which I am the bearer, and I have had a great many interviews with the Governors of Shimoda of late concerning the manner in which that letter should be delivered, as well as [to how] certain communications, which I wrote them I was charged with, should be made. They wished the letter to be delivered here in Shimoda, and the communications made to the Governors, while I demanded to go to Yedo, have an audience of the Shōgun, and then deliver the letter, and afterwards make the communications to the proper minister.

The Governors now produce an Imperial mandate, under the "seal and signature Royal," commanding them to receive the President's letter and bring it to Yedo, and they are now quite dumfounded that I refuse to yield to the mandate.

Tuesday, June 23, 1857. To-day received an official and also a private letter from Mr. E. E. Rice, "U. S. Commercial Agent at Hakodaté," announcing his arrival at that place, and that he had "hoisted his flag." He writes me that two ships under the American flag are there from Hong-Kong, and that the supercargo, Mr. Luhdorf, has some things for me, which Mr. Rice promises to forward to me if they are landed at Hakodaté, but he does not say one word about letters.

This is most tantalizing. I am now more than ten months in Japan, and have not as yet received a single letter from the United States. As no direct communication is allowed by sea between Shimoda and Hakodaté by Japanese junks, my supplies might as well be at Hong-Kong as there. I have been out of flour, bread, butter, lard, bacon, hams, sweet oil, and, in fact, out of every kind of foreign supply for more than two months. I am living on rice, fish, and very poor poultry, as no game of any kind has been brought to me for the last three months.

My health is miserable. My appetite is gone, and I am so shrunk away that I look as though a "vice-consul had been cut out of me." Where, oh, where, is Commodore Armstrong?

Saturday, July 4, 1857. I never felt more miserable and wretched than on this day. Ill in health and in want of everything but low spirits, of which I have an abundant supply.

I had a national salute of twenty-one guns fired in honor of the day by the Japanese, I paying the expense, which was less than two dollars. Dear New York! how I wish I could pass the day there among my friends. I have now abandoned all hopes of seeing Commodore Armstrong, and I accordingly have made an effort to send some letters through the Japanese to Hakodaté, hoping Mr. Rice may be able to forward them. My letters were very short and very guarded, as I do not doubt the Japanese will open them. Although the distance from here to Hakodaté is under six hundred miles by land, yet the Japanese consume thirty-five days in conveying a letter there.

Wednesday, July 8. Shinano no Kami started to-day for Yedo, for the purpose of reporting my refusal to deliver the letter of the President anywhere but in Yedo, or to any one but the Emperor. They assure me that it is quite preposterous to even think of an audience of His Majesty, as the laws of Japan forbid it. As it happens, they also told me that the Council of State could not write to any foreigners (the laws forbidding it), and as the council has written to me, I am shrewdly inclined to think that they will be found equally pliable in the matter of an audience.

Thursday, July 23, 1857. The cannon from the lookout hill was fired at noon to-day, and it caused such joy as only can be felt by those who have been living isolated as I have been for the last eleven months. Mr. Heusken ran like a deer to the top of the signal hill, and came back breathless and streaming with sweat to say that there was a ship in sight, about ten miles south of the harbor; that as the wind was not very fresh she would not come in for some time. He started again for Vandalia Point (the most southern point) to watch her approach. At four P. M. he returned quite downhearted; the ship had disappeared in the blue haze at a little after one o'clock, and had not reappeared; she appeared to be standing about N. E. We are now in doubt what it can mean, but think she must be bound here; else why approach so near?

Friday, July 24, 1857. Up at daylight, and off to the east hills that command a view of the bay of Yedo and the south Pacific. Alas! no ship could be seen. Whoever she was, it was clear that she was not bound to Shimoda. I never had anything to try my philosophy so harshly as this.

I am inclined to think that she was not the Flying Dutchman (as suggested nationally by Mr. Heusken) but simply a whaler, fishing along the coast. I wish the "blubber-hunter" had kept a few miles further from land, and spared us the excitement of hope and the bitter disappointment that followed.

Monday, July 27. Made a present of my third and last revolver to Déwa no Kami. I am sorry to hear of the death of Abé Isé no Kami at Yedo. He was the second member of the Council of State, and very influential.

He has always been represented to me as a man of great intelligence, and one that fully understood the power of the United States and other Western nations; and, above all, was convinced that the time had arrived when Japan must abandon her exclusive policy, or be plunged into the miseries of war. He is a great loss to the liberal party of Japan.

Friday, August 21. Happy day! I get a package with a dozen newspapers and some China letters from Mr. Rice. He writes me that he will forward my packages about October next by a Japanese schooner (American model) which will leave about that time. What a relief to have this slight glimpse of the outer world, although I do not get any American letters. This day is the anniversary of my arrival in Japan. One year here, and not a single letter from America! My last letters were dated February, 1856, eighteen months ago! How much may have happened in the mean time. Who among my old friends has death removed? I suppose my letters must be packed up in a box, which was not known to Mr. Rice, or he would have sent letters in place of newspapers. What has become of the American men-of-war of the East India squadron?

CHAPTER X.

VISIT OF THE PORTSMOUTH. — THE FIRST VICTORY.

MONDAY, September 7, 1857. At noon to-day the signal cannon again gave us the joyful news that a foreign ship was in sight. Mr. Heusken went over his old ground, and on his return informed me that a heavy ship was standing in for the harbor; that as the wind blew the colors end on, he could not make them out. It was a comfort to think that she was coming here, although we did not know what flag she wore; at all events, she was from a civilized land.

It is now one year and four days since I was left here by the San Jacinto, and full six months have run beyond the time that Commodore Armstrong promised to visit me. That it was not the Commodore was clear, as it was a sailing-ship. The wind fell provokingly light, and at seven P. M. the boom of a heavy gun came from the ship. Mr. Heusken volunteered to go to her, although she was some ten miles off. He accordingly started, and did not get back until one A. M.

Tuesday, September 8. The ship proves to be the United States sloop-of-war Portsmouth, Captain A. H. Foote,[1] eighteen days from Shanghai, where he left Commodore Armstrong in the San Jacinto, and where he has been nearly three months, at the distance of seven days' steaming from me. The Portsmouth did not expect to visit Japan when she left Hong-Kong, so that all my letters from home that have been received since April last (one still at Hong-Kong) have not come to me. She brought me letters from Captain Bell and the officers of the San Jacinto only. I was up all night eagerly reading the newspapers and the few letters she brought me.

The ship came up at noon, and at two P. M. the captain came to see me. He was much pleased when I showed him the Convention of June 17, and said that all would be surprised at my success. He told me that he had great difficulty in getting the Commodore's consent to come here, and I believe it was only obtained by some medical ruse by which the ship was ordered here for the health of the crew. Captain Foote told me he had the most stringent orders not to enter the harbor of Shimoda; that he was to stay the shortest possible

---

[1] Andrew Hull Foote, U. S. N., was born at New Haven in 1806, and entered the navy in 1822, becoming a lieutenant in 1830, a commander in 1852, a captain in 1861, and a rear-admiral in 1862. His capture of the Barrier Forts near Canton in China in 1856, and his services in the gunboats on the Mississippi and other inland waters during the Civil War, form part of one of the most noble records in the United States Navy.

time here, and an ungracious addendum was made that he would probably have to bring me away.

It appears that Commodore Armstrong has been occupied from December to June in protecting the British Colony of Hong-Kong, thus enabling Admiral Seymour to employ more of his force in active hostilities against the Chinese; he found himself able to send a ship to Manila to inquire about some Americans who are imprisoned there under a charge of murder; and he was also able to send another to Singapore to inquire into — what? — a case of salvage!!! However, let him pass with this addition. I informed Captain Foote that all my dispatches from the government were at Hakodaté, where they had remained since last May, and that as he was going there I asked him to touch here on his return and give me my letters. It would seem as though the Commodore had foreseen this request, for he positively ordered Captain Foote on leaving Hakodaté, to stretch out one hundred and fifty miles from land, while his direct route would have carried him about twenty miles south of Shimoda.

Captain Foote invited me to visit his ship tomorrow to receive a salute, and to dine with him. He then went over to the Go-yosho to look at the lacquer ware, Mr. Heusken attending him as his interpreter. Employed until a late hour of the night on my correspondence.

Wednesday, September 9, 1857. I told Captain Foote and his officers that I was deeply mortified that I could not invite them to dine with me, as in reality all I had to offer them was rice, fish, and tough chickens; they begged me not to mention it, as they had been fully prepared to find me suffering from privations, owing to the manner in which I had been neglected. Went on board at two P. M. and had my salute of thirteen guns from the heavy 68-pounders, which were loaded with full charges, and not with the usual reduced charge which is for saluting. A pleasant dinner in the cabin, with Captain Foote and his first lieutenant, Mr. Macomb, son of Major-General Macomb, of Plattsburgh memory.

I am to go with Captain Foote and his officers to visit the Governor to-morrow, and afterward dine in the ward-room. Returned home at five P. M., and went to work and wrote to a very late hour.

Thursday, September 10, 1857. To the Goyosho at eleven A. M., and had a pleasant visit which lasted about an hour. Captain Foote and his officers are very busy in making purchases, and they are delighted at only paying thirty-four and a half cents for what cost the San Jacinto one dollar. Mr. Heusken is constantly occupied with them, which retards my writing sadly.

Went on board ship at one P. M. and remained until five, having dined in the ward-room. The

Portsmouth appears to be a very happy ship. I learn from Captain Foote that he took Mr. C. W. Bradley with the Siamese treaty to Bangkok, and that the ratifications were exchanged. The Senate struck out the fifth article, which nearly lost the treaty, but the consul, Mr. Mattoon, accepted all the provisions of the article (which related to passports) as a police regulation. I am pleased to learn that the treaty is working admirably. Ships have already loaded for New York and San Francisco, and a large quantity of American tonnage is employed in the trade between Siam and China. Many of the finest American clippers have traded in this manner at the Menam.

Captain Foote has kindly permitted the purser to supply me with flour, butter, and pork from the ship's stores, I paying for them; and a great favor it is in two senses: First, to be able to get them at all; and, second, the price is only about half what they would have been at Hong-Kong. I cannot find words to express my thanks to Captain Foote and the officers of the Portsmouth for the generous manner in which they have divided their own private stores to help me in my distressed situation. Captain Foote supplied me with a quarter box of superior tea, two jars of lard, and a bag of prepared hominy. From the ward-room I received half a dozen fine Virginia hams, and five smoked tongues. I had nothing to give them in return but barren thanks.

Saturday, September 12, 1857. Mr. Heusken finished his copying at four A. M., and having made up our mail, he went on board the Portsmouth at five A. M. The wind being light, the ship did not get clear off the south point until three P. M.

The visit of the ship has thrown me into a state of intense excitement, as may well be imagined; I have not had three hours of consecutive sleep since the signal was fired announcing her approach.

Thursday, September 25, 1857. At the Goyosho this morning at eleven o'clock; the Governors informed me that they had received letters from Yedo relating to the President's letter. That after many anxious consultations it was finally settled that I am to go to Yedo in the most honorable manner; and after my arrival I am to have an audience of the Shōgun, and then present the letter of the President!!

I expected that something would follow this, — some objectionable proposition that I could not accept, which would throw the responsibility of the non-delivery of the letter on me, but nothing of the kind occurred. They wished me to agree to start and stop at certain hours and at certain places, saying that accommodations suitable for me could only be found at such places, etc.

I informed them that I should be willing to agree to such hours as might prove best, and to stop where I could be best accommodated; but I could not bind myself beforehand to any hour or march; that I must not only be free in my action, but that the escort attending me must be under my command exclusively. That they would find me, as a reasonable man, quite ready to adopt any proper suggestions on those points on the road, but I could not be bound up to comply with their regulations before I knew what might occur, etc., etc., to which they at once assented.

The manner in which I am to salute the Shōgun is to be the same as in the courts of Europe, *i. e.*, three bows. They made a faint request that I would prostrate myself and "knockhead," but I told them the mentioning such a thing was offensive to me. The Governors informed me that Shinano no Kami was ordered to Yedo for the purpose of assisting in the arrangements to be made for my visit. They said that a great deal was to be done in the way of preparation, and that it would probably require some two months to complete the arrangements. In the mean time, they will consult with me in preparing my retinue, etc., etc.

Monday, September 28, 1857. Shinano no Kami, with Moriyama Yénoské, started yesterday for Yedo. The commissary of Shimoda came today to take orders for procuring the men I shall want, and preparing their dresses.

I shall not take any of my Chinese with me, as the Japanese have a great dislike to the Chinese, and I do not wish to be associated in their minds with the Chinese or any other people. I shall therefore only be accompanied by Mr. Heusken and my two Japanese house servants from my family. My own train will consist of some forty porters bearing my luggage, cooking utensils, bedding, etc., etc., and by the following, who will all have the arms of the United States on their dresses, as the coat of arms is worn by the Japanese, *i. e.*, 20 norimono bearers, 1 sword; 12 guards, 2 swords; 2 standard bearers, 2 swords; 2 shoe and fan bearers, 2 swords; 2 grooms, 1 sword; 2 commanders of the foregoing. All except grooms and norimono bearers are to have silk dresses.

I am to be attended by the vice-governor of Shimoda, the Mayor of Kakizaki, the commissary of Shimoda, and by the private secretary of the Governor. They will have together a *tail* of some one hundred and fifty or more men, so that the whole train will form a body of not far from two hundred and fifty.

Wednesday, September 30, 1857. My health is much improved. I attribute this to my improved diet, as I am now well supplied with delicate China pork, my sow having littered thirteen pigs on the 5th of August last. I have no doubt that the agreeable termination of the vexed question of the reception of the President's letter has also been of great service to me, as it has removed an immense pressure from my mind. I cannot help hoping that I shall be able to do something satisfactory in the way of a commercial treaty before I leave Yedo.

Sunday, October 4, 1857. My birthday; I am fifty-three years old; my lease is rapidly running to its close; God grant that the short remainder of it may be usefully and honorably employed. My health is better than it was a month ago, but far, very far, from being as good as it was this time last year. Shall I ever see New York and my dear American friends again? Doubtful, but God's will be done, I can say truly and heartily.

Saturday, October 17, 1857. I have selected a variety of such things as I have that will probably be acceptable as presents to the Shōgun and the ministers at Yedo. They consist of champagne and sherry, wines, cordials, and cherry brandy, books of natural history richly illustrated, telescope, barometer, rich astral lamp, rich cut decanters, preserved fruits, etc. I am having these carefully packed up, and the Japanese prove to be very handy at such work. I have been almost daily occupied in seeing to clothing, etc., preparing for my people. The coat of arms is very neatly done, and the motto, "E pluribus unum," the eagle, arrows, and olive branch quite perfect. I am informed that the news of my visit has spread like wildfire over the country, and as they express it, "Millions will go to Yedo to see the grand entry of the American Ambassador." They will call me that name instead of Plenipotentiary, as the former has the grandest sound in their ears. They tell me that printed accounts of me, illustrated by drawings, are circulated by thousands.[1] These are not in the form of newspapers, but are analogous to the "broad sheets and little books" that preceded that mighty engine, the newspaper.

Tuesday, October 20, 1857. At last, and fourteen months after my arrival in Japan, I have received my letters and supplies from Hakodaté, from which place they were conveyed in a schooner to Yedo, and from thence they were sent to me in a Japanese junk. Thank God for them.

I received in all twenty-eight letters, but not one word from the Department of State about my treaty with Siam, or one word in answer to some of mine [to which] it was important to me to receive answers. All the letters from the Department were printed circulars except one, dated August, 1856, and relating to a debt contracted by two Americans, Reed and Dougherty, with the Japanese.

[1] These were the nishiki-yé or "brocade pictures," drawn on and printed from wooden blocks, and gaily colored, being zylographs. These pictures are usually made in three parts, which are pasted together, making one piece. They have been unusually numerous during the war between Japan and China in 1894 and 1895.

Saturday, October 24, 1857. I find that the President was strongly inclined to reward my services in making a commercial treaty with Siam by removing me from my office of Consul-General at Japan. It appears that the treaty reached Washington on the 17th of September, 1856, and on the same day the " New York Times " published what *it said* was the actual treaty. The President held that it was I, and I alone, who communicated it to the " Times," and was for my instant removal. This was only prevented by the friendship of Governor Marcy, and the untiring labors of my kind friend General Wetmore. The President appeared to think the best mode of proceeding would be to punish me first, and then call on me for my defense. This mode of procedure is quite common among oriental despots, but I am inclined to think that the Western rule is to hold every man innocent until he is proved to be guilty. Had the President, in his ardent desire to punish the guilty, given orders to compare the publication in the " Times " with the official copy in the State Department, he would at once have seen that the " Times " version could not have emanated from me, nor from any one who had an opportunity of copying the treaty.

Wednesday, October 28, 1857. Moriyama appeared at my house this morning, having just returned from Yedo. He brought a message from

Déwa no Kami, requesting to meet me at the Go-yosho at noon to-day. Moriyama brought me a box containing files of the "Singapore Free Press," "Illustrated London News," and "Java Bode," which were forwarded to me from Nagasaki on the 14th of August by Mr. H. Donker Curtius, by sea, and had (of course) passed by Shimoda and been taken to Yedo. Moriyama informed me that it was true that publications had been made concerning my visit, and added that the government had suppressed them, as they contained so many misstatements. On going to the Go-yosho, Déwa no Kami showed me various ground-plans of the building where my audience was to take place, and explained their views of the ceremonies to be had, etc.

I accepted the whole programme, with one exception. They proposed after my audience was over, and I had retired, that I should return to the Audience Chamber, not as the representative of the President, but in my private capacity; that instead of proceeding to the place I formerly occupied, I should stop at the place where I made my first bow; that the Shōgun would then address me, to which I was not to reply, but simply bow and retire.

It struck me that there was some petty scheme of glorifying themselves at my expense in this proposition, and I avoided it by saying that I could

THE FIRST VICTORY. 179

not divest myself of my character of Plenipotentiary which had been conferred on me by the President, and that so long as the President pleased, I must maintain that character.

They were evidently chagrined at this, and tried to persuade me to alter my decision, assuring me that it was meant as a personal honor to me, etc., etc. I replied that I was grateful for the intention, and that if the Shōgun wished to see me at a private audience I would cheerfully attend him, but that it must always be in my official character.

To-day I am told that Shōgun is not the proper appellation of their ruler, but that it is Tai-kun.[1] Shōgun is literally "generalissimo," while Tai-kun means "great ruler." The genius of the people shines out in this. For more than a year I have spoken and written Shōgun when referring to their ruler, and they never gave me any explanation; but now, when I am on the eve of starting for Yedo, they give me the real word.

My departure is fixed for Monday, November

---

[1] This term, now long obsolete in Japan, comes into view again in Korea, where the Tai (wen) kun or father of the king has been so active in politics for a generation past. The term Tai-kun ("Tycoon") was first assumed by the Yedo ruler in dealing with the Koreans in the seventeenth century. The term Shōgun or army commander is of very ancient use, though the first Tai Shōgun or Great General who also exercised *civil* functions was Yoritomo, in 1192.

23. They proposed Friday, November 20, but as that would cause me to pass Sunday among the hills, I declined it and fixed on Monday, which will cause me to pass my Sunday at Kawasaki, a town about fifteen miles from Yedo, on the banks of the river that brought up Mr. Bittinger, chaplain of the Susquehanna, when he made his dash at Yedo in 1854.[1]

Friday, October 30, 1857. To-day is the anniversary of the first visit paid to me by the Governors of Shimoda, and according to appointment Déwa no Kami visited me, attended by one of the vice-governors, the Mayor or Prefect of Kakizaki, the commissary of Shimoda and his private secretary, besides a large train of officers, guards, etc., etc., but the above were all that were admitted into my private room. After an hour of pleasant chat, we sat down to a very good dinner provided in our style, and they did full honor to my cheer, both solids and fluids.

As soon as this was done, the dishes were removed, and I gave them a second one in Japanese style. Still they ate, but nature has its limits; they did what they could, but fell far short of their first performance. They left me at five P. M., full of fun and good cheer. Their conduct at table would have passed in any society of New York, Paris, or London.

[1] Perry's *Narrative*, p. 419.

An enormous umbrella has been added to the paraphernalia of my *tail* for Yedo.

Saturday, October 31. I am truly grateful for improved health. I begin to recover a little of my lost flesh.

Wednesday, November 18. I have got everything packed up and ready for my journey to Yedo, which is to begin on Monday next, the 23d. Visited the Prince of Déwa at Nakamura, to take leave of him before my setting out, according to Japanese custom. The Governor gave me a copy of a treaty made with the Dutch in January, 1856. It is only a recapitulation of the substance of the Dutch Convention of November, 1855, except that it withdraws the right of the Dutch to lease the grounds and buy the buildings at Déshima.

Friday, November 20, 1857. Went to the Goyosho at the special request of the Governor, who gave me copies of additional articles made with the Dutch October 16, 1857, and with the Russians on the 24th of the same month. The only points of importance in these articles are those contained in my Convention of June 17.

CHAPTER XI.

THE TRIUMPHAL JOURNEY TO YEDO.

MONDAY, November 23. At eight this morning I start on my journey to Yedo.

I went on horseback; the morning was very fine, and the idea of the importance of my journey, and the success that had crowned my efforts to reach Yedo, gave me a fine flow of spirits. The American flag was borne before me, and I felt an honest pride in displaying it in this hitherto secluded country.

At Nakamura, about one mile from my house, I joined the main cavalcade, and we started in the following order: My avant-courier was Kikuna, a military officer with a rank corresponding to captain; he had his horse, and norimono, and the usual bearers and attendants, but before him went three lads, each bearing a wand of bamboo, with strips of paper attached to the top; they cried out alternately, "Shi-ta-ni-iro!" that is, "Sit down," "sit down;" they kept some four hundred yards in advance, and their cry sounded quite musical.

Next to Kikuna came the American flag guarded by two of my guards. Then I came on horseback with six guards; next my norimono, with its twelve bearers, and their head man, bearers of my shoes, etc.; then Mr. Heusken on horseback with two guards, then his norimono bearers, etc. Next followed a long retinue bearing packages containing my bedding, chairs, food, trunks, and packages containing presents; my cook and his following.

The vice-governor of Shimoda followed with his train, then the Mayor of Kakizaki, and lastly the private secretary of the Governor of Shimoda. A Dutch interpreter was carried in a *kago* in Mr. Heusken's rear. The whole train numbered some three hundred and fifty persons. All the bearers of luggage, etc., etc., were changed every two ri, or about five miles, and I was glad to see that these men were all paid for their labor.

My "Standard Bearer" was clothed in a long kabi-ya, or gown made of brown and white calico of a particular pattern and open at the sides like a herald's coat, from the hip downward. My guards were clothed in silk dresses, and had the arms of the United States on the right and left breasts of their upper garment; each man wore two swords.

The norimono of Japan appears to have been made after the model of the iron cages said to have been invented by Cardinal Balue, in the reign of Louis XI. of France. They are so low that you cannot stand upright in them, and so short that you cannot lie down at full length. To one who has not been accustomed to sit with his legs folded under him, and the whole weight of his body pressing on his heels, the posture is more painful than can be easily imagined. I previously had a norimono made for me, which was six and a half feet long, like a palanquin of India, which enabled me to avoid the tortures of the Japanese norimono.

The packages containing my bedding, clothing, etc., were covered with black cotton cloth with the arms of the United States neatly put on them. The other packages were nicely put up, and had a little pennon with the United States arms flying from a short bamboo, which was placed upright on each package.

My norimono bearers were dressed in dark blue, with the arms of the United States on the back; these were picked men, twelve for me and eight for Mr. Heusken, and very tall for Japanese.

My men wore a peculiar ornament, which is prohibited to any below the bearers of princes. It is made of cotton cloth, gummed very stiffly, and folded back and forth in folds about three inches wide. It is about thirty inches long, and has one end stuck in the girdle at an angle below the right shoulder, with the upper end projecting a little beyond the right side of the body; across the upper end two white strips run diagonally across all the folds.

The motion of the body causes the folds to open and close, something like the action of a fan, and is considered as being very beautiful by the Japanese.

My route to-day was only fifteen miles. It continued along the river of Shimoda, the ground gradually rising, and the river diminishing to a mere thread of water, until we crossed a hill some four hundred feet high which separates the watershed of Shimoda from the valley of Nashimoto. Our midday halt was at Mitsukuri. The last part of the ride gave us the sight of some noble cypress and camphor trees; one of the latter was of enormous bulk, and the Japanese said it was many hundred years old. Nashimoto is a small village of about one hundred houses, very prettily situated. My quarters for the night were in a temple which commanded a most beautiful view of the hills and valley, and of the village which lay some one hundred and fifty feet abruptly below us.

I have remarked, that throughout the Catholic and Pagan world the most picturesque positions are always selected for churches and temples. I found that much attention had been paid to the path, for it cannot be called a road, over which I passed to-day. Bridges had been built over every stream, the pathway mended, and all the bushes cut away so as to leave the path clear. At the temple I found that a bathroom had been built for my special use, and every attention paid to my comfort.

Tuesday, November 24. Started at eight A. M. Our route was over the mountain Amagi,[1] which is some thirty-five hundred feet above the level of the sea. The path was very difficult; so much so that I was compelled to leave my horse and enter my norimono, and it was no easy matter to carry that, even with eight men bearing it, as the road was sometimes at an angle of 35°, while the zigzags were some of them not so long as the pole or beam of my norimono, which is twenty-two feet long. Amagi is clothed with noble trees, consisting of cypress, pine, camphor, and others of the laurel family, besides many of whose names I am ignorant. The orchidea were numerous, and offer a rich harvest to the experienced botanist. We halted on the top of Amagi, whence we had a fine view of Shimoda, Oshima and its volcano, with the Bay of Suruga, the Gulf of Yedo, etc., etc. The descent is not quite so abrupt as the ascent was, and about two thirds of the way down I mounted my horse once more. As I descended, the valley opened and gave some beautiful views. On the south side of Amagi I saw a very pretty cascade. Passing through a village, I saw some camellias

---

[1] Amagi San or Yama is 4700 feet high, and has given its name to one of the warships in the Imperial Navy that was in the battle off the Yalu River, September 17, 1894.

which were already in full bloom, both white and red, but the flowers were all single.

Passing through the village of Yu-ga-shima to go to my quarters at a temple, I turned to the right from the road, and in a few moments I had my first view of the mountain Fuji-Yama. It is grand beyond description; viewed from this place, the mountain is entirely isolated, and appears to shoot up in a perfect and glorious cone, some ten thousand feet high, while its actual height is exaggerated by the absence of any neighboring hills by which to contrast its altitude. It was covered with snow, and in the bright sun, about four P. M., it appeared like frosted silver. In its majestic solitude it appeared even more striking to me than the celebrated Dwhalgiri of the Himalayas, which I saw in January, 1855. I found the temple at Yu-ga-shima prepared for me in the same manner as that at Nashimoto.

Wednesday, November 25, 1857. Left Yu-ga-shima at eight A. M., and as our road lay over a plain, I mounted on horseback. As I proceeded, the plain widened until, in many places, it was three miles across it. The scene was very pleasing. The plain was covered with a heavy crop of rice, of which the harvest had just commenced, and it reminded me of the golden wheatfields of old Ontario. The houses of the people, the mode of cultivation, the dress of the people, and all minor particulars were exactly like Shimoda. We halted at noon at a hamlet called Ogiso; and when I mounted my horse I passed on in company with Kikuna and Mr. Heusken more rapidly than my attendants could do;[1] this brought me to the town of Mishima at three P. M. This town is on the Tōkaidō, or great road of Japan, and is the route traveled by the Dutch when they go to Yedo. I may here remark that the Dutch have not been to Yedo for the last ten years, their tribute having been delivered at Nagasaki to the Japanese.

The Dutch thus avoided the great expense of the journey; but this has not relieved them from the presents they made on the occasion of those visits, as they are regularly demanded and given at Nagasaki.

Mishima contains about nine hundred houses, and the description of it by Kaempfer in 1696, after making due allowance for high coloring, will apply to it now. It had a fine temple, situated in a fine square, and surrounded by noble trees, but it was totally destroyed by the great earthquakes of December, 1855. I went to see its ruins, and in my walk I was surprised at the numbers of the people, which were apparently far more numerous than the

[1] One of the villages passed through by Mr. Harris was that of Hō-jō, where originated the famous family of the same name. At Kamakura, during the thirteenth and early part of the fourteenth century, they ruled Japan as Regents in the name of the "Puppet Shōguns." *M. E.* chapters xiv. and xv.

whole population of the place. On asking for an explanation, I was told that the time of my arrival was known many days ago, and that all those who could procure permission had come to Mishima to see me, and that some had come more than one hundred miles. The people were perfectly well behaved, no crowding on me, no shouting or noise of any kind. As I passed, all knelt and cast their eyes down as though they were not worthy even to look at me; only those of a certain rank were allowed to salute me, which was done by "knocking head" or bringing the forehead actually to the ground.

Thursday, November 26, 1857. As our march to-day is a weary one, I start at half past seven. I stop in the suburbs to visit a temple. It is approached by a noble flight of eighty-five stone steps. There was nothing to mark the difference between this and a Chinese Buddhist temple except that the Japanese affair was less gaudy and much cleaner than its Chinese fellow.

We were now on the great road of Japan; it is from thirty to forty feet wide, and is bordered by very noble cypress, pine, fir, and camphor trees. Many of the cypresses are of extraordinary size. The typhoon of September 22, 1856, made sad ravages among these fine trees. I found marks of its effects almost every hundred yards. We soon began to ascend the spurs of Hakoné; the road up the mountain is paved with flat stones, and from the total absence of wheel carriages, or of horses that are shod with iron, the stones are quite polished, and so slippery that it is dangerous riding a horse over them. The ascent is bad, but not so vile as that over Mount Amagi. Near the top of the mountain I was taken to a temple built by Iyéyasŭ, the founder of the present dynasty of Tai-kuns. From the top of Hakoné we had a fine view of the city and Bay of Suruga. Fuji-Yama was quite near, and altogether a different affair from the glorious view at Yu-ga-shima.

A short distance on the north side of Hakoné, and about one mile from the top, stands the village of that name. Here is the celebrated pass into the Yedo district, and a rigid search is made of every norimono, and each person is examined as to his passport. Here the vice-governor of Shimoda, after a vast deal of circumlocution, informed me that when the great Princes of the Empire passed here, the door of the norimono was opened, and an officer looked into it without stopping the bearers; that it was a mere ceremony, but the ancient laws required it, etc., etc. I replied that as I was not a Japanese subject, and being, as I was, the diplomatic representative of the United States, I was free from any such search; that they knew what was in my norimono, and could inform the officers at the pass that there was nothing forbidden in it.

The vice-governor tried for some time to change my determination, and at last proposed that I should ride through on horseback, and then permit the search of the empty norimono. I decidedly declined this, telling him that it was the search under any form that I objected to. He then said that we must stop until he could send to Yedo for instructions, which would only take five days. I told him I should not wait five days nor five hours; that if the search was insisted on, I should at once return to Shimoda. The poor vice-governor was in great tribulation, and finally went to the guard-house, and after a delay of two hours returned with word that it was all settled, and that I should pass unmolested.

Owing to the loss of time, I did not reach Odawara[1] until long after dark, but I was not sorry for the delay, as the effect of my train with an immense number of flambeaus, made from bamboo, presented a curious and novel appearance, as it wound and turned in the descents of the mountain, making a figure like the tail of an imaginary fiery dragon. Beyond the walls of the town I was met by the officials with an army of lanterns of all imaginable sizes, shapes, and colors, all decorated with the arms of the owners.

[1] The seat of the powerful *second* Hō-jō family which ruled Eastern Japan in the days of the Ashikaga Shōguns. Chamberlain's *Hand-Book for Japan*, p. 98.

It was so late when I arrived that I could not see much of the town. I was told it contains seven hundred houses, while Kaempfer gave it one thousand in 1696. If his account was correct, the town has lost three tenths of its houses during the last one hundred and sixty years.[1]

I should here remark that the principality of Idzu ends at Mishima. Idzu, in which Shimoda is situated, is one of the poorest provinces of the empire. It is so mountainous that only a very small portion of it can be cultivated, and it has no resources to support any large population. It has no town of ten thousand inhabitants, and the mountain Amagi cuts off the rest of the world from it, except by a painful and troublesome journey over it. The Japanese showed their astuteness in getting Commodore Perry to accept Shimoda for the Americans, as they were completely isolated by land, and they could easily keep away any undue number of Japanese craft. In fact, since I have been at Shimoda I have never seen one hundred and fifty vessels at one time in that harbor; while the Japanese assured me that a short time before my arrival it was not unusual to see from three to four hundred vessels at a time, and that during a gale of some days seven hundred vessels had been there at one time.

Friday, November 27. Left Odawara at half

[1] The town now contains 14,000 inhabitants.

past eight, and at noon halted at Oiso.[1] We were ferried over the river Banriugawa, which is now some two hundred yards wide, but in the rains of May and June it is over one mile wide.[2] The land on either side is a mere bed of sand, and the river is filled with quicksands. These sands, and the great width of the river during the floods, joined to the very low banks, render the bridging of the stream very difficult. This river with the broad sands and low banks reminded me of the river Sone in India.

Reached Fujisawa[3] at six P. M. From Odawara to Fujisawa it is almost one continuous village, as the hamlets are only separated a few hundred yards from each other. Kaempfer speaks of the crowds of travelers, priests, pilgrims, nuns, and beggars which thronged the Tōkaidō when he was in Japan. Nothing of the kind was seen by me. I have not as yet seen a dozen travelers on the road, nor met any of the great trains that attend the princes when they travel. In the towns and villages the shops are all closed except the cook shops. The people are collected in large numbers in front of their houses, and are silent and motion-

---

[1] Oiso was more famous in Yoritomo's days in the twelfth century than now, though the entirely modern Japanese practice of sea-bathing gives it new importance. Neesima died here January 23, 1890.

[2] Banriu gives its name to an Imperial ironclad warship.

[3] Famous for its monastery, temple, legends. *S. and H.* p. 62.

less as I pass. The authorities of each village conduct me to the bounds of their village, where they are relieved by those of the next. They salute me on leaving by a prostration, which is also made by my new conductors. The road has not only been repaired and put in order for my reception, but it is *actually swept* only a few hours before I pass over it. The cross roads and paths leading to the Tōkaidō are closed by ropes stretched across them. At the entrance of each village small cones formed of earth are erected, each having a small green sprig in the top of it. This is in honor of me. It reminds me of the " Shiva Lingas " [1] of India.

All the people I see are clad in their holiday costume, but as noted at Mishima it is only those of rank that salute me. All below that rank kneel and avert their eyes from me. At each place where I halt, the front of the house is decorated with long cloths festooned over the gates and doors, and of the Imperial colors, *i. e.*, black and white stripes, and a stake is always found placed to which my flag-staff can be attached.

As I mounted my horse after being ferried over the Banriugawa, my vicious brute of a horse both bit and kicked me. The little finger of my left

[1] Although in his Siam journal Mr. Harris refers to the phallic emblems seen by him near Bangkok, he does not seem to have noticed any in Japan, where the worship of the phallus or lingam was once quite general, being organically a part of Shintō or the indigenous faith. See *The Religions of Japan.*

hand was very painful, and I ordered some leeches to be applied. The doctor approached with great trepidation, while large drops of perspiration stood on his forehead. I asked what ailed him. He said that he never approached any person of such exalted rank before, and he was terrified at the idea of drawing blood from me. He was told to forget all about rank, and to apply his remedy as quickly as possible.[1] The leeches are very small, and of course are not very efficient. Excellent leeches are found in every part of the tropical East. A tank like those of Pulo Penang would be a pretty fortune to a man if he had it in New York. I have known the bites of those leeches to bleed for twenty-four hours.

The doctors of Japan are of two classes, the one following the European mode so far as they understand it; the other continues the old Chinese practice. Their medicines are generally of a simple kind. No violent chemicals are used, and calomel is unknown. Rhubarb and gentian are their internal remedies, while the moxa or cautery, with scarification, is applied externally in local inflammations, rheumatism, etc. Topical bleeding by leeching and cupping is also used. Vaccine matter was introduced by the Dutch a few years ago.

[1] A study of the leeches of Japan has been made by Mr. C. O. Whitman, of Milwaukee, formerly Professor of Biology in Japan, in the *Quarterly Journal of Microscopy*, London.

I was informed that about one tenth of the population have been vaccinated. They do not inoculate the small-pox. Still the ignorance of the Japanese of the true mode of treating the diseases of children, in particular, is shown in the frightful statement made to me by the Prince of Shiano, that, out of one hundred children born, no more than thirty reach the age of twenty years. My surgeon, having finished his labor, retired a proud and happy man: happy that he had pleased me, and proud that he had been called on to attend a person occupying my position.[1]

Saturday, November 28, 1857. Left Fujisawa at seven A. M. The road is very pleasant as the plain gradually widens as we approach Yedo. The Tōkaidō from Odawara runs quite near the shore, except where it crosses the peninsula of Sagami. See many marks of the typhoon of September, 1856, along the road. Fuji-Yama begins to improve in appearance as we recede from it. The

[1] To the doctors, more than to any one class, is Japan indebted for her modern renascence. The new civilization may be said to rest upon medical science. Long before Perry's arrival the physicians taught by the Dutch at Nagasaki, and scattered all over the country, began the creation of the public opinion which welcomed Western ideas. See the *Religions of Japan*, chapter xii. In 1891 there were 579 hospitals, 42,348 physicians (mostly practicing according to European science), 33,359 nurses and midwives, 2706 pharmacists, 11,849 druggists, besides excellent schools of pharmacy and medicine. Small-pox is nearly eradicated, and the proportion of infants reared is vastly greater than in 1857

villages are larger and more closely connected than on yesterday's route. The people, all in holiday costume, are kneeling on mats in front of their houses as I pass.

At noon, stop at Kanagawa, at a pretty honjin placed at the water side. This is an interesting spot to me, as it was the scene of Commodore Perry's negotiations. From my house I look across the bay to Yokohama, the place where his fleet was anchored. I was much surprised by the sight of three ships of European build and rig, which with two schooners were lying about midway between Kanagawa and Yokohama. These ships have been purchased from the Dutch by the Japanese, as the beginning of a navy. To the Northeast from Kanagawa I saw the steamer which the Dutch presented to the Japanese.

Kanagawa has the air of a flourishing town, and has much increased since Kaempfer described it. It is the nearest harbor to Yedo, and must become a place of great importance whenever Yedo shall be opened to foreign commerce.[1] I left Kanagawa with regret, and pursued my road to Kawasaki [2]

[1] Population of Kanagawa in 1889, 11,345. Of Yokohama in 1892, 143,754; of the Empire of Japan December 31, 1893, 41,386,265.

[2] Mr. Harris passed over the road later made famous by the attack on Mr. Richardson (to whom the Japanese have erected a monument) by the clansmen of Satsuma, and the story of the Japanese Rip Van Winkle, Urashima Tarō. See Chamberlain's *Hand-Book for Japan.*

where I shall pass Sunday. Ever since I have been in this country I have refused to transact any business on that day, or even to receive a message from the Japanese. They now fully understand my motives, and they respect me for them.

The village authorities are now preceded by a body of policemen, each bearing an iron rod some half an inch thick and six feet long. Four or five iron rings are attached by eyes to the top of the rod, which make a loud jingling noise as the foot of the rod is struck on the ground by the policeman at each two or three steps. They alternate the time of striking the rod on the ground by a regular measure; and this, with the different tones of the rings, makes a species of music.

The number of people seen increases. They are all fat, well clad, and happy looking, but there is an equal absence of any appearance of wealth or of poverty, — a state of things that may perhaps constitute the real happiness of a people; I sometimes doubt whether the opening of Japan to foreign influences will promote the general happiness of this people.[1] It is more like the golden age

[1] Whatever be the facts as to "happiness," it is certain that Japan's increase in actual wealth, population, and popular rights and privileges, since the introduction of the ideas and methods of Christendom, is amazing. *The Résumé Statistique de L'Empire du Japan* (published annually in Tōkiō by the Imperial Cabinet) for 1894 shows this most eloquently.

of simplicity and honesty than I have ever seen in any other country. Security for person and property, universal frugality and contentment, seem to be the apparent condition of Japan at present.

Sunday, November 29, 1857. The first Sunday in Advent. I read the whole service for this day with Mr. Heusken as my clerk and congregation. I experienced some peculiar feelings on this occasion. It was beyond doubt the first time that ever a Christian service on the Sabbath was read audibly in this place, which is only thirteen miles from Yedo, and this, too, while the law punishing such an act with death is still in force.

I now learn beyond doubt that the solitude of the great road is caused by positive orders issued by the government, prohibiting any travel over the road during my journey; and as my route for each day was fixed some time before, they could make their arrangements, and by my punctuality the stoppage of traffic was only for one day on each day's route.

Monday, November 30, 1857. To-day I am to enter Yedo. It will form an important epoch in my life, and a still more important one in the history of Japan. I am the first diplomatic representative that has ever been received in this city, and whether I succeed or fail in my intended negotiations, it is a *great fact* that will always remain, showing that at last I have forced this singular people to acknowledge the *rights of embassy*. I feel no little pride, too, in carrying the American flag through that part of Japan between the extremity of Cape Idzu and into the very castle of the city of Yedo.

I left Kawasaki a little before eight A. M. and was ferried over the river Rokugo,[1] which even now is both broad and deep. I proceeded to-day, after much deliberation, in my norimono. My wish was to go into Yedo on horseback, and the vice-governor eagerly encouraged that idea. *This excited my suspicion*, and after much difficulty I discovered that none but the " daimiōs " or princes of the highest rank can enter Yedo in their norimonos; all below that rank enter the city on horseback or on foot. This fact, coupled with the Japanese idea of seclusion and respectability being equivalent terms, determined me very reluctantly to proceed in my norimono.

The distance from Kawasaki to Shinagawa is seven and a half English miles, and the houses form almost a continuous street the whole way.

At Shinagawa our procession was re-formed; the vice-governor now led the way, and all my coolies, etc., were kept in line, and the whole cavalcade was nearly half a mile long. They proceeded with a slow and stately step along an unpaved street,

[1] Spanned since 1876 by iron bridges.

some forty to fifty feet wide, and bordered with wooden houses, none more than two stories high and mostly covered with tiles. Every Japanese town is divided into streets of one hundred and twenty yards long, and this district is responsible for the conduct of all in it. It has a captain called the "O-tono," and he has policemen under him. From Shinagawa, I found that these divisions were marked in an unmistakable manner: a strong stockade is erected each one hundred and twenty yards across the street, and has a pair of wide and strong gates. These gates are shut at a certain hour in the evening, and a wicket of some two feet square is opened for the passage of those who have the right to pass after the closing of the main gates. At many places in Yedo this stockade is double; that is, a second one is erected some fifteen yards distant from the regular one. When both the stockades are closed it makes quite a strong defense against anything but artillery, and is admirably calculated to stop the advance of a mob, or to secure the arrest of criminals. Again, Yedo has between eight and nine thousand of these streets, so that after a certain hour, it is cut up into that number of little forts. From Shinagawa, the people no longer knelt, nor did they avert their eyes.

The authorities made their prostrations as before, but the people remained standing. As the authorities were changed every one hundred and twenty yards, there was a constant "knocking of heads." A large proportion of the assemblage wore two swords, showing they were of some rank, and almost all had on the kami-shimo, or dress of ceremony. The number admitted into the streets through which I passed formed a rank of five deep on each side of the way; every cross street had its stockade closed to prevent too great a crowd, and as I looked up and down those streets they seemed a solid mass of men and women. The most perfect order was maintained from Shinagawa to my lodgings, a distance of over seven miles. Not a shout or cry was heard; the silence of such a vast multitude had something appalling in it. Lord Byron called a silent woman "*sleeping thunder*."

I calculated the number of persons that lined the street from Shinagawa to my residence at one hundred and eighty-five thousand. I called the distance seven miles, that each person occupied two feet of front in his lines, and that the lines were five deep on each side of the way. This calculation excludes all those who were in the cross streets or on the tops of the houses. In front of the lines of the spectators stood men about ten feet apart, each armed with a long white stave like a marshal's staff in the courts of New York. These men wore clothes of various colors, some green, some blue, black, gray, etc., while the coats of arms were so various that it easily appeared that they were the retainers of persons of rank, who "kept the ground" in the vicinity of their residences.

The people all appeared clean, well clad, and well fed. Indeed, I have never seen a case of squalid misery since I have been in Japan. A large number of officers of police attended the procession. In addition to his two swords, each one bore an iron truncheon about two feet long and one inch in diameter, a savage and dangerous weapon in the hands of a passionate or violent man; but there was no use for them, nor any apparent need of the constant cry of "Satu! Satu!" "Keep back! Keep back!" which was shouted forth by the street-keepers.

In this manner I went on, passing over seven bridges; the fifth was the Nippon Bashi, or bridge of Japan. It is from this bridge that all distances are reckoned in this country. After passing the bridge some few hundred yards, we went in a nearly N. N. W. direction, and after a while we reached a broad moat, on the opposite side of which rose a stone wall, varying from twenty to forty feet high, according to the make of the ground. The road followed this ditch for more than a mile, when my bearers started on a full run, rushed through a gateway, across a court, and ended by bearing me into the house. This was doing the matter in the most honorable Japanese manner. Mr. Heusken had to leave his norimono at the outer gate.

As I got out of mine, I was warmly welcomed by my old friend the Prince of Shinano, who conducted me to my rooms, and pointed out the arrangements made for my comfort. It will sound queerly when I say that these consisted of a bedstead, some chairs and tables, though the Japanese never use one of the articles. Their rooms are destitute of a single article that we would call furniture. The universal mat serves as chair, couch, table, and bed. Their food is served on stands or trays from three to ten inches high, and is contained chiefly in wooden bowls, lacquered. Porcelain is only used for drinking tea and saké from.

The bath-room was close to my sleeping apartment. I had set apart for my special use a bedroom, sitting-room, and dining-room. Mr. Heusken's rooms adjoined mine, and consisted of a bed and sitting room. In addition to this I was shown my reception-rooms, which could be increased to any size by merely removing the sliding doors. In fact, every Japanese house may in a short time be converted into a single room by this simple and expeditious process.

The building is very large. It is government

property, and was formerly used as a college.¹ It is situated within what is called "The Castle;" that is, it is the outer one of four circles, rather irregular ones, the centre one of which is the residence of the Tai-kun. My house stretches to the road that runs along the ditch, and on the opposite side it fronts on a wide street. From my rooms I see the stone wall before mentioned and the buildings occupied by two of the brothers of the Tai-kun. It is the "Court" part of the city, and none but persons of rank reside in it.

This over, the Prince informed me that the government had been in a fever of anxiety all day for fear of some accident; that the people were wild with curiosity to see my entry, and that had the government not used the most stringent measures, the people would have rushed to Yedo "by millions" (those are his numbers) to see me; and finally, that all of the inner gates of the city had been closed ever since the previous night to keep

¹ In this structure, originally the "Office for the Examination of Barbarian Books," *i. e.*, from Europe and America, lay the germ of the present magnificent Imperial University of Tōkiō, with its colleges and faculties of Law, Medicine, Engineering, Literature, Science, and Agriculture, the calendar of which for 1893-94 shows a grand total of 1396 students and 565 living graduates. The edifice in which Mr. Harris lodged was on the west side of the old Kai-Séi-Jō inclosure near the Kudan, fronting the Castle moat, and not far from the Shimidzu gate. Significantly, coming from Shimoda (low field), the district in Yedo where he lived was named Kanda (high or divine field).

away the crowd, and thus prevent accidents; that they were all much rejoiced at my safe arrival, etc.

He then informed me that as I came as the representative of so great a nation, the government had appointed eight persons of distinguished rank as "Commissioners of the voyage of the American Ambassador to Yedo." I did not exactly understand what was meant by this move. I was assured that it was solely in honor of me, and that nothing connected with their duties could give me any umbrage, etc., etc. I told him that with this explanation I had no objection to make at present.

The Prince then gave me a list of the commissioners, which was as follows: —

No. 1, Toké, Prince [1] of Tamba.
" 2, Hayashi, Prince of Daigaku.
" 3, Tsutsu, Prince of Hizen.
" 4, Kawasé, Prince of Saiyémo.
" 5, Inouyé, Prince of Shinano.
" 6, Uyédono, Mim-bu Shoyu.
" 7, Nagai, Prince of Gemba.
" 8, Tsukagoshi, Tosuké.

[1] The word Kami, here translated "Prince," means lord, ruler, rector. Hayashi was one of the regents of the University or Daigaku. None of the daimiōs were "princes" in any real sense of the word, that term being properly reserved to sons of the Emperor. Further, very few of the daimiōs were of any *personal* importance, the power which they were supposed to wield being in reality held and used by able men of low rank, who made the public opinion of the clan of which the average daimiō was the figurehead.

THE TRIUMPHAL JOURNEY TO YEDO. 207

Numbers 2 and 6 were commissioners with Commodore Perry at Kanagawa in 1854.

I was then informed that the next morning an ambassador from the Tai-kun would wait on me to congratulate me on my arrival, etc., etc.

The Prince of Shinano having been informed by me that my first official step after my arrival would be to write to Hotta, Prince of Bitchiu, informing him of my arrival at Yedo, that I was the bearer of a letter from the President of the United States to his Majesty the Tai-kun, and asking when I could have an audience of his Majesty for the purpose of delivering that letter, etc., etc., he now asked if I could send that letter by him at once. As the letter had been previously prepared at Shimoda, and only required to be dated and sealed, that matter was soon dispatched. A sumptuous repast after the Japanese fashion was now served to me and Mr. Heusken. Mr. Heusken's stands or trays were four inches high; the trays for my use were ten inches high.

After dinner was over, I told the Prince that it was my wish to pay all the expenses of my table, etc., etc., and that such was the fashion of all parts of the world. That otherwise I should not feel at liberty to order such articles of food as best suited me; that it would be a point of delicacy to eat whatever was sent without making any remarks, etc., etc. He replied that I could not be permitted to pay for anything sent to me, but he thought there would not be any objection to my people buying anything I might wish to have prepared by my cook that I had brought from Shimoda. This was just what I wished, and gave me full satisfaction. At last the Prince left me to repose after the fatigue and excitement of this (to me important and eventful) day.[1]

[1] While the Hon. John A. Bingham, of Ohio, was Minister of the United States in Tōkiō, he met one of the old officers of the Bakafu, who communicated a very pleasant account of the reception of Mr. Harris in Yedo, the route traveled, the preparations, details, etc. See *Foreign Relations of the United States for 1879–80*, vol. i. pp. 629–636.

CHAPTER XII.

THE AMERICAN ENVOY'S AUDIENCE OF THE SHŌGUN.

TUESDAY, December 1, 1857. The "Commissioners" of my voyage to Yedo paid me a visit of ceremony this morning. Their various retinues amounted in the aggregate to some hundreds; each one had his pikes, or ensigns of his dignity, borne before him, and led horses followed his norimono. The caparisons of the horses bore the coats of arms of their noble owners. Among others, each following had fan bearers, slipper bearers, cane bearers, etc., etc. Each one had his kami-shimo, or dress of ceremony, brought with him in neat lacquered boxes, and his portfolio was neatly wrapped up in silk and slung over the back of a particular bearer.

After they arrived, they went at once to rooms where they put on their kami-shimos, and then they proceeded to the audience chamber. As soon as they were ready I was informed, and I also went there, attended by Mr. Heusken, the Prince of Shinano, and a long following of Japanese.

On my entry, I found them drawn up in a line and standing. I took my place in front, and then we exchanged profound bows. Toké, Prince of Tamba, was their spokesman. He began by saying that to do proper honor to me as the representative of a great nation, his Majesty the Tai-kun had sent them to congratulate me on my arrival at Yedo, and to inquire after my health. To this he added the personal respect of himself and of his colleagues. I made a suitable reply, and then each of the Commissioners was separately presented to me.

As Hayashi, Prince of Daigaku, and Uyédono Mim-bu Shoyu were presented, I was told that they were among the Commissioners who negotiated with Commodore Perry at Kanagawa. The Prince of Hizen assisted in making the Russian treaty.

As soon as these particular presentations were over, I told them that I was happy to become acquainted with persons of their distinguished merit, and that I hoped our intercourse would prove mutually agreeable. They returned this compliment. Then followed more stately bows, and I retired, attended as on my entry. The Commissioners are rather intelligent-looking men taken together, while some of them bear faces that are capital introductions to your respect.

The Prince of Shinano informed me that the arrival of the "Ambassador" of the Tai-kun was delayed by the wish of his Majesty to examine personally the present which by the laws of etiquette of Japan was to be presented to me by the Taikun, and he then added that after it had been examined in the palace, it had to be taken to the Great Council for their examination. In answer to my inquiries, I was told that the Tai-kun cannot make or receive the smallest presents until they have been examined and approved by the Council of State!!! That single statement convinced me that the Tai-kun was a mere "lay figure" of government, and that he did not possess a single particle of political power. He is even more restricted than was the Doge of Venice by the "Council of Ten."

A little after midday I was told of the arrival of the "Ambassador," and on entering the room of audience I found him to be Toké, Prince of Tamba, who is a person occupying a high position at Court, and, so far as I could understand the matter, somewhat analogous to the office of Chamberlain at the courts in the Western world. In the toko (or alcove), and placed on a tray of white wood, stood a box some three feet high, which was tied with a broad green silk braid. I took my place near the toko, while Toké stood opposite. We then saluted each other, and the prince said that his Majesty, knowing that I had come from a far distant land, had sent him to inquire after my health, and whether I had made my long journey without accident. He then added that his Majesty had sent "a small present" for my acceptance. This ended, the Prince went three steps down the room, and from that place paid his personal compliments to me, and made inquiries after my health. This over, he returned to his first standing, and I made a proper reply to the kind message of his Majesty, and returned my thanks for this mark of his kindness. As I spoke of the present, I turned towards the box and bowed. When I began to thank the prince for his personal civilities, he again retreated the three steps, so that he might occupy a lower position when hearing what I said in relation to himself than the one he stood in while hearing what I said in relation to the Tai-kun. As soon as the interpretation of what I said was finished, he again returned to his original place, and we exchanged bows; and thus the ceremony ended.

When I reached my private apartments, the present was brought in. On opening it, it was found to contain four trays of Japan bonbons, made of sugar, rice flour, fruit, nuts, etc. They were arranged in the trays in a beautiful manner, and the forms, colors, and decorations were all very neat. The quantity was about seventy pounds of weight. I am sorry I cannot send them to the United States, but they will not keep for so long a voyage.

In my conversations with the Prince of Shinano to-day he enlarged on the difficulties that he had overcome, and the great labor he had performed to enable me to come to Yedo; he spoke of his anxious days and sleepless nights; that care and anxiety had taken away his appetite, so that he had become lean in his person; and that his blood had frequently gushed from his nose, from his great agitation; that he had done all this from his friendship for me, etc., etc.

Something of this had been before hinted at, but never so fully expressed as now. I replied that I was duly grateful to him for his friendship for me, but as he appeared to be under a great error as regarded my visit to Yedo, I must now fully explain myself on that point. I told him that I came to Yedo as the representative of the United States, and not in my private capacity; that the United States did not ask anything from the government of Japan *as a favor;* that it only demanded its rights; and that nothing would be accepted on the ground of favor; that my mission had for its object the good of the Japanese Empire; and that it was no favor to me or to my country that they should listen to my advice, but that it was the Japanese who should feel grateful to the President for the friendship he had shown to Japan, by the messages with which I was intrusted; that for myself, individually, I had no wish to come to Yedo, and that I only came here because my official duty required it; that I hoped he now fully understood not only my object in visiting Yedo, but that he would clearly see that it was not any favor to me, either in my private or in my official capacity, to receive me at Yedo.

The Prince was quite chapfallen at this, as it was the evident wish of the Japanese that I should look on my reception here as an unprecedented favor to me, both personally and officially; and thus they would establish a claim on my gratitude which might be of great use to them in the negotiations that might be commenced here.

However, the prince confessed that my view of the matter was a just one, and that he had only looked at the question from one point of view, and that point was on the Japanese side.

Wednesday, December 2, 1857. This morning, at half past ten, I felt a smart shock of earthquake, not severe enough, however, to do any damage. In the afternoon I received a letter from Hotta, Prince of Bitchiu, Minister of Foreign Affairs, informing me that he had received my letter and communicated its contents to his master the Tai-kun, and that his Majesty had fixed on Monday next, the 7th instant, for my public audience.

The Prince of Shinano is considered as my host (I do not know but keeper would be a more correct term), and he visits me daily. To-day he informs me that the great Council of State has heretofore consisted of five members, but since it had been determined to receive me at Yedo, the number had been increased to six, and that the Prince of Bitchiu, in addition to his position of first member of the Council, is now created "Minister of Foreign Affairs," and that all correspondence with foreign envoys will be conducted in his name.

Thursday, December 3, 1857. Wrote to the Minister of Foreign Affairs inclosing copy and translation of the President's letter to the Tai-kun. I also wrote him that I would pay him a visit of ceremony whenever he should be ready to receive me. In the evening I received an answer to my letter, and he wrote that he would be happy to receive my visit to-morrow. Had my usual visit from Shinano no Kami, and a good deal of conversation ensued. He was very anxious to have me make promises not to visit about the city, saying that Yedo contained a great many bad people, who might insult and maltreat me,[1] and thus the government of Japan would be plunged into serious difficulties with that of the United States.

I replied that I could not make any promises that would circumscribe my undoubted rights

[1] The Japanese officer had stronger grounds for this supposition than Mr. Harris imagined. "At this time, two young men conspired against his [Mr. Harris's] life, but they were arrested and shortly after died in prison." Inazo Nitobé's *United States and Japan*, p. 65. See later on in the Diary.

under the laws of nations; that I had no fears for my personal safety, as I had gone boldly and freely through many cities of the East where the population was of a much worse character than that of Yedo, and where I had no official character to protect me; that they must and might rely on my age and discretion that I should not do anything to cause them any embarrassment; but I must be left free to act in all respects according to the dictates of that discretion, and that I could not give them any pledge or promise of any kind that might afterwards be used by them to limit me in my freedom of action, etc.

I also told him that exercise in the open air was the daily practice of all Western people, and was necessary to the preservation of health; that I wished the government to point out some place, either in the wide streets or in a ba-ba,[1] where Mr. Heusken and I could take the requisite exercise.

This appeared to cause much trouble, but it was so just and reasonable that he could not urge anything against my demand, except his fears of the populace. I told him he might remember that when I demanded the removal of the guards from my residence at Shimoda he had told me that the people of Shimoda were the worst in Japan, and that the presence of the Japanese officers at my

[1] Horse-course, or place of military exercises.

house was absolutely indispensable to protect me from outrage by day and robbery at night; that notwithstanding his remonstrances on that occasion, I had insisted, and the guards were removed full eleven months ago, and that he well knew that nothing unpleasant had occurred since; that I had no doubt his fears about the conduct of the good people of Yedo were equally unfounded. Poor Shinano looked confused when I referred to the Shimoda affair, and in his reply said that what he then told me was by express orders of the government, but that I might rely on the truth of what he now stated about the people of Yedo. He concluded by saying he would report my wishes to the government, and hoped to have the matter arranged to my satisfaction.

Friday, December 4, 1857. I start on my visit to the Prime Minister at ten A. M., the Prince of Shinano acting as my escort. My retinue is composed in the same manner as it was on my entry into Yedo, excepting my luggage, cook, etc., etc.

I went southwardly over the same road that I came on my entry for about one mile, when we crossed the moat on a new bridge about one hundred feet long, and passed through a gate into a square of some fifty or sixty feet formed by stone walls about twenty-five feet high; a gate in the wall running at right angles with the gate of entrance gave us exit from the quadrangle, and we entered into the third inclosure of the castle by a broad street, having the outer wall on our left and a line of houses on our right. After a short time we turned to our right, or westward, still proceeding through fine streets lined with the houses of the daimiōs and kami, etc.

These houses were all built of wood, roofed with tiles. The streets were unpaved and scrupulously clean. The street-keepers were the retainers of the princes, and each wore the arms of his master. The crowd was not so great as in passing through the city; still, vast numbers were collected, especially when we came to the frequent open spaces or squares. The observers were the servants and retainers of the nobles, and gave a lively idea of the magnitude of the households of those personages. The buildings on the street have projecting windows like the houses at Cairo and Alexandria.

Through the grass screens to these openings we saw plenty of fair faces, and it would appear that Mother Eve's failing is fully inherited by her daughters in Yedo. Every possible part of the window, from its sill to the top, was plastered with a female face. As no part of their dresses could be seen, I am unable to describe them.

We passed by a causeway and short bridge over a canal; here the water had a fall of about six feet, and appears to prove that the city is built on ground that rises gradually from the shore of the bay. We reached the house of Hotta Bitchiu no Kami, or Hotta, Prince of Bitchiu. All the norimono, except mine, were stopped at the outer gate; my bearers mended their pace at some hundred and fifty yards from the gate, and by the time they reached it they were at a full trot, dashed through the gate, across the court, and plumped me down close to the edge of some clean mats that had been placed there for my reception.

On getting out of my norimono, my "shoe bearer" gave me a new pair of unsoiled patent leather shoes, which I put on. The Japanese of all ranks enter a house in their stockings alone, leaving their straw sandals outside; and there is a good reason for this, for, as I have before noted, the mat serves as chair, couch, table, and bed. In the vestibule, some thirty persons dressed in kami-shimos were seated in Japanese fashion, and saluted me by bringing the forehead down to the mat. I passed to the right, and soon met the Commissioners of my voyage, who saluted me, and, through Toké, Prince of Tamba, inquired after my health, etc., etc. I was now conducted into a room where I found chairs, made after our pattern, for Mr. Heusken and myself, with comfortable braziers filled with burning charcoal. In a few moments two tables were brought in, on which were placed pipes, tobacco, and fire. Soon afterward the Japanese great tea-luxury was served to me. It is made of very fine tea reduced to a powder, on which boiling water is poured,[1] and forms what may be called a tea gruel. The taste was much better than the looks.

As soon as I had drunk my tea I was asked if I would then see the Minister, and on my replying in the affirmative, the sliding doors were opened, and here I met the Minister. We saluted each other in silence, and he then led the way into a fourth room, where I found two chairs on one side, and ten black lacquered stools on the other; we again saluted each other, when the Minister courteously motioned to me to be seated, and, waiting until I was seated, he sat down himself. The Commissioners of my voyage now entered the room and again saluted me, after which they also took their seats on the black stools.

The Minister courteously inquired about my health, and after my reply and the requisite counter-inquiry, he expressed much admiration at the long voyage I had made through so many different countries, for he perfectly understood what is called the overland route to India. I made the proper answer, adding that I considered myself as a fortunate person, as I was the first foreigner who had ever visited the great city of Yedo in a diplomatic capacity.

Tables were now brought in by servants, who

[1] Hence the name cha no yu, tea of hot water.

carried them elevated as high as possible, marching with a stately step and with a measured cadence. Then followed pipes and tobacco, tea, and trays of refreshments. The trays of the Minister and myself were of the same height, both being some inches higher than those served to the others. The Minister courteously urged me to partake of his refreshments, and begged me to excuse his not smoking, as he never used tobacco. He afterwards said he did not offer me saké, as he understood I did not drink wine or saké when I could avoid it. After some little conversation, I presented him with a copy of my intended address to the Tai-kun on the day of my audience, adding that I had made it very short so that no unnecessary topics should be introduċed. The Minister requested leave to withdraw for a short time, in order to have the paper translated. He accordingly left me with Shinano no Kami, the Commissioners of my voyage going with the Minister. The interior of this house exactly corresponds with the one I occupy.

The agitation of the Japanese interpreter is beyond anything I ever saw; he trembled all over his body as though he had an ague fit, while large drops of perspiration stood like beads on his forehead.

My seat was placed nearest the toko, and I was warmed by a lacquer and copper brazier. In place of ashes, the brazier contained pulverized spar of a snowy whiteness, neatly formed into a representation of the celebrated Fuji-Yama, the top being opened like the crater of a volcano to admit the coals.

In about half an hour the Minister returned and told me that my address was quite satisfactory, and at the same time he handed me the Tai-kun's reply, showing clearly that his Majesty would utter exactly what the Council should dictate! The Minister informed me that, as the interpreters could not be admitted into the Imperial presence, he had furnished me with a copy of the reply; so that by having it translated, the presence of the interpreter would not be required.

My business being ended, I rose, and we again bowed, the Minister following me to the same spot where we first met, where we again bowed; beyond that I found my Commissioners, who again saluted me. The two who had made the treaty with Commodore Perry inquired very kindly after him, and requested me to inform him of the fact whenever I might write to him. In the vestibule I found the same persons seated, who *salaamed* to me as on my entry, and from thence I once more entered my norimono.

The Minister is about thirty-five years old, short in stature, of a pleasant and intelligent countenance, and his voice is low and rather musical.

AUDIENCE OF THE SHŌGUN.

Sunday, December 6, 1857. This is the second Sunday in Advent; assisted by Mr. Heusken, I read the full service in an audible voice, and with the paper doors of the house here our voices could be heard in every part of the building.

This was beyond doubt the first time that the English version of the Bible was ever read, or the American Protestant Episcopal service ever repeated in this city. What a host of thoughts rush upon me as I reflect on this event. Two hundred and thirty years ago, a law was promulgated in Japan inflicting death on any one who should use any of the rites of the Christian religion in Japan. That law is still unrepealed, and yet here have I boldly and openly done the very acts that the Japanese law punishes so severely!

What is my protection? The American name alone. That name, so powerful and potent now, cannot be said to have had an existence then, for in all the wide lands that now form the United States there were not at that time five thousand men of Anglo-Saxon origin.

The first blow is now struck against the cruel persecution of Christianity by the Japanese, and, by the blessing of God, if I succeed in establishing negotiations at this time with the Japanese, I mean to boldly demand for the Americans the free exercise of their religion in Japan, with the right to build churches, and I will also demand the abolition of the custom of trampling on the cross or crucifix, which the Dutch have basely[1] witnessed for two hundred and thirty years without a word of remonstrance. This custom has been confined to Nagasaki; had it been attempted at Shimoda, I should have remonstrated in a manner that would have compelled the Japanese to listen to me. I shall be both proud and happy if I can be the humble means of once more opening Japan to the blessed rule of Christianity.

My Bible and Prayer-Book are priceless mementos of this event, and when, after many or few years, Japan shall be once more opened to Christianity, the events of this day at Yedo will ever be of interest.

Monday, December 7, 1857. I started for my audience about ten o'clock with the same escort as on my visit to the Minister, but my guards all wore kami-shimos and breeches which only covered half the thigh, leaving all the rest of the leg bare. My dress was a coat embroidered with gold after

[1] This custom of trampling (fumi) on a yé (engraved copper plate with representation of the crucifix) was abolished by the Japanese government in 1853, the year before Perry's second arrival. As the *Kindai Geppio* states, "From this year, the practice of fumi-yé at Nagasaki was abolished." Most of the American sailors shipwrecked on the Japan coasts, and cared for by the government until shipped away, seem to have had no compunctions about treading on the copper plate, thereby proving they were not Portuguese. See Hildreth's *Japan*, p. 503.

the pattern furnished by the State Department, blue pantaloons with a broad gold band running down each leg, cocked hat with gold tassels, and a pearl-handled dress-sword.

Mr. Heusken's dress was the undress navy uniform, regulation sword, and cocked hat. Our route was by the same street that I have mentioned on my visit to the Minister, but we crossed the moat by a bridge that was about half a mile from my house; the gateway with the quadrangular building was precisely like those described in my journal of the 4th instant. So also the appearance of the streets, buildings, people, etc., was exactly the same. On arriving at the second moat, all were required to leave their norimonos except the Prince of Shinano and myself. We crossed the bridge, passed the gate and quadrangle, and pursued our course, and everything was so exactly like what I then saw that nothing but the assurance of Shinano could convince me that I was in a different quarter.

When we arrived within about three hundred yards of the last bridge Shinano also left his norimono; and our horses, his spears, etc., etc., with the ordinary attendants, all remained. I was carried up to the bridge itself; and, as they say, further than a Japanese was ever carried before, and here I dismounted, giving the President's letter, which I had brought in my norimono, to Mr. Heusken to carry. We crossed this bridge, through the same quadrangle as before, and at some one hundred and fifty or two hundred yards from the gate I entered the audience hall. Before entering, however, I put on the new shoes I had worn on my visit to the Minister, and the Japanese did not even ask me to go in my stocking-feet.

As I entered the vestibule I was met by two officers of the household. We stopped, faced each other, and then bowed; they then led me along a hall to a room where, on entering, I found the two chairs and a comfortable brazier. I should here note that tobacco is not served among the refreshments of the palace. I again drank the "tea gruel."

The breeches are the great feature of the dress; they are made of yellow silk, and the legs are some six to seven feet long! Consequently, when the wearer walks, they stream out behind him, and give him the appearance of walking on his knees, an illusion which is helped out by the short stature of the Japanese and the great width, over the shoulders, of their kami-shimos.

The cap is also a great curiosity, and defies description; it is made of a black varnished material, and looks like a Scotch Kilmarnock cap, which has been opened only some three inches wide, and is fantastically perched on the very apex of the head; the front comes just to the top edge of the forehead, but the back projects some distance behind the head. This extraordinary affair is kept in place by a light-colored silk cord which, passing over the top of the "Coronet," passes down over the temples and is tied under the chin. A lashing runs horizontally across the forehead, and being attached to the perpendicular cord, passes behind the head, where it is tied.

My friend Shinano was very anxious to have me enter the audience chamber and rehearse my part. This I declined as gently as I could, telling him that the general customs of all courts were so similar that I had no fear of making any mistakes, particularly as he had kindly explained their part of the ceremony, while my part was to be done after our Western fashion. I really believe he was anxious that I should perform my part in such a manner as to make a favorable impression on those who would see me for the first time. I discovered also that I had purposely been brought to the palace a good hour before the time, so that he might get through his rehearsal before the time for my actual audience. Finding I declined the rehearsal, I was again taken to the room that I first entered, which was comfortably warm and had chairs to sit on. Tea was again served to me.

At last I was informed that the time had arrived for my audience, and I passed down by the poor daimiōs, who were still seated like so many statues in the same place; but when I had got as far as their front rank, I passed in front of their line and halted on their right flank, towards which I faced. Shinano here threw himself on his hands and knees. I stood behind him, and Mr. Heusken was just behind me.

The audience chamber faced in the same manner as the room in which the great audience was seated, but separated from it by the usual sliding doors; so that although they could see me pass and hear all that was said at the audience, they could not see into the chamber. At length, on a signal being made, the Prince of Shinano began to crawl along on his hands and knees, and when I half turned to the right and entered the audience chamber, a chamberlain called out in a loud voice "Embassador Merican!" I halted about six feet from the door and bowed, then proceeded nearly to the middle of the room, where I again halted and bowed. Again proceeding, I stopped about ten feet from the end of the room, exactly opposite to the Prince of Bitchiu on my right hand, where he and the other five members of the Great Council were prostrate on their faces. On my left hand were three brothers of the Tai-kun prostrated in the same manner, and all of them being nearly "end on" towards me. After a pause of a few seconds I addressed the Tai-kun as follows:—

"May it please your Majesty: In presenting

my letters of credence from the President of the United States, I am directed to express to your Majesty the sincere wishes of the President for your health and happiness, and for the prosperity of your dominions. I consider it a great honor that I have been selected to fill the high and important place of Plenipotentiary of the United States at the court of your Majesty, and as my earnest wishes are to unite the two countries more closely in the ties of enduring friendship, my constant exertions shall be directed to the attainment of that happy end."

Here I stopped and bowed.

After a short silence the Tai-kun began to jerk his head backward over his left shoulder, at the same time stamping with his right foot. This was repeated three or four times. After this, he spoke audibly and in a pleasant and firm voice what was interpreted as follows: —

"Pleased with the letter sent with the Ambassador from a far distant country, and likewise pleased with his discourse. Intercourse shall be continued forever." [1]

Monday,[2] December 7, 1857. Mr. Heusken, who had been standing at the door of the audience chamber, now advanced with the President's letter, bowing three times. As he approached, the Min-

---

[1] Here ends the record in "Journal No. 4."
[2] Here begins the record in "Journal No. 5."

ister for Foreign Affairs rose to his feet and stood by me. I removed the silk cover over the box, opened it, and also raised the cover of the letter so that the Minister could see the writing. I then closed the box, replaced the silk covering (made of red and white stripes, six and seven), and handed the same to the Minister, who received it with both hands, and placed it on a handsome lacquered stand which was placed a little above him. He then lay down again, and I turned towards the Tai-kun, who gave me to understand my audience was at an end by making me a courteous bow. I bowed, retreated backward, halted, bowed, again retreated, again halted and bowed again, and for the last time.

So ended my audience, when I was reconducted to my original room, and served with more tea gruel. A good deal of negotiation had been used by the Japanese to get me to eat a dinner at the palace, alone, or with Mr. Heusken only. This I declined doing. I offered to partake of it, provided one of the royal family or the Prime Minister would eat with me. I was told that their customs forbade either from doing so. I replied that the customs of my country forbade any one to eat in a house where the host, or his representative, did not sit down to table with him. At last the matter was arranged by ordering the dinner to be sent to my lodgings.

I had not been long in the room last mentioned before I was requested to meet the Council of State. I found them in the place where the daimiōs had been seated, but who had now left the room. Hotta, Prince of Bitchiu, spoke, and in the name of the Council congratulated me on my arrival and audience, and then said his Majesty had ordered a present to be offered to me, which was then in the room, at the same time pointing to three large trays each holding five silk kabiyas thickly wadded with silk wadding. I thanked the Council for their kind inquiries, and desired them to return my thanks to his Majesty for his present.

After this, bows were exchanged and I turned and left the room, going towards the vestibule, but a few yards from it I halted and turned, when the Council of State again formed line, and took leave of me by a deep bow. At the vestibule, I met the two officers who had first received me, and I exchanged bows with them, and then left the palace and proceeded to my norimono, and returned home by the same route I had come by.

The Tai-kun was seated in a chair placed on a platform raised about two feet from the floor, and from the ceiling in front of him a grass curtain was hung; when unrolled, it would reach the floor, but it was now rolled up, and was kept in its place by large silk cords with heavy tassels. By an error in their calculation, the curtain was not rolled up high enough to enable me to see his head-dress, as the roll formed by the curtain cut through the centre of his forehead, so that I cannot fully describe his "crown," as the Japanese called it. I was afterwards told that this mistake arose from their not making a proper allowance for my height, as had my eyes been three inches lower I could have seen the whole of his head-dress. This may or may not be so. The dress of the Tai-kun was made of silk, and the material had some little gold wove in with it, but it was as distant from anything like regal spendor as could be conceived; no rich jewels, no elaborate gold ornaments; no diamond-hilted weapon appeared; and I can safely say that my dress was far more costly than his. The Japanese told me his crown is a black lacquered cap, of an inverted bell shape. The dress of the Tai-kun was differently shaped from those of his courtiers, and appeared like loose robes, while his breeches were of a reasonable length. The material was far inferior to the glorious "Kincabs" of the Benares looms.

I did not see any gilding in any part, and all the wooden columns were unpainted. Not an article of any kind appeared in any of the rooms, except the braziers, and the chairs and tables brought for my use.

At the right side of the last gate I entered, a square pagoda or tower of three stories was erected.

There was the same absence of military display as on my visit to the Minister.

Soon after reaching my quarters the dinner followed. It was very handsome according to Japanese rules, and the centre-pieces were beautifully got up. Miniature fir-trees, the tortoise and stork, emblems of longevity, with tokens of welcome and respect, were prominently exhibited.

I merely looked at it, but was unable to eat a morsel, as I was seriously ill. I had taken a violent cold; had much inflammation of the lungs, and now a violent ague fit attacked me. I was glad to send for the doctor [1] of the Prince of Shinano, — a very intelligent man, that I had frequently seen at Shimoda. Finding I had already taken cathartic medicine, he prescribed tisanes, put in hot water, to drink freely of hot couju or rice gruel, and to put on as many clothes as I could pile on my bed, so as to promote perspiration.

Tuesday, December 8, 1857. Still quite ill, though better than yesterday. Write to the Minister for Foreign Affairs that I have some important communications to make which deeply concern the interests of Japan, which I will communicate to him, or to the whole Council of State.

I omitted to state yesterday that the dinner sent

[1] This gentleman, and the other physicians who later at Shimoda attended Mr. Harris, had been trained by the Dutch surgeon at Déshima, Nagasaki.

to me was placed on some forty to fifty trays made of unpainted wood.[1] These trays were eleven inches high for me, and about five inches for Mr. Heusken. The dinner was served in the usual lacquered cups.

I was told that the trays and other utensils, after having been used by me, could never be used by any other person, and therefore they were made of unvarnished wood; this being the custom of Japan when presenting food to persons of exalted rank, etc., etc.

The fan used at the audience differs from that used on ordinary occasions; it does not open and fold like ordinary fans, but is permanently fixed, and is about three inches across the top. The handle also is longer than that of the ordinary fan.

Gave the letter for the Minister to the Prince of Shinano, who came to me this afternoon after his visit to the Castle. He told me that all who were present at the audience yesterday were amazed at my "greatness of soul," and at my bearing in presence of the mighty ruler of Japan; they had looked to see me "tremble and quake," and to speak in a faltering voice. He added that the Americans were a very different people from the

---

[1] So also chop-sticks of unpainted wood are furnished at dinners, so that after use they may be broken up and destroyed, — a method and process that is well suited to fastidious folk who are disturbed at unskillfully washed knives and forks.

Dutch. I insert this because he told it to me, and I let it pass for what it is worth, but I am hugely inclined to think that there is some admixture of "soft sawder."

Thursday, December 10, 1857. We had a shock of earthquake yesterday at nine A. M., quite light. Better to-day. Show the presents I have brought for the Tai-kun; they consist of the following articles: —

Twelve quarts of champagne, twenty-four pints of champagne, twelve bottles sherry, twelve bottles of assorted liquors, one rich astral lamp, three rich cut globes, with extra chimneys, etc., etc. Two very rich cut glass decanters, one telescope, one barometer aneroid, two volumes "Museum of Natural History" with one thousand plates, five Bramah's patent locks. Trays to place these articles on must be made before they can be presented.

The Prince of Shinano tells me that the person who gave maps of Japan to Von Siebold did not perform the hara-kiri,[1] but was crucified, and that a number of other persons lost their lives by their conduct on that occasion.

Crucifixion is performed as follows: The criminal is tied to a cross, with his arms and legs stretched apart as wide as possible; then a spear is

[1] *T. J.* p. 387. In 1826 P. F. von Siebold accompanied the Dutch to Yedo, where, after his companions left, he remained until January 18, 1830, most of the time in prison.

thrust through the body, entering just under the bottom of the shoulder blade on the left side, and coming out on the right side, just by the arm-pit. Another spear is then thrust through, from the right to the left side, in the same manner. The executioner endeavors to avoid the heart in this operation. The spears are thrust through in this manner until the criminal expires, but his sufferings are prolonged as much as possible. Shinano told me that a few years ago a very strong man lived until the eleventh spear had been thrust through him.

No man is put to death in Japan until he has confessed his guilt. After conviction, if he asserts his innocence, he is put to the torture until he confesses, or dies, or faints. In the last case he is removed to his prison and brought to the question on another day, and this continues until he either confesses his guilt or dies under the torture.[1] Had a long argument on the injustice of the torture as a means of eliciting truth.

[1] This is still the Chinese procedure, as illustrated in the case of the two Japanese students delivered up to the Chinese authorities by the American consul at Shanghai by order of the Secretary of State. See *Harper's Weekly* for December 1, 1894. Torture was abolished in Japan on the adoption of the new law codes in 1877.

CHAPTER XIII.

PRELIMINARIES TO THE TREATY-MAKING.

SATURDAY, December 12, 1857. Again visited the Minister for Foreign Affairs; everything attending this visit was so exactly like my first visit that I have nothing to note except what relates to the conference I had with him. The Commissioners of my voyage assisted the Minister on this occasion.

My private papers on "Japan" contain an exact copy of what I said on this occasion, therefore I do not copy it here.

It related to the changed condition of the world by the introduction of steam; that Japan would be forced to abandon her exclusive policy; that she might soon become a great and powerful nation by simply permitting her people to exercise their ingenuity and industry; that a moderate tax on commerce would soon give her a large revenue, by which she might support a respectable navy; that the resources of Japan, when developed by the action of free trade, would show a vast amount of exchangeable values; that this production would not in any respect interfere with the production of the necessary food for the people, but would arise from the employment given to the actual surplus labor of Japan, etc., etc. ; that foreign nations would, one after another, send powerful fleets to Japan to demand the opening of the country; that Japan must either yield or suffer the miseries of war; that even if war did not ensue, the country would be kept in a constant state of excitement by the presence of these large foreign armaments; that to make a concession of any value, it must be made in due season; and that the terms demanded by a fleet would never be as moderate as those asked by a person placed as I was; and that to yield to a fleet what was refused to an ambassador would humiliate the government in the eyes of all the Japanese people, and thus actually weaken its power. This point was illustrated by the case of China in the war of 1839 to 1841, the events succeeding that war, and the present hostilities.

I told him that by negotiating with me, who had purposely come to Yedo alone and without the presence of even a single man-of-war, the honor of Japan would be saved; that each point should be carefully discussed; and that the country should be gradually opened.

I added that the three great points would be: first, the reception of foreign ministers to reside at Yedo; second, the freedom of trade with the Japanese, without the interference of government officers; and third, the opening of additional harbors.

I added that I did not ask any exclusive rights for the Americans, and that a treaty that would be satisfactory to the President would at once be accepted by all the great Western powers.

I did not fail to point out the danger to Japan of having opium forced upon her, and said I would be willing to prohibit the bringing it to Japan. I closed by saying that my mission was a friendly one in every respect, that I had no threats to use; that the President merely informed them of the dangers that threatened the country, and pointed out a way by which not only could those dangers be averted, but Japan made a prosperous, powerful, and happy nation. My discourse lasted over two hours, and was listened to with the deepest attention and interest by the Minister. He asked some questions occasionally, when he did not fully understand what was said.

When I had finished, the Minister thanked me for my communication, and said it should be communicated to the Tai-kun, and have that consideration which it merited, and that it was the most important matter ever brought before the government. He added that the Japanese never acted as promptly on business of importance as the Americans did; that many persons had to be consulted; and therefore I must give them sufficient time for those purposes. This was to prepare me for the usual delay of the Japanese in everything.

I replied I wished them to fully consider all I had said, and that I should be very glad to give any explanations of details whenever it should be asked.

Sunday, December 13, 1857. The second Sunday in Advent; read the service with Mr. Heusken. I have told the Japanese that I performed my religious worship, in order that they might not say they had no knowledge of it.

Monday, December 14. I have had a long and unpleasant debate about my diplomatic rights, on the Japanese insisting on their right to appoint persons to guard me from insult, injury, fire, etc., etc.

I replied that I had come to Yedo alone, therefore I wished the government to place proper persons in the house; but that it must be done by my request, and not as their right. I had in view the great importance of my not doing anything that might be quoted as a precedent whenever foreign ministers shall come here to reside. This matter has been agitated for a number of days, and at last I carried my point, and the matter was settled as follows. He wrote me a letter stating that the Japanese government admitted my full and complete control of the premises occupied by me, and that no person could enter the place without my permission.

I wrote in reply, first quoting his letter, and added that I wished the government to supply me with a proper number of persons to protect me from accidents, carefully adding, "But in so doing I do not admit the right of the Japanese government to place any person in my house, under any pretense whatever, without my consent."

Wednesday, December 16, 1857. In reply to my request for some place where I could exercise on horseback, the Japanese offered me a piece of ground adjoining my house, about five yards wide and some thirty yards long!

They then offered me another spot, about one hundred feet long by seventy-five feet wide. This I also rejected. To-day the Prince told me that they had set apart a ba-ba, not far distant from my place, and wished me to send Mr. Heusken, or to go myself and see it. Mr. Heusken examined it, and reported that it was a regular military ground, over three hundred yards long, and from fifty to seventy-five yards wide, and that it would answer my purpose. On this I accepted it, and in the afternoon I went to it. It is on a plateau elevated some fifty feet above my residence, and directly opposite to a bridge and gate leading to the residence of the brothers of the Tai-kun. It is inclosed with a hedge and large trees. Large numbers of the people collected around the hedge and the streets by which I went to the place; they were perfectly quiet, the only noise being that of the street-keepers with their eternal "Satu! satu!" "Keep back! keep back!"

To-day I sent a present of a few bottles of wines and liquors to the Minister of Foreign Affairs, with a copy of Bhent's "Coast Pilot." In my letter to him I called his particular attention to the book, and that it contained an accurate account of every harbor in the United States, West Indies, and South America; that such books were printed by private individuals, and sold freely to all that wanted them; that the government encouraged such publications, as they increased the facilities of foreign commerce, which was one of the great elements of our prosperity; and that I considered it as a very proper book to place in the hands of the Minister for Foreign Affairs in Japan.

Tuesday, December 17, 1857. A fine ride in the ba-ba to-day. The Japanese wish me to agree to go to the ba-ba only two days in the week, and that for a single hour, as they require it every day for the exercise of their soldiers. I replied that, if the place was wanted for that purpose, I must of course give it up, and, as the times they named were unreasonable, I would hereafter take my exercise along the street running along the moat. This did not suit at all, and at last it was settled that the ba-ba should be at my disposal from three P. M. every day of the week except Sunday.

I may be said to be now engaged in teaching the elements of political economy to the Japanese, and in giving them information as to the working of commercial regulations in the West.

This is attended with more labor than can be well imagined, for I not only give them ideas for which, as they are new, they have no adequate terms, but the interpreter does not understand the Dutch terms when he hears them; thus I am sometimes employed for hours in trying to convey a very simple idea. It requires an incalculable amount of patience to prevent my throwing the matter up in despair. But I know that every word I utter, every new idea I succeed in conveying, is at once carried to the Council of State. So I persevere in the hope that my labors will at last produce fruit, if not for me, at least for my successor.

Friday, December 18, 1857. After an incredible amount of talk and difficulty the Japanese have given me a map of Yedo. I am not to give it away, or suffer it to be copied.

Sunday, December 20. The last Sunday in Advent; read service as usual. Yesterday had an earthquake, not very sharp. Quite unwell these three days.

Monday, December 21. To-day the Commissioners of my voyage call on me for the purpose of receiving information.

The chief point of their inquiries related to the object of sending ministers to foreign countries; their duties; their rights under the laws of nations. All these questions were as clearly answered as possible.

I added that when a Minister gave serious offense to the court to which he was appointed, the government might suspend intercourse with him, and order him to leave the country; that the usual mode was to complain of his conduct to his own government and to request his recall. The Commissioners asked questions also respecting commerce, and what I meant by trade being carried on without the interference of government officers. This I also succeeded in explaining to their full satisfaction. They said they were in the dark on all these points, and therefore were like children; therefore I must have patience with them. They added, that they placed the fullest confidence in all my statements.

I gave them a written paper containing the basis of a commercial treaty, which I explained to them article by article, and told them I wished that paper might be taken into serious consideration.

I then gave them champagne, which they appeared to understand and to like.

Friday, December 25, 1857. Merry Christmas! I little thought on last Christmas to pass the present one in Yedo. If I could pass one in Pekin it would make my different places of passing the day a remarkable list.

I ask every day when I may expect an answer to my great communications.

The invariable reply is, that a great many persons are to be consulted: the brothers of the Taikun, all the daimiōs, and some other great men; that letters have to be written, and answers received; and then the old story, "The Japanese do not decide important affairs until after long deliberation."

Wrote to the Minister for Foreign Affairs, transmitting a memorandum, pointing out the most obvious articles that will form the elements of foreign commerce, and showing how these articles may be increased in production, etc.

Sunday, December 27. Snow, and a gloomy day. I cannot get one word out of the Prince of Shinano as to my prospects of success, nor a hint as to the existence or non-existence of any obstacles. This state of uncertainty, joined to indifferent health, greatly depresses my spirits.

Thursday, December 31, 1857. An earthquake to-day. I have not had a visit for three days from the Prince of Shinano. This, joined to the uncertainty that hangs over my negotiations, causes me to pass this the last day of the year in a melancholy manner.

I fondly hope that the year now about to commence will give me more frequent opportunities of communicating with the outer world than I have enjoyed during the present one; in truth, I was most shamefully neglected by the navy in the East.

Friday, January 1, 1858. I desire to return thanks to Almighty God for permitting me to see the beginning of a new year.

With my poor health, and over half a century of years, I cannot promise myself that I shall see another. I am thankful that I have been able to accomplish so much as I already have done for the honor of my country during the past year, and I hope I shall be able to effectually open this country before the present one closes. I was visited in honor of *my* New Year's Day by the Princes of Toké and Shinano; both came in dresses of ceremony, and brought me some trifling presents. Had some very pleasant conversation, but nothing was said on business.

Saturday, January 9, 1858. To-day the Prince of Shinano visited me for the first time in three days. I determined to bring about a crisis, and therefore began by saying that it was now twenty-nine days since I had made some very important communications to the Minister of Foreign Affairs, of which no official notice had since been taken; that they would not even name a period within which I should have a reply. That such treatment could not be submitted to; that the President had sent me to Yedo on a most friendly mission, having solely the benefit of Japan in view; that the United States asked nothing for themselves; that the trade of Japan was no object to us; that all we cared for was that our ships could make repairs and get supplies in their harbors, and that we had already got that point; that they must open their eyes, and then they would see that I neither asked nor would I accept any favors from Japan; that ten days ago I offered to give them explanations on any points on which they needed information; and would reply saying that their treatment of me showed that no negotiations could be carried on with them unless the Plenipotentiary was backed by a fleet and offered them cannon-balls for arguments. I closed by saying that, unless something was done, I should return to Shimoda.

Poor Shinano listened in evident trepidation, and earnestly assured me that no slight to the President or insult to me was intended; that, as tomorrow was my Sunday, and I would not do business on that day, he could not answer me before the next day, at which time he told me I should be satisfied.

This was apparently a bold step on my part, but from my knowledge of this people I felt that I ran no kind of danger of breaking off my negotiations by what I did, and that the more I yielded and acquiesced the more they would impose on me; while by taking a bold attitude, and assuming a threatening tone, I should at once bring them to terms.

Monday, January 11, 1858. A visit to-day from the Prince of Shinano. He began by saying that he had reported all I had said to him, at our last interview, to the Minister of Foreign Affairs; that the Minister admitted that I had just cause of complaint, but that the position of the government was most difficult; that *they* were *enlightened*, and knew that what I had recommended was truly for the best interests of Japan; but their conviction alone was not sufficient; they had to convince the brothers of the Tai-kun, the daimiōs, the military and literary classes, of the wisdom of following my advice; that the Minister and his colleagues had labored constantly, night and day, to secure the consent of the persons referred to; and that a brother of the Tai-kun was in Kiushiu, and they had to write to him and get his reply; and finally he said that on Friday, the 15th, he would inform me the day when I should have an answer.

This was much to my satisfaction; and I told the Prince that, so long as I had specific days fixed, then I could wait with patience. I endeavored to draw from him some hints as to the probable color of the answer I should receive, but I could not elicit anything; either he has "great powers of silence," or he actually was ignorant of the matter.

Friday, 15th January. To-day, according to promise, the Prince of Shinano visited me. He said the Minister of Foreign Affairs would give me an answer to-morrow, or at a later day, as best suited me; and, as the matters were of the highest importance, he desired to have a conference with me. I accepted at once the day and place of conference.

Saturday, January 16. Again to the Minister's; retinue, roads, and the appearances in the streets exactly as they were on my two previous visits to him, except that there was not so many people in the streets to look at the cortége as it passed. Foreigners will soon cease to excite curiosity here.

I was received in the usual manner by the [Minister], except that I thought his smile was warmer this morning than before; to-day it was more than skin-deep. The Minister soon opened the conference by saying that the communication I had made verbally to him, together with the written memorandum I had sent to him and the information I had communicated to his princes, had all been laid before his Majesty the Tai-kun. His Majesty desired first to thank the President for his very kind advice, and for the friendship he had thus shown for Japan. The Minister then proceeded to give me his Majesty's answer.

The demand for the residence of a Minister at Yedo is admitted. The place of his residence and the rights he is to exercise shall be settled by negotiation.

The right of free trade is granted. Commissioners shall be appointed to settle the details of trade.

Three harbors having already been opened, and as Japan is a small country, the number cannot be increased; but as Shimoda is not found to be suitable as a harbor, another shall be given in place of it, but the number may not be increased beyond three. After the Minister had ended, I told him I was much concerned at his Majesty's decision about harbors; that it was impossible for me to make a satisfactory treaty under such restrictions. I pointed out to him the west coast of Japan, bordering on the Japan Sea. From Hakodaté to Nagasaki, following the coast line, it is quite four hundred ri (one thousand English miles), yet in all that distance not a single harbor was opened; that many American whaleships were in the Japan Sea, and it was very important for them to have a convenient harbor in that sea; that his Majesty had spoken of the small size of the Empire, but an examination of the maps of the principal parts of the world would show that Japan had a coast line far greater than the average states. I therefore earnestly recommended a reconsideration of that part of his Majesty's decision.

I was informed that the Commissioners to negotiate with me would be appointed immediately, and that the first interview should be held day after to-morrow, and that the negotiations should be conducted at my quarters. I then handed the Minister a copy and translation of my full powers, and pointed out to him the necessity that the powers of the Japanese Commissioners should specify that they were appointed to negotiate with me, and not a mere general power. I requested that a translation of the Japanese full powers should be handed to me before the meeting.

I also told the Minister that, as soon as we had gone through the formality of exchanging our full powers, I would hand the Commissioners a draft of such a treaty as would be satisfactory; that they could have it translated into Japanese, and after having duly considered it we could then proceed with our negotiations; that this course would greatly facilitate our negotiations, and thus save valuable time; adding that I had nothing to conceal, no secret motives or wishes, and therefore I could proceed in this frank and open manner. The Minister said that my course was very praiseworthy, and that it gave him much satisfaction.

I have the draft of a treaty which I drew up before leaving Shimoda, and I was anxious to take the initiative in presenting a draft, as, had the Japanese presented one, it would have been difficult if not impossible to reject it entirely, and to try to amend one of their performances would have made a piece of literary or diplomatic patchwork that would have excited the laughter of all who might have the misfortune to be compelled to read it. I could not learn the number or names of the intended Commissioners. I was told the Prince of Shinano would be one, but nothing further.

CHAPTER XIV.

THE HERMITS INSTRUCTED IN MODERN WORLD LIFE.

MONDAY, January 18, 1858. To-day I rigged out in full dress, in honor of the signatures of the President and Tai-kun, which are to be exhibited to-day. I learn to-day that I am to have only two Commissioners to deal with. This pleases me, as it will prevent much interruption. Although the Commissioners will have full powers, yet in reality I shall be negotiating with the whole Council of State. The Commissioners will hear my arguments, and then request time to consider them. They will repeat what I have said to the Council, who will consider the matter, and then dictate what the Commissioners shall say. I feel just as sure of this as though I had been told it by themselves. The Commissioners are Inouyé, Prince of Shinano, and Iwasé, Prince of Higo.

At one P. M. the Commissioners appeared; they were attended by two secretaries to take down every word that was uttered.

We saluted each other standing. I then gave my full powers to Mr. Heusken, who handed it to the

Prince of Shinano, who opened it, looked at the President's signature and the seal, and then passed it to his colleague, who also examined it and then returned it to Mr. Heusken, who handed it to me. The full powers of the Japanese Commissioners were then given to the vice-governor of Shimoda, who handed it to me. I opened it and looked at the Imperial seal and signature, and then returned it. Those who have read Commodore Perry's account of his Japanese expedition will remember that the Japanese would not let their full powers go out of their hands, pretending the Imperial seal was so sacred it could not be handled by any but a Japanese, and, of them, only by those to whom it was specially directed.

The seal was in vermilion, about two and a half inches in diameter, and composed of the old Chinese "Seal character." This over, I handed the Commissioners a Dutch translation of my draft of a treaty. I told them that, as this treaty might contain words not well understood by their interpreters, I suggested that the work had better be done in one of the rooms of the house where we were, so that, if any words or phrases were not understood, they could at once have recourse to Mr. Heusken for explanation, and thereby not only would the translations be facilitated, but greater exactness would be secured. They assented at once to my suggestion; they added, that as soon as they had time to examine the translation and consider it, they would again meet me, but that it would require some days to do both. I requested the Commissioners not to read the treaty piecemeal, as it was translated, as the various articles had such relations with each other that they must be read together and not separately; that to read it as it was translated would give very erroneous ideas, and thus perhaps prejudices might arise that it would be difficult afterwards to remove. They at once assented to this. The original draft of the treaty will be found among my private "Japan papers."

Saturday, January 23. To-day the translations were finished. In order to be sure of the translation being correct, I had the Japanese translator read from the Japanese copy and translate orally into Dutch to Mr. Heusken, who held the Dutch version. It has been an immense labor, but my great anxiety has been that the Japanese should fully understand what I proposed to them.

A visit from the Prince of Shinano to-day. Some time ago I told him that, if he saw a dog that had any white hair about him, he might be sure the tip of the dog's tail would be white also. This he repeated, of course, at the Castle, and it appears that each of the nobles set his retainers to search for a dog which should have some white about his body, while the terminal color of his tail should be black, or at least not white. Many thousands of dogs have been examined, and as yet no exception to my rule has been found. This has given me a reputation for universal wisdom that is quite amusing from its simplicity.

I have omitted to note that I made presents of wines, cordials, sardines, preserved salmon and lobster, and Bramah locks to all the Commissioners of my voyage. These presents exhausted all the articles I brought from Shimoda.

The Tai-kun was much pleased with my presents, and uses the astral lamp constantly. He sent me a return present of a very handsome cabinet.

The Commissioners each sent me a present of a piece of brocade silk, twenty-four inches wide and three and a quarter yards long, the pattern of a pair of such breeches as are worn by the highest ranks only.

Monday, January 25, 1858. To-day, at two P. M., we fairly opened our negotiations.

In this journal I shall confine myself to the leading facts of actual transactions, omitting the interminable discourses of the Japanese, where the same proposition may be repeated a dozen times; nor shall I note their positive refusal of points they subsequently grant, and meant to grant all the while; nor many absurd proposals made by them, without the hope, and scarcely the wish, of having them accepted: for all such proceedings are according to the rule of Japanese diplomacy, and he who shows the greatest absurdity in such matters is most esteemed. They do not know the value of a straightforward and truthful policy; at least they do not practice it. They never hesitate at uttering a falsehood, even where the truth would serve the same purpose.

The preamble to the treaty was accepted, as was the first article so far as to agree to receive a Minister and Consuls. They wished the Minister to reside between Kanagawa and Kawasaki, and only come to Yedo when he had business; nor should the Minister or Consuls travel anywhere in Japan except on actual business.

They then proceeded to read from a book what I will abridge and insert merely to remind me hereafter of their mode of doing business.

They began by saying that they had carefully considered the draft of the treaty I had given them. The Empire being small, it had been determined that not more than three harbors should be opened; that Shimoda should be closed, and a large harbor should be given in place of it. The opening of any harbors to Commodore Perry was a great concession, and was made with much difficulty. Thus far, American ships have only been furnished with supplies, and not with Japanese goods. Now, in consequence of the President's letter, and the very important and friendly communications of the Plenipotentiary, it has been determined to open trade with the Americans on the same terms as were contained in the treaties just made with the Russians and Dutch!!! They offered Kanagawa and Yokohama in place of Shimoda, and, after all the daimiōs are satisfied with the effects of trade, another harbor should be opened. Trade to be conducted as provided for in the Dutch and Russian treaties. Americans cannot be allowed to travel in Japan, and must be confined to strict limits.

They here paused, and I replied that, by the ninth article of the treaty of Kanagawa, anything granted to other nations accrued at once to the Americans, and therefore did not require any treaty stipulations;[1] that, as to those treaties, the conditions of them were disgraceful to all parties engaged in making them; that, so far as trade was concerned, those documents were not worth the paper on which they were written; that, were I to sign any such conditions, the President would recall me in disgrace. I then demanded that the promise of the Tai-kun "that freedom of trade should be granted" should be made good. I added that it was mere trifling to offer to me conditions that had already accrued to us months ago; that the propo-

---

[1] This, the "most favored nation" clause, was inserted in the Perry treaty at the suggestion of Dr. S. Wells Williams, who stated this fact in a letter to the editor.

sition to shut out the Minister from residing in Yedo, or wherever he pleased, was highly offensive, and that it would be far better for them to refuse to receive him than to couple his reception with such conditions; and that the Minister and Consuls must have all the rights enjoyed by such persons under the laws of nations; that I asked nothing more for them than those rights, and that I could not take any less.

Monday, January 25, 1858. The Commissioners were not prepared for this; it quite upset their plan so nicely prepared for them by the Council of State, and they were embarrassed exceedingly. They began to repeat the old story: "Japan has been closed for more than two hundred years; the people are not prepared for such great changes as you propose; they must be introduced by degrees, and as the people learn to know you better, then we can act more freely," etc.

I replied that, under such regulations as they proposed, trade was impossible; that Americans might be in Japan for fifty years, and make no advances towards a better acquaintance; that intercourse under such circumstances, so far from removing prejudices, would increase them, for the Japanese would learn to despise the Americans as much as they do the Dutch.

That, from all I had observed in Japan, I was convinced that the people were actually anxious to have a free intercourse with us, and, if objections existed anywhere, they were confined to the daimiōs and the military, two classes of people that in all countries were opposed to any improvement in the condition of the great body of the people.

The Commissioners frankly admitted that I was right in my last statement, adding that a large class called the literati, or expectants of office, being entirely ignorant of everything out of their own land, were also opposed to opening the country. In explanation of this I was told that every person who had mastered the four books of Confucius,[1] and could pass the requisite examination, received a small pension from the government, and that, as officers were wanted, they were selected from this class. They added that colleges were established at Yedo, and in each of the provinces of the empire; that the only books used were Confucius and the History of China; that no sciences, arts, history, or polite literature, or in fact anything but Confucius and Chinese history, were taught in those institutions.

The Commissioners here had a long and animated conversation together.

After it ended, the Prince of Shinano asked me

[1] On the Chinese ethical system, Confucianism in its modern form, philosophy in Japan, see *The Religions of Japan*, New York, 1895, and Dr. George Wm. Knox's papers in *T. A. S. J.* vol. xx.

if I would hear a private, confidential matter, which he wished to communicate to me. I replied, "Most certainly." He then said that, of the sons and brothers of military men, none enjoyed any rank except the eldest son; that they all received a military education, being taught the art of war, the use of weapons, etc.; they had no pay, nor any prospect of advancement in life; they were supported in idleness by the head of the family, as their position forbade their devoting themselves to any useful avocations, and they had no hope of honorable employment. Their only distinction consisted in their right to wear two swords. From these habits of idleness many of them fell into bad courses, became dissipated, drunken brawlers and bullies; and that, when their conduct became too outrageous, they were disowned and cast off by their families.

In this condition, they form a class called "Rō-nin,"[1] which corresponds to bravo, bully, rowdy, and loafer. The government has just discovered a plot among these "Rō-nin" against the

[1] Literally wave-man. When the retainer of a daimiō was set afloat or adrift, or even resigned the service of his master, he was free to act as he pleased, but there was not necessarily any disgrace in being a rō-nin, and, as a matter of fact, not a few rō-nin were peaceful and honorable gentlemen. My own interpreter in Fukui, a cultivated scholar, one of the first samurai who gave up the wearing of two swords (presenting his longest one to myself), was a rō-nin.

American Ambassador (what they intended to do to me I could not learn),[1] and the government had that morning arrested three ringleaders of the conspirators, and had them now in prison; that it had given the government the greatest possible anxiety; for, should anything happen to the Ambassador, it would be the cause of serious difficulties with the United States, besides disgracing the government of Japan in the eyes of all the civilized world; he then added that a large body of men was now employed in patrolling around my house and in all the neighborhood, and that at night they would be in all the various courts and open spaces of the house. He then gave me the names of these three Yedo rowdies. They are as follows: —

Horeye Yosi Nosuke [Horéi Yoshinosŭké].

Nobu-ta nee [Nobutani] Tui-ro. To-zo.

The Commissioners now resumed, and said, from what had been told me, I must see that the residence of foreign ministers in Yedo would be certain to cause disturbances, and therefore it was far better for them to reside at Kawasaki or Kanagawa.

---

[1] Mr. Harris's life was in real danger, for the purpose of these Rō-nin was nothing less than to assassinate him. Between 1858 and 1870, many foreigners, probably several score in all, were wounded or murdered by these cowardly swashbucklers, Mr. Heusken being one of the first victims. See Nitobe's *United States and Japan*, pp. 65, 75, 76. The soshi, such as fired at Li Hung Chang at Shimonoséki in March, 1895, was the successor of the murderous rō-nin.

I thought it a most suspicious circumstance that these " Rō-nin " should have remained perfectly quiet for the whole fifty-five days I have been in Yedo, and should only stir at the very nick of time that the question of the residence of foreign ministers in Japan was to be agitated, and that they should be arrested on the morning of the very first day that the conferences were to be opened; therefore I concluded that if the whole matter was not an actual " Arrowsmith," it was very much like one.

I replied to all this that they did not know the material of which foreigners were composed, if they supposed that the acts of three, or three thousand " Rō-nin " would keep them away from Yedo; that I considered it as too trifling a matter to call for any serious reply.

The Commissioners were again in a quandary at my suggestion. They took up my draft, and gave a general answer on each article. The demand for Americans to have Japanese coin, or for Japanese to receive American coin, was rejected in a most decisive manner.

It was emphatically declared that no sales could be made except through Japanese officials. In this manner they went through the treaty, rejecting everything except article 8. This article I had inserted with scarce a hope that I should obtain it. It provides for the free exercise of their religion by the Americans, with the right to erect suitable places of worship, and that the Japanese would abolish the practice of trampling on the cross. To my surprise and delight, this article was accepted! I am aware that the Dutch have published to the world that the Japanese had signed articles granting freedom of worship, and also agreeing to abolish trampling on the cross. It is true that the Dutch proposed the abolition, but the Japanese refused to sign it.

In the Dutch treaty of January, 1856, an article provides that "within the buildings at Deshima the Dutch may practice their own or the Christian religion." The extraordinary words "their own or the Christian religion" are copied from the treaty as sent to me by the Dutch Commissioner, Mr. John Henry Donker Curtius, from Nagasaki; and it is also in the copy of the same treaty which was furnished me by the Japanese.

I have copies of every article ever made by the Japanese with the Russians, Dutch, and English, and the above is the only article that relates to religion. I told the Commissioners, as we were about to adjourn at five P. M., that it was useless to proceed with the further consideration of the treaty, until they would consent to grant the Minister the rights he enjoyed under the laws of nations.

Tuesday, January 26, 1858. Commissioners

come at half past two P. M. They open the business by saying that I had misunderstood them yesterday; that they did not refuse the right of the Minister to reside in Yedo, but only recommended Kawasaki or Kanagawa as a more suitable place for his first residence. They therefore accepted the article as it stood, so far as it relates to the Minister. They wished, however, that the treaty should not go into effect until January 1, 1861 (it stood July 4, 1859, in my draft). I replied that to suspend a treaty for three years was an unheard-of thing, and showed a most unfriendly spirit on their part. They hastily replied that they did not mean the treaty, only that the Minister should not be sent before that time. I answered that was even worse than the other; that the object of sending a Minister was, that he could promptly settle any small difficulties that might arise; whereas, if they were neglected until word could be sent to America, they might grow into grave and serious matters. I added that the proposition manifested a spirit quite at variance with the preamble of this treaty. They then asked me to give them my secret promise that the Minister would not be sent before that time. I told them that such a promise was beyond my power, as it was the President and not the Plenipotentiary that had that matter in his power. They then requested me to write to the President, making known their wishes on this head. I told them I would write to the Secretary of State, who would make their wishes known to the President, and this satisfied them.

They then insisted that the consuls should not have the right to travel in Japan "except on business." I pointed out to them that to accede to such a clause would put every Consul at once in the power of each local Governor, who would have the right to inquire into his business, etc.; that, if the Consul wished to make a journey for his health, he could not do so, with other objections. They said that, as the treaty was to be read by all the daimiōs and great nobles, they did not wish to have it appear that every Consul had the right to travel in Japan; that the words "on business" were proposed as a mere cover to conceal the extent of the rights actually conceded; and that no Governor or other official should ever inquire into the nature of the business on which a Consul might be traveling. I said that implied that the Consul would be willing to tell a falsehood when he wished to travel and had no official business; that such conduct was not according to our customs; that a liar was looked on with the greatest contempt; besides which, it was a sin by our religion for a man to utter a falsehood.

Finding we could not agree at present on this point, I requested them to lay it aside for the present and proceed with the other articles, which was agreed to.

Article 2 provides that the President will act as the mediator of the Japanese when asked to do so,[1] and that American men-of-war and consuls should assist Japanese vessels and their crews so far as the laws of neutrality permitted.

There is nothing in this article that requires a treaty stipulation, but I inserted it to produce an impression on the government and people, and it had that effect. This article was accepted without hesitation.

Article 3, the Sebastopol of the treaty, was now taken up, and the debate continued until the hour of our adjournment. In the draft as proposed by me, I claimed Hakodaté, Shinagawa, Osaka, Nagasaki, another port in Kiushiu near the coal mines, Hirado, and two ports on the west coast of Nippon,[2] making together eight harbors; and I also claimed the cities of Yedo and Miako should be opened.

They went over the old ground of objections so often stated before. In answer I said that, to secure the peace, honor, and prosperity of Japan, a satisfactory treaty must be made; that the freedom of trade was an essential part of such a treaty, and without harbors it was absurd to talk of trade.

[1] The mediation of the United States, so effective in the Chino-Japanese war of 1894-95, was asked for by the Chinese.

[2] Nippon is the name of the whole Empire, Hondo of the main island.

I repeated the remark I had made to the Minister of Foreign Affairs, that there was a distance of four hundred ri on the west coast in which not a harbor was opened. The discussion continued until dark, when the Commissioners said that my arguments were so important they must have a day to take them into consideration, and therefore they could not meet me until the day after to-morrow, thus making good what I have before noted, that in reality I am negotiating with the whole government, and that the Commissioners can only repeat what has been told them, and report what I say.

The two Japanese secretaries are constantly employed in taking down every word that is uttered.

Thursday, January 28, 1858. The Commissioners arrive at half past one P. M. They go to the Castle in the Council of State at nine A. M., and leave at one, eat a hasty meal, and then are ready for business. They opened proceedings by saying that half the daimiōs were at Yedo, and the other half in the provinces, and that when the half in the provinces returned to Yedo, the other half went to the provinces also; that the government was compelled to consult the daimiōs on all important matters, and, if the government attempted to carry any important measure against their advice, it would cause "confusion," *i. e.* rebellion; therefore the government must defer to their opinions. The answer of the Minister of Foreign Affairs on harbors was final. No doubt more will be opened by and by, but not at present. *The merchants and common people are no doubt in favor of opening the country*, but the *daimiōs* and *military* oppose it.

The civilians at the head of the government understand these matters better. They have learned a great deal since you have been in the country; therefore they are in favor of a treaty which they see will make the country prosperous, and the government rich and powerful.

This is not a refusal to open more harbors, it is only a statement of the condition of the country. Coals have been discovered within three ri of Nagasaki, so that the other harbor asked for in the island of Kiushiu is not wanted. The island of Hirado is small and poor, and only produces porcelain; therefore a port in that island is not needed. Miako is not the true name of that city; it is Kiōto. The meaning of Miako is "capital."

(This is another instance of the extraordinary secretiveness of the Japanese; for more than three hundred years they have permitted foreigners to call it Miako instead of Kiōto![1])

Kiōto is comparatively a poor place; the population, instead of being five hundred thousand, as stated by Kaempfer, does not [number] two hundred and fifty thousand. It is merely a city of

[1] The term miyako is a common noun, meaning simply the place where the Mikado or Emperor lives; that is, the capital.

priests and temples. No large manufactures are carried on, nor any lacquer ware made there. Silk is not woven in more than twenty houses. (They spoke almost contemptuously of the Mikado, and roared with laughter when I quoted some remarks concerning the veneration in which he is held by the Japanese. They say that he has neither money, political power, nor anything else that is valued in Japan; he is a mere cipher.)

As to Shinagawa, it is no harbor, as no large ship can come within two and a half ri of it. Kanagawa is the nearest to Yedo of any harbor, and that is already opened to you. The Kanagawa post-house is seven and a half ri from the Nippon Bashi. Osaka is fifteen ri from Kiōto.

To my surprise, after the beginning of this speech of theirs, they wound up by offering me the harbor of Niigata, in the province of Echigo, on the west coast of Nippon. The city has a large river running through it, and contains sixty thousand inhabitants. On further inquiry I [learned] that only nine feet of water was found on the bar of the river, and from their charts the outer harbor is more like an open roadstead than a harbor.

They assured me that no good harbors, like Hakodaté, Nagasaki, and Kanagawa, could be found on the west coast;[1] that all the harbors were so

[1] The best harbor on the west coast of Hondo is Tsuruga, in Echizen, now the sea-terminus of the railway from Kiōto. It is

filled up with sand that vessels of large size could not enter them. They added that, if a better harbor than Niigata could be found on the west coast, it should be given in exchange for it. On these terms I took Niigata. I then told them that my way of doing business was plain and straightforward, and to give them proof of my friendly feeling and to facilitate our business, I would withdraw the claim to Hirado, one harbor on the west coast, another in Kiushiu, making three harbors withdrawn.

That, to give ample time to prepare for these changes, I would fix the opening of the various places as follows: Yedo to be opened January 1, 1863 (with Shinagawa); Osaka, July 4, 1861; Niigata, July 4, 1860; Kanagawa, July 4, 1859; and Shimoda should be closed January 1, 1860; Nagasaki to be opened July 4, 1859.

In answer to their often-repeated assertion that all these places would be opened "by and by," I replied that between nations verbal assurances had no value; that it was written stipulations alone that were considered as of any value; that a written promise to open a harbor in four years would be far more satisfactory than a verbal promise to open it in two years.

The Commissioners said they did not see how

the seaport of the city of Fukui, and has a population of twelve thousand. *M. E.* pp. 418, 419.

the difficulties to Yedo and Osaka could be overcome; they thought it impossible; they therefore required a day to think of it, and would meet me on Saturday.

Saturday, January 30, 1858. Meet at the usual hour. They promptly offer to open Yedo and Shinagawa, but the Americans to reside at Kanagawa and Yokohama; the Americans only to purchase articles in a small way at Yedo. They have a class of large merchants called Toyas, who keep immense establishments, and are ready to buy anything and to any amount. These merchants will open establishments at Kanagawa where the Americans can buy and sell what they desire. They have entered into a long argument showing that the residence of Americans in Yedo for the purpose of trade was unnecessary; and then to my great surprise they added that the American may buy where he can best suit himself as to quality and price, and sell to whom he pleases *without the intervention of any government officer*. This is a complete abandonment of the leading principle of the Dutch and Russian treaties, and is one of the chief points which I have so long contended for.

I now entered into arguments tending to show that to expect Americans to go to Yedo from Kanagawa and to return the same day (thirty-seven and a half miles), and to do business in Yedo, was a physical impossibility; that such a regulation would prevent their selling anything in Yedo; that to limit their sales to the Toyas was in fact creating a monopoly in favor of that class; that every person of rank and wealth resided a part of every year in Yedo, while the families of all these classes resided there; that the quantity of foreign articles sold at Yedo alone would, at the beginning of the trade, be more than [in] all the rest of the Empire; that most of the articles were not even known by name to the Japanese; that they must first see them, learn their use, etc., and, after one person had purchased a thing, it would be the means of inducing others to buy the same article; that to do this the Americans must bring their goods to Yedo to show them, and this of course involved the necessity of their having their warehouses and residences in Yedo; that it was idle to think of trying the experiment of free trade, so long as the Americans were excluded from Yedo and Osaka, two of the greatest cities of the Empire, etc. I offered to withdraw Shinagawa as a port, and that American ships should not go above the harbor of Kanagawa; but for this I must have Yedo and Osaka open for trade.

Monday, February 1, 1858. Meet the Commissioners at the usual hour. They open business by the following proposition: "The permanent residence of Americans shall be at Kanagawa; and after 1st January, 1863, one street shall be opened in Yedo for the temporary residence of Americans to buy and sell." Nearly three hours were occupied in making and discussing various propositions regarding Yedo, the Japanese making strenuous resistance to any concessions beyond the above. I finally made them the following proposition: —

"On the 1st [of] January, 1863, the city of Yedo shall be opened to Americans for the purposes of business; the place they shall occupy for their business shall be settled by the American diplomatic agent and the government of Japan." The Japanese take until to-morrow to consider this proposition.

Tuesday, February 2. Meet at the usual hour. The Commissioners object to the word "business," and wish the word "trade" inserted in lieu of it. As this, in its literal sense, would deprive the American of cook, clerk, medical aid, and in fact of all assistance, I objected to it; at the same time I told them the word used by me would not justify the residence in Yedo of any persons who were not either directly engaged in trade, or in the employ of such persons. After a vain attempt to come to an understanding, I propose to lay Yedo aside for the present and to take up Kiōto and Osaka. They produce a map of Kiōto (the map in Kaempfer is an exact copy).

The Commissioners said that there were insurmountable objections to opening Kiōto to the Americans as a place of residence, which were connected with their religion; that, if it were only extremely difficult, they would say so, but in reality what I asked was impossible; that it was no place of business, as the American Minister could satisfy himself whenever he should visit the city; to attempt to open the place for the permanent residence of foreigners would excite a rebellion; that they were sure, when I reported this to the President, that he was too good a friend to Japan to insist on a thing which was of no real value, and would at the same time introduce anarchy and bloodshed into Japan. They made the most solemn asseverations that what they said was true.

They then offered to open Sakai, a town containing one hundred and fifty thousand souls, situated on the Bay of Settsu, and distant by land only three ri from Osaka, the second city of the Empire. Osaka lies on a river, and by that route it is five ri from the bay. Ships going to Sakai or Osaka anchor nearly at the same spot; but, owing to shoals or mud-banks, ships like the Americans' cannot come nearer than one and a half ri to Sakai, or two ri of the mouth of the river leading up to Osaka. Osaka has never been opened to foreigners as a residence, and its proximity to Kiōto renders the opening of it to them very objectionable to the Japanese. If I do not like Sakai, they offer me Hiōgo on the same bay, and lying ten ri to the westward of Osaka River; it is about the same size as Sakai, but it has a bold shore and a good artificial harbor, built many hundreds of years ago at a vast expense.

I insisted on having Osaka opened for the permanent residence of Americans. A long time was passed in debating a proposition of theirs that Americans should reside at Sakai, but have the right to visit Osaka, to buy and sell there, and to rent houses for that purpose, etc., but not to sleep in Osaka. I strongly insisted on the unfriendly and inhospitable appearance such an article would bear, and told them I could not understand why they should have greater objections to opening Osaka than they had to opening Yedo. I said that difficulties would constantly arise under such an arrangement, and gave as an illustration that, suppose an American late in the day should be taken suddenly and violently ill, and quite unable to return to Sakai, the authorities of Osaka, acting under stringent orders, would place the sick man in a norimono and send him off to Sakai. On the road the man dies; the Americans, indignant at such inhumanity, would make a very strong and possibly exaggerated statement of the transaction; this would be sent to the Minister, and copies to the United States; a very serious difficulty might thus arise between the two nations. As to the vicinity to Kiōto, I was willing to let the lines run at the full distance from that city, so that difficulty was imaginary.

I also told them to remember that the seventh article of the treaty claimed for every well-conducted American who had resided one year in Japan the right to travel as freely as the Japanese. The Commissioners told me that the seventh article and the opening of Kiōto were two impossibilities; that they could not be granted without producing rebellion. Many other propositions of the treaty were excessively difficult, but still might be carried into effect, but the two points were absolutely impossible, and here they made a very sensible remark: they said, if foreign nations would go to war with them on account of those two points, they must make the best they could of the calamity; but under no circumstances was war from abroad so much to be feared as intestine commotion.

Lamps had been introduced by me, and as we had been steadily at work, the Commissioners told me I had fairly beaten them out in my powers of endurance, and they must therefore beg to be excused for the evening. I urged them to reflect seriously on what I had laid before them, remarking that the present was the turning-point of the treaty, and that one false step might utterly destroy our labors. No meeting to-morrow.

CHAPTER XV.

THE STRUGGLE FOR THE OPENING OF THE PORTS.

WEDNESDAY, February 3, 1858. This morning, at an early hour, the Prince of Shinano called to have some private conversation. He said there was an intense excitement among the old party at the Castle; that the concessions already made had greatly exasperated them, and he feared, if I persisted in insisting on Kiōto being opened, and on the right of the Americans to travel in the country, I should run a great risk of losing the whole treaty; that what had already been conceded excited his wonder, for when I arrived at Yedo he did not dream that I could use any arguments that would secure so much. He said, "Better secure what you have obtained than wish for the attainment of what is of little or no value, even if you do get it." He said that if we would be patient, and let the present treaty work its work quietly among the people, he had no doubt the two disputed points would be granted without difficulty by the time named for the opening of Yedo; that the two points were not refused by the government, but merely postponed to await a favorable period for carrying them into effect. He closed by saying that he was very unhappy, and implored me to consider the wisdom of following his advice.

I gave him to understand that, if all the other parts of the treaty were arranged to my satisfaction, I should try to suit them on the two points.

Meet at eleven A. M. A long debate on the seventh article. At last I offer to withdraw the objectionable clause provided they would open Osaka as a place for the permanent residence of Americans. I also offered to limit the boundaries at Osaka in the direction of Kiōto to two ri.

The Commissioners inform me that my request to have a salute fired in honor of the birthday of Washington had been acceded to, and that I should be conducted to the battery on the 22d inst., when a salute of twenty-one guns should be fired.

They added that Commodore Perry had made them a present of a brass howitzer gun; that they had made many after that model; and that the salute should be fired from their copies of the American gun.

Meet again at two P. M., and take up the articles *seriatim;* 3 and 4 accepted. Article 5 relates to the currency, and contained a clause giving the Japanese government an agio of six per cent. on all foreign coin paid to them, and prohibited the exportation of Japanese coin. To my utter astonishment they gave up the six per cent., and permitted the free exportation of their coin!! and also declared that all foreign coins should pass freely in Japan. They *did* astonish me.

Wednesday, February 4, 1858. Article 4 gives to the United States government [the right] to land, free of duty, stores for the use of its fleet at Kanagawa, Hakodaté, and Nagasaki. By this I have secured the choice of three good harbors for our naval depot in the East, in a country that has the most salubrious climate in the world, where the men cannot desert, and with a power that is sufficiently civilized to respect our rights; and, above all, not a power with whom we might have a rupture, like England. I consider this clause of immense importance, as now the depot can be removed from that wretched place, Hong-Kong, and the stores out of the power of England. We finished our day's work with article 5, and adjourned until the 6th inst.

Saturday, February 6, 1858. We take up article 3. To my surprise, they proposed to build a lazaretto outside the walls of Osaka for the use of any Americans that might suddenly be taken sick while on a visit to Osaka from Sakai, and still excluded Americans from a residence in the city. I was indignant. I have noted the terms on which I agreed to withdraw the two difficulties in the way of the treaty, and it was fully understood *that* was the basis on which the matter was to be arranged. I told them that their proposition was so very offensive that I would not consent to have it again interpreted to me. I taxed them roundly with bad faith, and gave them notice that I renewed the clause in article 7 (right to travel), and also the claim for Kiōto. The Commissioners stammered and boggled for some time, partially admitting that the proposal was none of their making, and that they would consult over it (*i. e.* report its rejection at the Castle); they then proposed to take up the articles of the treaty.

Article 6 agreed to.

Article 7 postponed until article 3 is settled.

Articles 3 to 15, inclusive, all agreed to, with some slight verbal alterations not calling for any remark.

Article 16. The family name of the Tai-kun is Minamoto[1] Iyésada. The article provides for the exchange of ratifications, and they proposed, if I were willing, to send an ambassador in their steamer to Washington *via* California for that purpose! I told them nothing could possibly give me greater pleasure; that, as the United States was the first Power that Japan ever made a

[1] All the Shōguns, from the first Minamoto Yoritomo, have been of Minamoto name or stock. Iyésada took the first syllable of his name from the founder of the Tokugawa dynasty, Iyéyasŭ (1542–1616), who was made Shōgun in 1603.

treaty with, I should be much pleased that the first Japanese Ambassador should be sent to the United States. The article was accordingly altered, and also amended so as to make the treaty go into effect if, from any unforeseen accident, the ratifications should not be exchanged by that time. The regulations of trade, except the tariff, were informally accepted. I gave them notice that I wished to introduce a clause giving the right to American ships to employ Japanese as seamen on board American ships, giving bonds to return the men to Japan within three years, except in cases of death or desertion. The Commissioners agree to meet me on Monday at eight A. M., and to work the whole day. Adjourn at seven P. M.

Monday, February 8, 1858. Meet, according to agreement, at eight A. M. The Commissioners propose various articles on the subject of Osaka, and at last the following is agreed on: "On the 1st of January, 1863, the city of Yedo, and on the   day of   , 18   ,[1] the city of Osaka, shall be opened to Americans for residence and trade. The special place within which they may hire houses in each of these two cities, and the distance they may walk, shall be settled by the American diplomatic agent and the government of Japan." The Japanese showed me maps of Sakai and Osaka.

[1] The blanks are in the MS. record. Osaka was not opened until January 1, 1868.

Sakai produces twenty-two articles, among which are metal work, silk stuff, arms, rattan work, etc., etc.

I inform them [that] I wish both Sakai and Hiōgo, the latter for its good harbor, and the former from its proximity to Osaka. They positively refuse both places. I then claim Hiōgo, according to their original offer to me of either. They reply that [that] offer was made by them in lieu of Osaka, and that I did not include Sakai or Hiōgo in my original draft. After much debate, I tell them I shall withdraw the claim, as they will be quite willing to open Hiōgo by the time Osaka is opened. We at last fix the dates on which the various places shall be opened : —

Kanagawa, July 4, 1859.
Nagasaki the same.
Niigata, January 1, 1860.
Yedo, January 1, 1862.
Sakai, January 1, 1863.
Osaka, January 1, 1863.

Adjourned at one P. M. for their dinner, and meet again at two P. M. The whole of this [afternoon] was spent in a vain attempt to fix the boundaries of the various places. They were so unreasonable and so inconsistent that I could not help suspecting the champagne which I sent to them had not operated favorably. Adjourned at five P. M. to meet tomorrow at eight A. M.

Tuesday, February 9, 1858. Meet at nine A. M. Take up articles regulating trade. In the treaty with the Russians, the regulations were imperfect and oppressive. Fines of the most outrageous character were imposed, and ship and cargo both were confiscated for light offenses, and the innocent were thus punished for offenses in which they neither participated, nor had any knowledge of, or power of preventing. I pointed out the injustice of such laws to the Commissioners, and they admitted the force of my objections. They said they were entirely in the dark on the subject, not having any experience to guide them.

They said I had evidently taken much pains in drawing up the new code now before them, that they thanked me for my kindness, and, as they had perfect confidence in my integrity, they would accept it.

They then examined the figures of some fines that had been changed, at their request, from kobangs to dollars, and found them all right. I now took up the tariff.

I began by stating the objections to all tonnage dues, and showed that they only served to check commerce, were unequal in their operation, and injurious to revenue.

I then stated the objections to export duties, saying that it was a burden on the industry of their own people, was vexatious to the merchant, led to great expense to prevent smuggling, and was not of much benefit to the revenue. I then quoted the example of England and the United States, two of the greatest commercial nations in the world, neither of which levied tonnage dues or export duties. I closed by saying that commerce could bear a certain burden and no more, and, whether that was collected under one or three forms, only a certain tax could be paid; and concluded this branch by urging the simplicity and economy of collecting their revenue from imports alone. I then took up the tariff and explained the various classes, and my reasons for making different rates of duties, etc., etc. They say the tariff is out of their province, and must be submitted to the Chamber of Accounts. They also inform me that the 14th instant is their New Year, and they cannot meet me again before the 17th; that they usually take seven days for these holidays, but on account of my long detention here they will only take three.

It was agreed that clean copies of the treaty should in the interim be drawn out, and the amendments and alterations translated into Japanese.

Friday, February 12, 1858. The Prince of Shinano visited me to-day. He said they were all very busy in preparing their annual reports for the close of the year, but that he would pay me a short private visit.

He soon after introduced the boundaries of the opened places, and the right of consuls to travel in the country, and, from his frequent mention of the daimiōs, I am prepared to have difficulties with them on these subjects.

Saturday, February 13. Busy in writing. I find I have omitted any notice of the "Rō-nin" since the 25th of January. On that and the following night I was much annoyed by the noise kept up by the "grand rounds" who patrolled every half hour. As soon as the point of the residence of the Minister in Yedo was settled, the rounds and noise ceased. This adds to the belief always held by me that the whole matter was a mere "Arrowsmith" got up to frighten me, and, failing of its purpose, it was then abandoned.

Sunday, February 14, 1858. Japanese New Year's Day. The streets are filled with the long trains of the daimiōs and nobles going to the Castle to pay their compliments and carry presents. This reminds me of the New Year's festivities in New York.

Monday, February 15. The Tai-kun sends presents of boiled cakes on New Year's Day to all those he wishes to honor; but hearing I did not eat those cakes, he sent me a large basket of oranges from Kiishiu.[1] The present came yesterday, but I

---

[1] Kiishiu, or the province of Kii, is the great orange orchard of the Empire.

declined receiving it on that day, it being Sunday, and I was glad of an opportunity of showing the Japanese that not even for the Tai-kun would I alter my strict rule for that day. I receive presents of fans from Higo no Kami and others.

Ash Wednesday, February 17. The Commissioners, instead of meeting at noon, as they had appointed, did not arrive until near five P. M. They commenced by giving a history of my negotiations from the day of my audience up to the 9th instant, repeating many parts three or four times, and constantly referring to the daimiōs, and their opposition to any change in the ancient customs of the land by permitting the residence of foreigners in Japan, etc.; this lasted for more than an hour without their giving me any information as to what they desired. I plainly saw there was a hitch somewhere.

They then proceeded to say that on the 11th instant the treaty as it then stood had been submitted to the daimiōs, and instantly the whole Castle was in an uproar; some of the most violent declared that they should sacrifice their lives before they would permit such great changes to be made; the Council of State had labored incessantly to enlighten these men, — had pointed out to them not only the policy but necessity there was to make the treaty, if they would avert the ruin of the kingdom, etc.; they had brought over some, but others still remained obstinate; that the government could not at once sign such a treaty except at the expense of bloodshed; that they were sure the President did not wish to bring any such evil on Japan.

I at last discovered that they wished to delay the signing of the treaty until a member of the Council of State could proceed as "Ambassador to the Spiritual Emperor" at Kiōto and get his approval; that the moment that approval was received, the daimiōs must withdraw their opposition; that they were content to take the treaty substantially as it stood, having only some slight verbal alterations to suggest, and solemnly pledged their faith that the treaty should be executed as soon as the ambassador returned from Miako, which would require about two months.

Having concluded this extraordinary conversation, I asked them what they would do if the Mikado refused his assent. They replied, in a prompt and decided manner, that the government had *determined not to receive any objections from the Mikado.*

I asked what is the use, then, of delaying the treaty for what appears to be a mere ceremony. They replied that it was this solemn ceremony that gave value to it; and, as I understood, that being known that the Mikado [had been] thus gravely appealed to, his decision would be final, and that all excitement would subside at once.

They proposed that we should go on with the treaty until it was completed and engrossed; that I should amuse myself by going about, and, if I wished to make a trip to Shimoda, the government would send me down and bring me back in their steamer. In answer I said that what they had told me was unprecedented in the history of negotiations; that it was much like the acts of children, and unworthy of wise statesmen like those who ruled Japan; and that it was trifling with a serious matter; that it would be sure to give the President great concern; that it would have been far better not to have negotiated with me at all than to refuse to sign a treaty, which had cost so much labor, for so very trifling a reason, etc.

I added that the mere *act* of signing the treaty might be kept as secret as they chose, as I should not divulge it in Japan. They replied that it was impossible to keep anything secret that passed between us (and I have no doubt they spoke truly); that they were acting in good faith, and I might rely that the treaty should be executed. I finally told them that I had no power to compel them to execute the treaty, that I could not then give them an answer to their proposition, but I proposed to put that matter aside for the present and proceed to complete the treaty, but they must clearly understand that I did not agree to accept the delay asked for.

This was agreed to, and they opened the treaty with the first article, over which they wasted time (and with an evident intent to do so) until eight o'clock, when they said they were weary, and begged to adjourn until day after to-morrow.

Their plan evidently is, to spin out the time, until I either assent to their wish, or the ambassador has returned from Yedo.

I have before noted that they had agreed to fire a salute on Washington's birthday. They now informed me the salute would be fired between Shinagawa and Kawasaki, some eight miles from my residence, adding that was the nearest place where cannon could be fired. In answer I said I could not go so far as that; that, if they had any objections to firing the salute, I would withdraw my request; that a salute under such circumstances would be anything but an honor; that I had heard howitzers fired every week since I had been in Yedo; that I was so accustomed to such sounds that I could very well judge of the distance; and that the firing had frequently been within sixteen streets of my residence, one mile. They said that must have been the guns of the daimiōs. They then said they could themselves fire the salute. I replied they of course could fire when they pleased, but I should not consider it as being fired in honor of the day. They then proposed that Mr. Heusken should ride to the place. I answered that he was not the representative of the United States. They said the discount of six per cent. was to be paid by me until the new treaty went into effect.

Thursday, February 18, 1858. I have no entries in my journal of my having gone out of my house for any purpose, except on official business, since December 17, 1857. In fact I have not gone out of the inclosure of the premises but once since that date, and that was on the occasion of my visit to the Minister of Foreign Affairs on the 16th of last month. My reasons for this seclusion have been twofold.

I have frequently referred to the fact that the Japanese connect the idea of seclusion with high rank, and that the one is the measure of the other. The government had proclaimed me to be, from my official position, a person of *exalted* rank, as they termed it, and caused all the ceremonies of my journey from Shimoda here to correspond with that idea. I felt that my influence with this singular people greatly depended on my maintaining that opinion.

I also knew that a large majority of the daimiōs were violently opposed to the object of my mission, and that some were exceedingly violent. I apprehended that, were I to go out frequently for recreation, I should meet the trains of some of these persons, and that difficulties might arise from their claiming from me some acknowledgment of their rank that I might not be willing to concede; or that, from my ignorance of their complicated etiquette, I might unwittingly give umbrage that might create much angry feeling among this class, who, from an *esprit du corps*, would embrace the cause of their brother daimiōs, whom, they might suppose, I had wantonly insulted, thereby creating difficulties to the object of my mission, give power to the opposition, and embarrass the government of Japan. I have taken exercise by walking some miles every day in the court on which my rooms open. I walk from three to eight miles per diem, yet my health has sensibly suffered and I am become exceedingly thin. I also feel the want of food properly prepared, as my Japanese cook is extremely deficient in many points.

The Prince of Shinano visited me to-day, and we had a long talk over business. He says that I may rely that the government is acting in good faith, and is anxious to make a treaty with me; that the mission to Miako will be successful in obtaining the assent of the Mikado; and that, when that assent is promulgated, the opposition of the daimiōs will instantly cease. The prince informed me that, of the eighteen great daimiōs, four were in favor and fourteen opposed to the treaty; that, of the three hundred daimiōs created by Iyéyasŭ,[1] thirty

---

[1] The Japan of Tokugawa days (1614–1868, or from the capture of the Castle of Osaka by Iyéyasŭ to the seizure of the Impe-

THE OPENING OF THE PORTS. 293

out of every hundred were in favor, and the remainder opposed; that the government was con-

rial palace and person in Kiōto by the coalition of progressive clans) was one of the most curious composites of feudalism in the much-feudalized Old World. When, in 1192 and later, the military classes dispossessed the kugé, or court nobles, of their land, offices, and titles, in whole or in part, the clan-leaders or daimiōs made the courtly titles their own, whether these titles had any real significance or not. Usually the daimiōs who had the ancient court titles (sixty or more in number in Mr. Harris's time), such as " no Kami," " Taiyu," " Daibu," etc., after their names and territorial titles, had no actual duties corresponding to these empty sounds. According to the *Yedo Manual*, the number of daimiōs " created by Iyéyasŭ," as Mr. Harris says, was two hundred and sixty-five, of whom eighteen were province lords, independent in domestic matters of the Tycoon, or overlord in Yedo; thirty-two were rulers of districts; and two hundred and twelve were lords of castles. The richest of the daimiōs was Maéda, the lord of Kaga, the next being Shimadzu of Satsuma. Their " revenue " was stated in terms of the rice product of which their domains were supposed to be capable, and on the basis of which they levied taxes; that of Kaga being 1,027,000, Satsuma 710,000, Chōshiu 369,000, Datté 350,000, Echizen 325,600; and of " the three titular brothers " of the Shōgun (Go San Ké), Owari 610,500, Kii 550,000, and Mito 350,000 koku respectively. A koku of rice, usually contained in two hiō or straw bags, amounts to 5.13 bushels. To be a daimiō, or " big name," one must have a revenue of 10,000 koku. The personal retainers of the Shōgun receiving land assessed under 10,000 koku were called shomiō, or " little names." In the first class of shomiō were those who rallied around the flag, or hata-moto, whose incomes were over 300 or less than 10,000 koku. In the second grade were the go kenin, or honorable retainers, whose income varied from 100 koku to that of those poor fellows (many of whom the writer knew personally) whose annual stipend out of the local rice-stores was but fifteen stantly working on these men, and when they could get them to listen they frequently convinced them;

hiō, or less than three koku. The *Yedo Manual* groups the daimiōs into thirty-nine clans or families, allied by blood, or by a very free system of adoption that deranges all our Western notions of propriety, — as Mr. Harris noticed. In the *Legacy of Iyéyasŭ*, a document of uncertain date, authenticity, and value, the daimiōs, beside being classed as kokushiu, riōshiu, and jōshiu, are called tozama and fudai, or outer and vassal rulers of territory, the former having declared their adherence to Iyéyasŭ only *after* the fall of Hidéyori and Osaka in 1614. The tozama lords rule' 'ıeir own fiefs, while the fudai could be ordered on and off each other's domains like pieces of chess by the Tycoon or overlord at Yedo. To the great Tokugawa clan belonged the "three princely families" (Go San Ké) and eighteen other fudai daimiōs. Nearly all the offices under the Bakafu were held by hata-moto or go kenin, though the rōju, or elders in the Council of State, and the higher offices were from the class of fudai daimiōs. Furthermore, there were thirty grades of court rank, one of which was attached to every office, real or imaginary. The highest could be given only after death. In the province and daimiate of Echizen, in which the writer saw the feudal system during a residence of ten months, these divisions of land, offices, titles, illustrations of the power or of the limitations of the overlordship at Yedo, were strikingly, often dramatically, and even ludicrously, manifested. The general term for the civil nobles of the old Imperial court was kugé, while that of the military classes was buké, the pure Japanese word being samurai. The literal meaning of this latter term, which included all persons eligible to the honor of wearing two swords, is "servant of the Emperor." By the Imperial Rescript of June 6, 1884, the orders of nobility were reformed, and out of the kugé, daimiō, and samurai was formed the general class of kwazoku, or "flowery nobility," in which are five grades, princes, marquises, counts, viscounts, and barons. In this nobility, besides the old names and houses, is a large number but many, like the obstinate of more enlightened countries, refused to listen to a word of reason, argument, or explanation. This last class will only yield to the opinion of the Mikado when it shall be promulgated.

I made the following suggestion to Shinano: Let us proceed, and complete the treaty as soon as possible, and have it engrossed and ready for signature. Then let the Council of State, or the Minister of Foreign Affairs, write me a letter saying that the Commissioners appointed to negotiate with me a commercial treaty between the United

of men, once of low rank, who for signal ability or meritorious services have been ennobled. The gentry have been renamed shizoku. The common people are héimin. In December, 1888, there were eleven princes, thirty marquises, eighty-two counts, three hundred and sixty-four viscounts, and ninety-six barons. In the Upper House of the Imperial Diet, created in 1889, thirty-seven members of the nobility sit by hereditary right; while, out of the remaining five hundred and forty-four, a limited number, not exceeding one fifth of the whole, may be chosen to serve seven years. In the list of eleven princes are four representatives of the old daimiō families, two of Satsuma, one of Takatsŭkasa, and one of Tokugawa. Among the marquises are a few old kugé families, but most of them are from the old territorial feudal nobility. It would not be difficult to show that, from the first attempt of the Bakafu in 1853 to sound public opinion by consulting the daimiōs concerning the question of making a treaty with the Americans, the evolution of representative institutions has gone steadily forward. Out of the rōju, or Council of Elders, in Yedo has grown by steady progress the Imperial Diet of to-day, which the Liberals insist shall be transformed still further from the German to the English type.

States and Japan had completed their labors, and that the treaty was now ready for signature; but, for certain important reasons, the signing of the treaty must be postponed for sixty days, on or before the expiration of which time the treaty as it now stood should be signed.

Thereupon I would return to Shimoda to prepare my dispatches for my government; that at the end of fifty days, if not before, the government should send their steamer to Shimoda for bringing me again to Yedo, for the purpose of executing the treaty. The Prince was much pleased with the idea, and told me he would communicate it to the government at once, and speak to me about it to-morrow. I do not see what I can do better under the peculiar circumstances in which I am placed. If I can get the written promise of the government that *the* treaty (not a treaty) shall be signed by a certain day, I do not see but it is as binding on them as the signature of the Commissioners to the treaty itself.

Friday, February 19, 1858. Toké, Prince of Tamba, sent me a beautiful present of a plum-tree in full bloom, having more than one thousand blossoms! The stock is four inches diameter at the bottom, and eighteen inches high. Nearly thirty grafts have been inserted in the stock, and these have grown up some twenty-four to thirty inches high, and, branching out, give more than fifty sprays. Not a green leaf is visible, but all the sprays are covered from end to end with fragrant white blossoms.

At two P. M. the Prince of Shinano visited me, and brought a beautiful china pot of bulbs of the daffodil family, in bloom; the Japanese name is "Happy Longevity," and it is a favorite New Year's gift. He tells me that their laws regarding mourning have been greatly modified during the last two hundred years. Formerly, an officer on the death of his father resigned his employments, and lived retired for three years. Now, he does not resign, and mourns for fifty days full mourning; that is, does not attend to any business, or shave his head or beard during that time: after the fifty days are expired he resumes his duties, and shaves, etc., but for one year he must not attend any festivities.

The daimiōs, who have sovereign rule in their dominions, are seven or eight of the original eighteen of that rank. The Prince of Kaga has the largest principality, and is the most powerful and wealthy of any of his class. Not even the Tai-kun may send a person into the dominions of these daimiōs without their consent "first had and obtained." The Japanese pretend that any officer of the Imperial government intruding without such leave would instantly be put to death.

Did not meet the Commissioners until nearly

five P. M. They informed me that the proposition I made to Shinano no Kami yesterday was accepted by the government, and that the letter pledging the faith of the government that the treaty should be executed within sixty days from this date would be signed by Hotta, Prince of Bitchiu, Minister of Foreign Affairs, and that the steamer should be sent to Shimoda ten days before that time to bring me to Yedo.[1]

We then took up the treaty for final consideration, and after much consideration the preamble was accepted. A long debate arose on the [clause]: "All diplomatic and consular officers shall have the right to travel freely in any part of the Empire of Japan." After much time wasted over it, I offered to strike out the whole clause, and leave those officers to claim their rights under the laws of nations. This they also objected to, wishing to restrain consuls to their consular districts, which I as strongly refused to do, or to insert any clause which might deprive them of a right they could claim under the laws of nations.

I had at one time serious [fears] that the whole treaty might be wrecked on this point. They went over the old ground of objections, the claims of the daimiōs to exclusive jurisdiction in their own principalities, then furious objections to any infringe-

[1] All these promises were fulfilled to the letter, as Mr. Harris's letters and dispatches show.

ment of their ancient rights, and the certainty that serious difficulties would arise from the clause. At last they said that they would consent to insert that the Minister and Consul-General should have that right, but to exclude other consuls. I at last consented to accept their proposition, but not to insert the words " other consular officers." At last they accepted it, after a struggle to get the insertion of a clause requiring the Minister and Consul-General to give notice to the government of their intention to travel, etc., etc., and also to strike out the word " freely " from the connection " may freely travel in any part," etc. Both propositions were rejected by me, and finally the clause was accepted as above amended. The counterpart for " Japanese Diplomatic Agent, etc., in the United States," was made to correspond with the grant to us. The whole article was now finally accepted.

Article 2. After an attempt to strike out the word "request" from the first paragraph, "The President of the United States will at the request of the Japanese government act as a friendly mediator," on inquiry, I found they had translated the Dutch word " versoek" " to beg." After an explanation of the true meaning of " request," they consented to take the clause as it stands in the original draft. The Commissioners now wished to adjourn, promising to meet me at noon tomorrow.

I am told that formerly, on the death of one of the daimiōs, numbers of his domestics or officers performed the hara-kiri, *i. e.* ripping themselves up; but that custom has been abolished.[1]

Earthquake at 11.30 P. M.

Saturday, February 20, 1858. Snow this morning. I am told the Prince of Kaga "goes on" like a lunatic about the treaty. He says, while the Tai-kun governs by the ancient laws he will be his subject; but when he departs from them his allegiance ceases. I do not by any means place full faith in what the Japanese tell me about these matters. I know enough of them to be aware that to lie is the rule, to tell the truth is the exception.

I am told the Tai-kun is in favor of the treaty, saying that he is convinced it is for the good of the country. The smaller daimiōs dare not openly oppose the government, but they shield themselves under the opinions of the greater daimiōs. They say that two papers will be presented to the Mikado, one in favor of the proposed treaty and the other against it; that, after examining both, he will approve of one, and that approval is binding on all; that even those most violently opposed to the treaty will say, if he decides in favor of the treaty, "God has spoken: I submit." This does

---

[1] The custom of jun-shi, or dying with the master, was a very ancient one in Japan, but was abolished only gradually. See *M. E. T. J., Religions of Japan,* etc.

not agree very well with the almost contemptuous manner in which the Japanese speak of this potentate.

I am told that large sums of money have already been distributed among the officers of the Mikado, and that still larger sums will be applied in the same manner.

Meet the Commissioners at two P. M., and continue until seven. A very discouraging meeting; the whole time was passed in noting down their proposed amendments to the first eight articles. Many of these are absurd, others childish, and some fatal to the working of the treaty.

Sunday, February 21, 1856. The first Sunday in Lent, and a lovely day. I am quite disheartened and low-spirited about the treaty. I greatly fear that I shall altogether fail in making a treaty that will be acceptable to the President.

To add to my difficulties, their Dutch interpreter is very imperfectly acquainted with the idioms of that language, while his self-sufficiency is in the exact ratio of his ignorance. The Japanese language does not possess either singular or plural, has no relative pronoun, nor is the use of the antecedent known; neither has it any possessive case. These defects require the constant repetition of nouns and verbs, and at all times make the meaning vague and obscure.

I never shall get to the bottom of the deceptions

of the Japanese. I now learn that the "three brothers of the Tai-kun" are merely titular brothers;[1] they are of the family, but the removes by birth carry them beyond the list of parentage as known by us. They are the Princes of Owari, Kii, and of Mito. These men are called the "first brothers" of the Tai-kun, and he also has three "second brothers," who are also merely titular relations.

Monday, February 22, 1858. Meet at nine A. M. Only Shinano no Kami present. I note the proposed amendments to the treaty offered by him, but do not enter into any discussions about the merits of them.

They are of various classes. Some are absurd, others mischievous, and not one that is of the least benefit to Japan by adding to her security or honor. The insertion of some would make obscure what is now clear, and many would excite laughter. The tone of all the amendments is unfriendly and haughty, and calculated to make the treaty unacceptable.

They have not as yet decided on the tariff; consequently the subject of tonnage dues, import and export duties, and fines was all passed over, they promising an answer to those points on the 24th. The next meeting is to be to-morrow at two P. M.,

[1] There is no simple term for "brother" in the Japanese language. See *The Religions of Japan*.

when both Commissioners are to be present. They promise to give me an amended copy of the letter which is to be written to me by Hotta, Prince of Bitchiu, after the negotiations are closed.

Tuesday, February 23. Met both the Commissioners at one P. M. I opened the discussion by saying that I had carefully considered all their proposed amendments; that some were a mere change of words, others rendered the meaning obscure; that many will open the door for disputes and difficulties; that the change of a word in one article sometimes required the alteration of many articles, as all must agree; that many of the amendments showed a very unfriendly spirit; and that the insertion of what they proposed would cause the treaty to be rejected. I closed by saying that such amendments as were reasonable or necessary should be adopted.

We then took up article 7, concerning the limits of the various ports, and to my agreeable surprise they accepted my proposal for Hakodaté and Nagasaki; they now give me Hiōgo for Sakai, and the boundaries are arranged. Niigata is postponed until it is determined whether that port, or another on the west coast of Nippon, shall be accepted; and, lastly, we settle on the Nagasaki boundaries. The treaty must be referred to for the particulars. We then took up their proposals in the order in which they relate to the articles, and rapidly disposed of them, so that at five P. M. the treaty was agreed on.

The regulations were then taken up. They accepted the penalties, and agreed that tonnage duties should not be levied; but they gave me notice that they should levy export and import duties. I then informed them that the levying of export duties would require an alteration of article 10, and the striking out of article 11 of the treaty, which they assented to.

They informed me that the report on the tariff and export duties could not be ready before the 25th instant. On the morning of which day they would hand me the tariff as they propose it, and meet me at one P. M. Thus closes this journal with an account of the most satisfactory day's business I ever had with them. They seemed to be in earnest, and acted promptly and reasonably.

Thursday, February 25, 1858. The Commissioners sent me their proposition for duties. With the exception of a few articles, they propose an import duty of twelve and a half per cent. and an export duty of the same amount on all articles exported, whether of Japanese or foreign production. Such an export duty would crush anything like prosperous trade.

Met the Commissioners at two P. M. Stated my objections to their tariff. I have been anxious not to have any export duties, but am forced to abandon the idea. We at last agreed on export duty, at five per cent., on all articles of Japanese production exported as cargo. The import duty is to be five per cent. on all articles required for ships, whalers, etc., and some other articles, including living animals of all kinds, bread and breadstuffs, and salted productions, etc.

Intoxicating drinks of all kinds, thirty-five per cent.[1] All other articles (except as below), twenty per cent. Gold and silver, coined or uncoined, with the clothing, books, furniture, etc., of persons who come to reside in Japan, are duty free.

The duties are to be subject to revision, if the Japanese desire it, five years after Kanagawa has been opened.

I informed them that ministers, consuls - general, etc., did not pay duty on any articles for their own use. They agree to write to the Governor of Hakodaté to act with Mr. Rice in selecting the place where Americans shall erect their buildings, etc., at that place, also, that Mr. Rice is to be furnished with Japanese money. I gave them Mr. Rice's complaints about high prices at Hakodaté, and they promised to inquire into it.

They still wish me to write to my government, asking that a Minister shall not be sent to Japan before January 1, 1861. They gave me notice

[1] See closing words of the final chapter of this book, showing how this proviso was later altered.

they should write me a letter requesting that copies of the treaty should be transmitted to the English and Russians by the Secretary of State.

We made some slight verbal amendments, and then agreed that a fair copy should be made for examination, prior to its being engrossed.

They still stick to the six per cent. discount on money in my case; rather small for a government that professes to have such a contempt for money.

Saturday, February 27, 1858. Last evening, gave clean copy of treaty to the Japanese.[1] To-day the Commissioners send me word they will require until Tuesday next, March 2, to examine, with the Council of State, the final draft of the treaty. If any doubt had existed in my mind that I was in reality negotiating with the Council, and that the Commissioners had no real full powers, this significant circumstance would remove it.

They tell me it will take the steamer two days to run from Kanagawa to Shimoda (not over seventy nautical miles). If this be true, it must be a very poor affair, and will hardly take their ambassador to San Francisco.

Busy yesterday and to-day in writing letters, —

---

[1] For the text of this treaty, with the appended regulations, as well as of the Convention of June 17, 1857, and subsequent treaties between Japan and the United States, see pp. 597–628 of *Treaties and Conventions between Japan and Other Powers.* Washington, 1887.

one to Mr. Rice, one to Mr. Donker Curtius, and other private letters to my friends in America.

Since the 16th instant, when the snow fell so deeply, the weather has been remarkably cold for the latitude of 36° until to-day. The thermometer has never risen above 33°, although the days have been generally fine. A fresh wind, N. W., bringing the frosty air from Kamchatka, has constantly blown.[1]

NOTE. — Mr. Tsuda Sen, who is well known to many Americans, and whose daughter, Miss Umé, was educated in Washington, D. C., in a letter dated May 27, 1892, writes: —

"I knew Mr. Harris personally. When he first came to Yedo, one of the Japanese phrenologists, named Yamaguchi Chiyéda, desired very much to meet him and see his physiognomy, but he could not meet him easily. One day, hearing that the Consul-General was to visit the temple at Asakusa, he disguised himself as one of the servants of the tea-house there. He saw Mr. Harris's physiognomy and said with wonder, 'There is no such man as he in Japan. He is an honest and virtuous man; and if we follow his opinion, it will profit the country much. He is a saint.' Every one hearing the words of the phrenologist felt very strangely, but I see that his words were true.

"At that time I served as an officer in the Foreign Department, and I often met Mr. Harris. I admired him because he did not change his views frequently, for he always spoke deliberately."

[1] Here ends Mr. Harris's Journal.

PART III.
SUCCESS, REPOSE, AND HONORS.

Heaven's ordination baffles the human.
PRINCE KITASHIRAKAWA.

Baron Ii was the man called to face these great problems (of foreign intercourse). Confident in the wisdom of his policy, he bravely opposed public opinion, and was hated even by his own kin. The result was the sacrifice of life to conviction. Yet this sad event not only saved our country from the misfortune that befell our neighbor China, but opened the pathway of civilization in our own land. This merit is attributable to none but to Baron Ii. COUNT FIELD-MARSHAL YAMAGATA.

As beats the ceaseless wave on Omi's strand,
So breaks my heart for our beloved land.
Poem by II KAMON NO KAMI.

The reason why we treat the United States as our good neighbor is because she has good will to our country, but also, as we believe, that the future queens on the Pacific are not to be found anywhere else except in the United States and Japan. We do not expect her to be our political ally; we only want to run with her in the race of civilization, as our beneficial friend, toward social and commercial enterprise. TOKUTOMI.

CHAPTER XVI.

JAPAN OPENED TO THE WORLD.

MR. HARRIS'S journals end with the record of February 27, 1858. Our brief story of his life from this time forth is made up out of his letter-books and from Japanese documents.

In those days the Japanese people understood very little of the nature of treaties. To most natives the Americans' demands for commercial privileges were interpreted to mean territorial invasion and ultimate occupation. Coming so soon after Great Britain's conquest of India, and the American humiliation of Mexico, this was nothing wonderful. The Japanese nobles and samurai were quickly divided into Exclusionists and Progressionists. The former, in vast majority, were led by the powerful daimiō of Mito; the latter had as yet no conspicuous leader to dare the assassin's sword.

The gravity of the situation was felt so keenly by the Shōgun and his Senators that an envoy was dispatched to Nikkō to lay a copy of the American treaty upon the mausoleum of Iyéyasŭ, and make inquiry of his august spirit. The learned professor Hayashi was sent to Kiōto to gain the

Mikado's consent to the treaty. After a month's loss of time, he returned to Yedo to report failure. Meanwhile the political cauldron began to boil as never before.

Mr. Harris, while in Yedo, refrained from correspondence with the Dutch Commissioner at Nagasaki, Mr. J. H. D. Curtius, until March 8, when, the treaty negotiations being over, he wrote: —

"The Minister for Foreign Affairs and President of the Council of State has written me a letter positively pledging the signatures to the treaty on or before the 21st of April."

To the same effect Mr. Harris had written, March 4, to the Hon. Lewis Cass, Secretary of State, inclosing a Dutch copy and an English translation of Hotta's letter for the archives in Washington.

Leaving Yedo in the Japanese government steamer March 10, Mr. Harris reached Shimoda on the 12th. Exhausted nature giving way, he sank unconscious into a nervous fever, which lasted for weeks. The idea of losing their friend at this crisis of affairs so alarmed the statesmen in Yedo that the Tycoon's own physicians, graduates of the unincorporated but efficient Dutch school of medicine at Nagasaki, were dispatched to Shimoda. It was intimated to them that their own lives would be in peril if the American's were lost. As on a former occasion in Yedo, the chief lady of the city, the

Tycoon's wife, sent Mr. Harris tempting delicacies prepared by her own hands. With a sword suspended, as it were, over their bowels, and possible seppuku in view, the doctors, aided by nature, saved their patient. The threatened symptoms of putrid fever passed away, and by April 1 the treaty-maker began to think of his return to Yedo, which was fixed for the 15th. Despite the remonstrances of his physicians, and so weak that he had to be carried on board the steamer, he made the journey by water. Arriving in the great city on the 17th, he found disappointment awaiting him. Hotta was still in Kiōto.

Long before this time, Mr. Harris, though still much puzzled, began to suspect that the Yedo government was an empty sham, and that the real ruler of Japan was the Mikado, whose approval of the treaty must be obtained in order to calm the country. Hotta, the Minister of Foreign Affairs, had departed for the "Blossom Capital," and was still laboring to obtain the true Imperial signature. In over two hundred years, only two missions from the Yedo government had been dispatched to Kiōto, success in both instances following within ten days. In this case Hotta waited, negotiated, exhausted all his resources, for fifty days, in vain. In the native histories the story is a long one about the vacillations of politics at the Court; one day, the Emperor's premier, declaring by edict "that full powers were given to the Bakafu to deal with the foreign question," and the next "the opinion of the Court undergoing a profound change." Of Mr. Harris, the native historian says that, rendered impatient by long waiting, "he threatened that, if his time was to be wasted in this way, he would proceed forthwith to Kiōto and arrange it [the treaty] himself." Hotta returned to Yedo June 1, and on the 5th Mr. Harris had an interview with him.

All this time Mr. Harris had used no menace or threats of force, though he had not failed to hint at contemporaneous events in India and China, and at the presence of large British and French fleets in neighboring waters. He showed how much the Japanese would gain by inaugurating foreign intercourse by a commercial treaty granted reasonably and freely, before they were compelled by force to make disastrous concessions. So far was this civilian, alone in Yedo, successful that, before leaving for Kiōto, Hotta, in the name of the government, had given in writing the pledge demanded by Mr. Harris, and in his letter of February 17, 1858, after stating "the necessity of delaying the signing of the treaty," promised "it should be executed before the expiration of sixty days."

On June 6, the day after his interview with Hotta, the two treaty Commissioners visited Mr. Harris, who, in his letter from Shimoda, July 8, to Mr. Cass, the Secretary of State, writes: —

"The Commissioners assured me that the Tycoon and Council of State were fully resolved to carry the treaty into effect; that they did not ask any alteration of its conditions, but required time to bring the daimiōs to reason. They said the government had the power to crush the opposition by force; that they shrunk with horror from the idea of bloodshed; that the time they asked for accomplishing their purpose was until the 27th of the seventh month (September 4, 1858); that if I would agree to this delay, the Council of State would write me a letter, in which they would pledge their faith and that of the Tycoon that the treaty should positively be signed on the date named above, no matter what might be the state of public opinion at that time."

Mr. J. H. D. Curtius, the Dutch superintendent of trade at Nagasaki, had arrived in Yedo six days after Mr. Harris, April 23, and, after an audience of the Shōgun, May 8, expressed himself ready to make such a commercial treaty as *would* be acceptable to the daimiōs.

Mr. Harris knew this, and knowing also that after *his* treaty should have been made the Dutch would gain all advantages under the "favored nation" clause, wrote in the same letter of July 8:—

"After mature deliberation, I determined to accede to the request of the Japanese, provided they would also pledge themselves in writing not to sign any treaty or convention with any power until the expiration of thirty days after the signing of the American treaty.

"This proposition was accepted by the Council of State, who subsequently wrote me a letter expressing the conditions already stated. I transmit herewith a copy of the Dutch version of that letter with an English translation of the same.

"This document may fairly be considered as a virtual execution and ratification of the treaty.

"The Minister of Foreign Affairs also delivered to me a large box containing a letter from the Tycoon addressed to the President of the United States. I was assured that no letter had been addressed by the Tycoon to any foreign power for more than two hundred and forty years, and that the answer to the letter of the King of Holland had been written by the Council of State."

With such documents in his pocket the treaty was practically won, and Mr. Harris returned to Shimoda June 18. Not since the great Iyéyasŭ, founder of the Tokugawa dynasty of Shōguns in Yedo, had in 1613 addressed through Captain Saris letters to King James I. of England, and later to the Stadtholder of the United Netherlands, had the Tycoon ever sent an autograph letter or his signature to a foreign power. Harried out of his dominions by the royal pedant, the Pilgrims, after political training in Holland, had, with other Englishmen and the republican Dutchmen, founded the great nation whose representative again set the Tycoon's pen in motion.

The Shōgun Iyésada, who had thus written to President Buchanan, had already resolved to summon to the helm a fearless soul who would quail at no storm. Two days after Hotta's return, the baron of Hikoné, better known as Ii Kamon no Kami, was appointed premier. With fierce patriotism, joined to an iron will and tireless energy, this able statesman girded himself to grapple with the two problems which confronted the Bakafu. The first was the choice of an heir to the childless Iyésada; the second was the question of foreign intercourse. The first was a vital matter in Japanese politics, but does not concern us except to note that the choice fell on Iyémochi, son of the daimiō of Kii.

Mr. Harris, though still a lonely exile, without a man or a ship at hand to back his claims, could not long remain a quiet hermit in Shimoda. Great events were happening in China, and so important have these been in the eyes of Englishmen that most European writers on the history of Japan utterly ignore the great labors of Townsend Harris in the education of a nation. His work and his moral influence are alike unknown to them and to the encyclopædias and dictionaries of biography. To most historians, so called, the four years from the time of Perry to Lord Elgin form a vacuum, and the historic page has a blank. The publication of Mr. Harris's own journals, written on the spot, and day by day, reveals both the facts and the truth.

Let it be noted, then, that Mr. Harris's success had been already substantially won before news of the humiliation of China by the allied forces reached Japan, even as it had been begun and was well on its way before even the European squadrons had gathered in this part of the world. To this day the unenlightened Englishman believes that the unique success of Mr. Harris, "not a diplomatist, but a plain, honest-hearted gentleman," was "due to the influence he obtained over the Taikoon at a time when the Taikoon and Council in Yedo were agitated and alarmed by our second war in 1857, as well as the subsequent opportune arrival of Lord Elgin with a British squadron at Yedo in 1858." [1]

As a matter of fact, Japan was already bound by the written promise of the Yedo government as early as February 17 to execute the treaty, nor was any attempt made to evade, revoke, or modify the instrument. It was only for the peace of the coun-

[1] This conjecture of Captain S. Osborne in *Japanese Fragments*, reëchoed in the British Blue Books and by Sir Rutherford Alcock thirty years ago, is reaffirmed in the *Life of Sir Harry Parkes*, vol. ii. pp. 20, 21, 24–26, 43. The Japanese historians do *not* agree with the English writers.

try, and in the hope of obtaining the Mikado's signature (which, however, came not until 1868), that the Tycoon's officers asked even for delay.

On July 23, 1858, the U. S. S. S. Mississippi arrived at Shimoda [1] with the news of peace in China, the suppression of the Sepoy mutiny in India, the capture of the Péi-ho forts by the British and French forces, and the coming of the allied fleets to Japan. In his brief letter to Hotta, July 24, Mr. Harris, after epitomizing the news, urged "the very great importance of having the treaty signed without the loss of a single day." On the 25th, Commodore Tatnall appeared in the U. S. S. S. Powhatan. On the 27th, at one P. M., Mr. Harris reached Kanagawa, and delivered his letter of the 24th.

For the first time, the Yedo government acted promptly and with independence, for the simple reason that there was a man at the helm who dared for his country's good. The memory of Ii Kamon no Kami (assassinated March 23, 1861), so long desecrated, is now cleansed from stain by the scholarly labors of Shimada Saburo.[2] Unwilling to risk his country's becoming like India or China, Ii, the regent and premier, dispatched the two

[1] See *Life of Matthew Calbraith Perry*, pp. 414, 415.

[2] A digest of the contents of Mr. Shimada's learned and judicial work, *Kaikoku Shimatsu* (Opening of the Country), *or, The Life of Nawosuké* (Ii Kamon no Kami), has been given by the writer in *The Literary World*, Boston, May 6, 1893.

Commissioners, Shinano no Kami and Higo no Kami, to Kanagawa by a steamer, which anchored near the Powhatan at midnight of July 28. Despite the rule against salutes after sundown, Commodore Tatnall received the two envoys on his ship with a salute of seventeen guns.

In a private interview with Mr. Harris, they conveyed to him the thanks of the Council of State for communicating important news. They urged that to sign the treaty now, after notification of its execution by September 4 had been sent to the daimiōs, would cause confusion, while by that time all opposition would probably cease.

Mr. Harris writes to Secretary Cass: " I replied that I did not demand any new arrangement; that I had merely informed them of the approaching danger, and had given them my candid advice as to the best course they could pursue; that if they did not agree with me I had only to return to Shimoda, and quietly wait the day fixed on for the termination of the business.

"The Prince of Higo then proposed that I should write a letter to the Council of State, in which I was to pledge myself that the French and English would accept the American treaty, and that, if it was refused, I would act as a friendly mediator on their behalf."

Mr. Harris declined to do this, as proposed, but he wrote a letter to the Council of State " stating my [his] belief that the American treaty would be accepted by the English and French, and that I [he] was willing to act as a friendly mediator should any difficulties arise. This proposition was accepted, and a letter to the foregoing effect written, a copy of which is herewith transmitted.

"The Commissioners went to their steamer for the purpose of translating the letter, which being complete, they returned to the Powhatan at three P. M., and the treaty was then signed. After the signatures had been affixed, Commodore Tatnall hoisted the Japanese and American flags together at his port, and saluted them with twenty-one guns."

This was joyful music to Townsend Harris. The guns were as many as had been his months of mental strain. The treaty was dated July 29 instead of September 4. On the 2d of August he wrote to Sir John Bowring of Hong-Kong:—

"Lord Elgin and Baron Gros will find their work all done to their hands when they arrive, and that a large fleet was not required as a demonstration."

With mighty squadrons, the British, French, and Russians came later and made treaties, and these were followed by twenty nations; but the treaty negotiated by Townsend Harris is the basis of them all. Mexico was the first country (November 30, 1888) to treat with Japan on equal terms.

Returning to Shimoda, and later making a voyage for a few weeks of recreation to China, Mr. Harris found himself by unanimous vote of the Senate, January 7, 1859, on President Buchanan's nomination, Minister Resident of the United States to Japan.

On the 30th of June, the Consulate was removed from Shimoda to Kanagawa, where the American flag was hoisted July 1, 1859. On the 7th of July, accompanied by a party of twenty-three fellow Americans from the U. S. S. S. Mississippi, Mr. Harris established the American Legation at the Shin Shiu Buddhist Temple, Zempukuji [Shrine of Virtue and Happiness], which had been founded A. D. 1232 by the famous teacher and missionary Icho. Here Mr. Harris remained during his whole stay in the city during the troublous times that followed the opening of the ports.

In Yedo, as American Minister, amid murders, assassinations, and incendiarisms, when all his colleagues had struck their flags and retired to Yokohama, Mr. Harris held his position alone, and kept the American colors flying. To him the only proper place for an envoy was in the nation's capital, as he believed Yedo to be. He assisted generously, and lent his interpreter, Mr. Heusken, to Lord Elgin and to Count Eulenberg, when the British and Prussian treaties were in course of negotiation. He felt keenly the murder of Mr. Heusken, which took place on January 14, and the slaughter on March 23, 1860, of the Premier Ii, who in a large sense of the word was a martyr.

At Mr. Harris's suggestion and advice, an embassy [1] left Japan for Washington via San Francisco, February 13, 1860, in the U. S. S. S. Powhatan, to exchange ratifications of the Harris and to obtain a fresh copy of the Perry treaty. The company of seventy-one persons was headed by Shimmi. Their welcome in the United States was enthusiastic, and, after their final audience of President Buchanan, gold, silver, and bronze medals were struck in honor of their visit. They recrossed the Pacific in a Japanese steamer commanded by Katsu Awa, who still lives as the venerable first organizer and historian of the modern Japanese navy.

Despite all alarms, Mr. Harris "stood on the burning deck," because he felt that his duty was in Yedo. As indemnity for the assassination of Mr. Heusken he demanded and obtained the sum of ten thousand dollars, which was duly paid to the sorrowing mother in Amsterdam. With intensest sympathy for the brave men of the Bakafu, who had to suffer and fall with the hoary system to which their loyalty was pledged, he helped with his kindly advice the Tycoon's ministers as he was able.

---

[1] See account in Nitobe's *The United States and Japan*, pp. 159–162.

Mr. Harris's letter of resignation to President Lincoln is dated July 10, 1861. He pleads ill-health and advancing years, and insists on retirement from public duty. In spite of the formal request of the Japanese to the American government that Mr. Harris might be kept in office, and of Mr. Seward's personal wishes that he should continue to represent his country, Mr. Harris persisted. In his answer of October 21, 1861, Mr. Seward wrote: —

"You will do me the justice, therefore [in view of his recommendation of Mr. Harris to President Pierce in 1855], to believe that I sincerely sympathize with you in your suffering from ill-health, and that I regard your retirement from the important post you have filled with such distinguished ability and success as a subject of grave anxiety, not only for this country, but for all the Western nations."

Before leaving Japan, Mr. Harris made a gift of one thousand dollars for the erection of the American Union Church at Yokohama, built in 1875, and standing on part of the old Perry treaty ground. In due time he handed the Legation of the United States of America, at the temple of Zempukuji, to his able successor, the Hon. Robert H. Pruyn, who held his post during the trying times of our Civil War. Mr. Harris left Japan when Americans felt almost like men without a country.

It was while returning home, in an agony of fear for the safety of the Union, that the loyal American, Townsend Harris, was directly and personally insulted by the captain of the British mail steamer flying the Confederate flag. Englishmen often wonder whether Americans "hate" them, and why.

CHAPTER XVII.

HOME AGAIN. — SOCIAL JOYS. — PEACEFUL END.

AT home in his beloved country and State, Mr. Harris paid a visit to his boyhood's home at Sandy Hill, N. Y. Then, returning to the metropolis, he found repose and honors. The polished and courtly gentleman was a favorite in New York society. Regaining the vigor of health, he enjoyed richly the hospitalities showered upon him. Among his especial intimates were General Prosper M. Wetmore, Judge C. P. Daly, General George W. Cullum, and Mr. T. Hooker Hamersly. Amid the darkest days of the Civil War, his faith in the ultimate success of the Union arms was unshaken. Judge Daly says: —

"Townsend Harris was a far-seeing War Democrat. He believed from the first that the Union would be maintained. His reply after every defeat of the Federal army was, 'We'll whip them yet.' He considered that our men had poor leaders."

He hailed with joy the appointment of Grant as general of all the armies of the Union. At Judge Daly's house, Mr. Harris presented to the hero the superb Japanese sword which the Shōgun had given him at his farewell audience in Yedo. The note offering the gift, and the reply, are reproduced from Mr. Harris's papers: —

UNION CLUB, NEW YORK, November 15, 1865.

GENERAL, — On the occasion of my audience of leave, his Majesty the Tycoon of Japan presented me with a *sabre d'honneur*, which gift President Lincoln kindly permitted me to retain.

It is my desire to transfer it to one of the bravest and worthiest of my countrymen, and the united voice of the whole world unmistakably points to you as the man I seek.

I pray you, sir, to accept this sword as a small mark of my deep sense of the great debt of gratitude which I (in common with all my countrymen) owe to you for your eminent services in saving my beloved country from the ruin that threatened her.

I have the honor to be,
    With profound respect,
        Your obedient and humble servant,
            TOWNSEND HARRIS.

LIEUTENANT-GENERAL GRANT.

HEADQUARTERS OF THE ARMY OF THE UNITED STATES,
WASHINGTON, D. C., November 23, 1865.

HON. TOWNSEND HARRIS:

DEAR SIR, — I have received the *sabre d'honneur* presented to you by his Majesty the Tycoon of

Japan, together with your note of the 15th inst. accompanying it. This present under ordinary circumstances would be highly appreciated; but coming with the assurances it does, not only of the intense loyalty of one of our country's foreign ministers during the darkest days ever any country passed through, but with the compliment paid to myself in that note, it will not only be appreciated by myself, but will be handed down to my children and their children with the note itself.

I am not vain enough to assume that you have selected the right person to become the recipient of this gift or token, but feel complimented to know that you should think so.

With assurances of my best wishes for your future welfare, permit me to sign myself,

Very truly and respectfully,
Your obedient servant,
U. S. GRANT,
Lieutenant-General.

Professor Brander Matthews, Mr. Harris's nephew, writes as follows: —

"He was at Rome with us in 1867, and in Paris at the Exposition. . . . After his return to New York, in 1867, he settled down and lived quietly, spending most of his time at the Union Club. . . . He disliked the noisy, fast, stock-exchange element of the Union Club. He used to say that he and two or three others 'talked sense' at one end of the room, and the rest of the club 'talked dollars' at the other end. He it was who started the library of the Union Club. He told me once that Mr. E. H. House [1] had been to see him, and I believe they corresponded while Mr. House was in Japan."

It was at the Union Club building, corner of Twenty-Second Street and Fifth Avenue, that the writer of this biographical sketch called on Mr. Harris in the autumn of 1875, meeting him for the first time. In this his seventy-first year he was in failing health, though still of imposing presence. Some of the younger and less reverent members of the club referred pleasantly to him as "the Old Tycoon." Faultless in dress, he wore in his buttonhole the tiny blue ribbon of the Order of the Black Eagle, which he had received from Prussia. He had been spending the winters in Florida, but suffered so much from the lack of comforts and conveniences of life in the land of oranges (those

[1] Mr. E. H. House was correspondent of the *New York Tribune* in Japan from 1870 to 1875, and from 1877 to 1880 was the proprietor and able editor of *The Tōkiō Times*. He also wrote valuable historical pamphlets on The Shimonoséki Affair, The Kagoshima Affair, and, after accompanying the army, The Japanese Expedition to Formosa. In his Japanese Episodes, and his articles in *Harper's Magazine*, *The New Princeton Review*, and especially in *The Atlantic Monthly*, he earnestly pleaded for justice to the Japanese, which he has, despite long sickness, lived to see done, or at least in course of inauguration.

being the days before palace hotels) that he henceforth resolved to winter in New York. He inquired eagerly as to how the Japanese regarded him, for he grieved heartily over the non-revision of the treaties, which, when making, he had expected to see revised in half a decade. I gave him two copies, one plain and one colored, of my Map of Tōkiō, with names, and notes, historical and explanatory, in English. These he thankfully appreciated.

Mr. Harris was one of the founders of the New York Society for the Prevention of Cruelty to Animals. He held also honorary membership in various European and American learned and scientific societies.

He died, after a short illness, February 25, 1878, and was buried in Greenwood Cemetery, Brooklyn, three days later.

Townsend Harris intended the treaty he made with the Japanese to be just, honorable, fair; to protect them in their ignorance; to remain in force only during their childhood of experience, but to be revised after July 1, 1872, "if desired by either party."

How Japan has for twenty years suffered "oppression by treaty," how the provisions have been altered in the interests of European nations and to the detriment of Japan, how her efforts at either revision or redress have been steadily repulsed, how her rights have been trampled upon and her wrongs multiplied by a delay, every hour of which is injustice, has been already told by able writers. Let now the Japanese speak for themselves through the editor of the "Tokumin no Tomo" (The Nation's Friend). In a recent number of this Tōkiō magazine a native writer says: —

"Why is the United States the true friend of our nation? We do not need to repeat the story of Commodore Perry at Uraga. Then, his procedure involved or manifested not a few elements of disturbance and confusion. We dare not give our gratitude to Commodore Perry for everything he did. We cannot do that. But let us consider the commercial treaty, which, though not in any sense perfect, yet contains the guaranties of our national interests, which restrict the English, Russian, German, and French powers so that they cannot go further in their arbitrariness than the limits specified in the treaty. In all this matter, who is the influential one? However many patriots there be who demand the revision of the treaties, they ought to shed tears of gratitude for Townsend Harris, the author of the Anséi (A. D. 1854–59) treaty. Is it not a fact that he gave us more freedom than we find in the treaties to-day, even when we have the National Diet, in which the nation's voice is heard? Though the present tariff is, on the average, less than five per cent., yet in the document drawn up by Mr. Harris this five per cent. tariff was limited to steam-machinery, lumber, ships' supplies, coal, flour, zinc, and lead. All kinds of liquors were to be charged thirty-five per cent., while all other things were to pay twenty per cent. These generous arrangements were made by our benefactor. Whether a high tariff is still necessary to our country or not is not now our question. At this moment, we desire only to express our satisfaction with his generous proposition at such a time, when the Shōgun's officers were effeminate and ignorant. Had he chosen, he could have done us a most terrible injury, like a lion ravaging sheep. Such an instinct the honest spirit of Townsend Harris commanded him to repress.

"Moreover, he said (in later years) concerning the fiction of law called *jigwai-hoken:* 'The extraterritoriality given to the people of the United States who are in Japan is against my conscience. Ah! am I not to see the day when these unjust treaties shall be abrogated before I die?' His deep sorrow in the bottom of his heart may be imagined. When we think of those ministers of European powers who have indulged their covetousness, taking advantage of a crisis in our national history as their opportunity; when we think of their selfishness and thoughtlessness in availing themselves of the alarm of our people and the timidity of the Shōgun's officers; when we think of their making our extremity their gain by overreaching us, — we know not what to say. All the more can we see the abounding friendship of the United States for the Land of the Rising Sun."

CHAPTER XVIII.

JAPAN AT THE END OF THE CENTURY.

ON the 8th day of May, 1895, we pen a final chapter. Two coincident events compel contrast between the hermit nation of Townsend Harris's day and the new Asiatic power of our own times. Then, deception and weakness hobbled behind a fence of shams. Now, truth and strength walk together in the highway. On this day, triumphant Japan and humbled China, at Chi-fu, ratify a treaty of peace. At this date, also, lies on our table Japan's ninth annual revelation of facts. The Imperial government now openly publishes, to the full measure of its ability to furnish, what once was wholly concealed. The "Résumé Statistique de l'Empire du Japan," issued yearly by the Emperor's Cabinet, is a manual of statistics that delights alike the critical student and the lover of truth. It is a storehouse of facts and a revelation of the national resources, such as Townsend Harris craved.

The presence of the alien on the soil of Japan shattered anarchy, and compelled national unity. In Kiōto, February 3, 1868, the era of Méiji and of united Nippon began. We may freely translate the chronological term Méiji as "enlightened appropriation" of the ideas and arts of Christendom. Yet neither by native genius and energy, nor by alien pressure and importation, were those results of peace, war, and diplomacy, which to-day astonish the world, attained; but rather by intelligent union of the two.

There is no actual mystery in this marvelous transformation of a nation. Japan has never ceased borrowing religions, arts, sciences, weapons, and instruments, despite the fact that her powers of assimilation amount to positive genius, while her ability to improve is marked. Two hundred years of Dutch leaven, the work of Townsend Harris, the presence of a small army of American teachers, missionaries, and engineers, numbering possibly twelve hundred, with "hired foreigners" from many lands, are facts in history which neither the admiring rhapsodist from afar, nor the conceit-swollen son of the soil, must forget. Under Divine Providence, Japan, with both natives and aliens as instruments, seems to have been chosen to reconcile in one the Oriental and Occidental civilizations.

In this end of the century, the Japanese do not like to be called in English "natives" even of their own country. This is owing to the bad translations and wrong associations of the word, which, in their first dictionaries, are those akin to ours of "aborigines" and "heathen." Similar other foolish notions will be corrected when they know the English language better, just as some of ours will be when we and the Japanese, who can teach us many things, shall have been better acquainted.

Even the title "Mikado" is obsolete in popular speech and writing. Instead of a hermit inside of a walled garden in secluded Kiōto, the chief ruler of the Empire is the active governor of his people. They speak of him as "the Emperor." We who talk English shall continue to honor him by his ancient title. The word "Mikado" separates the chief magistrate and the greatest servant of Japan from the crowds of "crowned" heads that are found in all continents except America.

In a thousand ways the Japanese have come to know their power, — artistic, manufacturing, commercial, political, and military. They are the one æsthetic nation of Asia. All the world knows that they love things beautiful, and especially the fine art of good manners. The Centennial year of 1876, at Philadelphia, first revealed to the American people the genius of their trans-Pacific neighbors. At the World's Columbian Exposition at Chicago, in 1893, the former glory was eclipsed. In 1876, these islanders, who were so far east of us as to come from the west, sent seventeen hundred and thirty tons of products to show and sell. In 1893, six thousand tons were sent to what was their fourteenth exhibition abroad since that at Vienna in 1873. At Philadelphia we saw a collection, at Chicago a selection. The American people were given fresh surprises.

The Japanese left on Wooded Island, in Jackson Park, one of the few existing memorials of the White City. On a small scale, three styles of architecture and as many epochs of national taste are represented in the edifice. The ground-plan follows that of the Phœnix Temple in Kiōto. The right wing shows how a Court noble's palace looked when the great cathedrals of Europe were rising, between 1000 and 1200 A. D. Nails, metal hinges, sliding partitions, and matting were not yet in use. In the left wing we see the advance of luxury in the times of Ashikaga, 1300–1600 A. D. Then papered walls, matting-covered floors, partitions, and ornamental building hardware had come into vogue. The main portion represents a typical nobleman's dwelling in Tokugawa days, from A. D. 1600 to 1850. The decorations on ceiling and wall, with most of the interior details, are historically correct. The splendid and varied products of the soil and waters, the art and handicraft of Japan, astonished all visitors. A new and more intelligent interest was awakened in the minds of Americans concerning the people who were hermits only a generation ago.

The ambition of the Japanese is not only to secure recognition of equality with civilized nations, but to take a place in the very front rank. With any inferior place they will not be content. Yet, except those who had personally aided them to win the secrets of the West, few foreigners were prepared for the exhibition which Japan gave the world of her commercial and military power in 1894. The struggle of modern times is a fight for trade. In this, with brains and pen, machinery and bayonets, the Japanese have won and are winning.

Cotton is still one of the kings. Almost the only muslin woven under Tai-kun or Mikado, until 1875, was by women on hand-looms at home. Now in fifty mills, working by steam or water power, millions of spindles, plus brain and hands, weave acres of snowy cotton cloth. Sending out their ships, wares, and consuls in every direction, the Japanese are now competing with the British for a lion-like share of the world's trade. They have already made vast progress in Korea, China, India, and Australia. Over one half of their commerce is with English-speaking nations. American raw cotton is now imported by thousands of bales. In bulk of trade with Japan the United States still leads all nations, but England still sells most goods. The island Empire, which was once poor and "hardly worth trading with," enjoyed in 1894 a total foreign trade of 230,000,000 yen, or about $185,000,000 in gold.

Old Japan of Mr. Harris's days has vanished,

AT THE END OF THE CENTURY.

and in New Japan life is more than worth living for the average man. Such popular freedom and advantages were never before known. Instead of the caste, monopoly, cramping laws, repressive customs, and cruel government of former days, the common people live in a new world of rights, privileges, and possibilities. New institutions, codes, and ideals have come in. The land is for the most part owned by the men who till the soil. The courts are open to every one, and justice is cheap and easy to obtain. Schools invite all to enter. Once only samurai could be soldiers; now the army and navy are filled without regard to class by enthusiastic conscripts. The men are well fed, well paid, well taught, and well nursed in time of sickness. The old sectional jealousies, sectarian bigotries, and political hatreds are vanishing. Wealth, comfort, happiness, national unity, and population are steadily on the increase. With over two thousand miles of railway, with telegraphs, lighthouses, post-offices, newspapers, savings banks, hospitals, and most of the appliances of modern civilization, life seems very rich and full to the lad and lass born in this "era of Méiji" (1868–1895+).

Japanese travelers and enterprising adventurers are now found in many countries. Immigrants by thousands dwell in Hawaii, the United States, Australia, Mexico, Korea, China, and in British, Russian, Dutch, Spanish, and French Asia. With her population increasing at the rate of over half a million a year, it is necessary for Japan to expand and colonize. Her desire and ability to do both are manifest. These facts explain in part also why so small a nation did not hesitate, when peace seemed no longer possible, to go to war with colossal China.

When in 1870 the Japanese abolished feudalism, they rejected also most of the ideas of government and society borrowed from China and from Confucius and his commentators, and adopted those of the Western World. China, her pride deeply injured, and disapproving of the change in her former pupil, at once became sulky, jealous, and hostile. Furthermore, with Great Britain, Russia, and France so earth-hungry and ambitious, and busily engaged in swallowing up Asia, and refusing to revise the odious treaties, it was necessary for Japan to arm for defense. Quietly and steadily, forts, arsenals, and dockyards were built and furnished. The finest arms and ships were bought in Europe, and hundreds of young men educated in the military and naval schools abroad. A truly national army was raised by conscription. All eligible male subjects were enrolled in the active or reserve forces.

With modern tactics, strategy, camps, and actual movements in the field, a high state of military efficiency was obtained. By 1893, it was possible and safe to dismiss foreign assistants, for steel warships could be built and armies drilled, equipped, provisioned, and led by natives. In 1894, two hundred and fifty thousand experienced soldiers and sailors, burning with patriotism, were at the service of the Mikado to resist robber nations, and to compel the respect of the Powers.

No cloud-sign of war, however, even as big as a man's hand, rose above the horizon in 1893. Industry thrived, literature bloomed afresh, and in politics progress was made toward true national unity. On the 9th of February, 1894, the silver wedding of the Emperor and Empress was celebrated with national rejoicings. Flowers, arches, processions, festivals, and congratulations made a picture of joy like that in the fairy tales. Two new postage-stamps were issued to commemorate the happy day. Both were of unusual size. They bore as symbols of felicity a pair of phœnix birds, the cherry-blossom or national flower, and the imperial chrysanthemum. The legend, "Imperial Wedding, 25th Anniversary," was printed in English and Chinese letters. Pink (2 sen) and blue (5 sen) were the colors chosen. For the first time the Imperial husband and wife rode side by side in an open carriage. By this public act Chinese prejudices were shocked, and advance was made toward Christian ideas of honor to woman.

The Mikado's son, Yoshihito, is the crown prince, born August 31, 1877. He is a bright and promising young man, who is likely to continue his father's policy of progress.

It was not a new thing in Asiatic history when China and Japan began hostilities in the summer of 1894, but it was in a wholly novel way. Each published a formal declaration, and appealed to the sympathies of Christendom. Japan proceeded according to international law, and with scientific and Christian-like methods. A superb hospital corps, trained nurses, the Red Cross Society, and the absence of privateers were noticed. In old Japanese times the wounded in battle committed suicide, were left to die on the field, or received only blacksmith surgery. These days are over.

What caused the war? Which side began it? Why was China so ready to provoke while so poorly prepared for war? Why was Japan so alert, eager, well prepared, and so quickly and steadily successful?

The bone of contention was Korea.[1] Japan first, followed by the United States and the other Powers, made treaties with Chō-sen, recognizing her as an independent and sovereign state. Notwithstanding this, the Peking government attempted to keep Korea under Chinese influence and power. Early in 1894, a widespread rebellion

[1] So all scholars now spell the name.

broke out in the southern provinces of Korea, which the King was unable to put down. The pro-Chinese faction in Séoul asked for Chinese aid to help suppress the rebels, called Tong Haks. China was only too ready to do so; but, by sending troops before notifying Japan, the Chinese, in the first place, broke the treaty of 1885. By speaking of Korea, in the dispatch to Tōkiō, as " our subject state," the Peking government struck at the treaties and at Korean sovereignty. The Mikado at once sent his envoy, Mr. Otori, to Séoul, accompanied by General Oshima's mixed brigade, to inquire of the King in person whether Korea was an independent state. The answer was "Yes." The Japanese now made a proposition to the Chinese government to undertake jointly the reform of Korean finance and polity. Pending the peaceful settlement of this and other questions long in debate, notice was given that the dispatch of any more Chinese troops into Korea would be considered an act of war.

China refused the proposition of Japan, demanded the recall of her soldiers, and began to send on more ships and men. The Japanese, not to be surprised or outnumbered, hurried forward an army corps. The Naniwa sunk the Chinese transport Kow-shing because her crew refused to surrender. The first land battle was fought on the 27th of July, when the Japanese infantry, after victory in the open field, drove the Chinese out of A-san.

War was declared by both Sons of Heaven on either side of the Yellow Sea, August 1. Reinforcements from both countries were poured in, meeting at Ping-yang. In the great battle fought September 16 the Chinese were routed. The naval trial of valor and skill between steel-clad men-of-war, in which the Japanese were victorious, took place the next day. When the sun rose on Korea the first day of October, it shone on no Chinese. One of the finest of modern armies was pursuing a mob in Manchuria. The war soon became a monotonous and one-sided story of the success of "pigmies" against "tigers" and "giants." The sun-banner waved in Continental Asia over a territory larger than the Japanese Empire.

For twenty years China had been draining her treasury to fortify the sea-gates leading to her capital. Hundreds of millions of dollars had been spent in building and arming the forts at Port Arthur, Wéi-hai-wéi, and at the mouth of the Taku River. While the First Army of Japan was fighting in Manchuria, the Second Army captured Port Arthur.

The Third Army took Wéi-hai-wéi. The Fourth Army occupied Pescadores Islands and Formosa in March and April. The Chinese sued for peace. By the treaty made at Shimonoséki, Premier Ito and Li Hung Chang, acting as plenipotentiaries, Formosa becomes part of the Japanese Empire; and Korea promises to follow, according to her ability, the example of Japan in improvement and reform. Will China now accept that one civilization before which all others must fall?

Japan, one of the great powers of the world, is now recognized in the fraternity of civilized nations. The two English-speaking peoples led the way in treaty revision. After twenty-two years of protest and discussion, the Japanese have won their case. On the 26th of August, Lord Kimberly and Viscount Mutsu in London, and on November 22, 1894, Secretary Gresham and Minister Kurino at Washington, signed the new treaties. These abolish what is called extra-territoriality. What the Japanese at first granted so quickly and gladly they repented of longest and most bitterly; but soon consular courts in Japan will be no more. The Senate of the United States, on the 8th of December, 1894, ratified the American treaty, which will go in force before the opening of the twentieth century. How Mr. Harris, whom the Japanese called "The Nation's Friend," would have rejoiced to see this act of justice done!

INDEX.

Abé, Isé no Kami, 112, 165.
Adams, Will, 33.
Agriculture, 67, 72, 156, 158.
Alcock, Sir Rutherford, 318.
Amagi San, 186, 190.
Ambassador, 32, 206.
American influence in Japan, 2, 32, 223, 310.
Anséi era, 43, 115, 319.
Architecture, 77, 116, 118, 218.
Armstrong, Commodore, 21, 22, 35, 36, 49, 50–52, 56, 146, 149, 152, 157, 163, 167, 168, 169.
Army, 344.
Art and handiwork, 27, 154, 159, 175.
Ashikaga, 191.
Aston, Mr. W. G., 30, 151.
Audience of the Tai-kun, 228–230.
Audience question, 161, 162, 163, 172, 173, 178, 179, 221, 222.

Bakufu, 118, 121, 208, 294, 295, 323.
Balestier, Mr., 18, 25.
Banriu, 193.
Bathing customs, 80, 159, 185.
Beggars, 74–76, 193.
Bedell, Bishop G. F., 12.
Bell, Captain, 21, 22, 36, 39, 40, 41, 57, 168.
Bingham, Hon. John A., 208.
Bittinger, Rev. E. C., 180.
Bolivar, 8.
Books, 121, 143, 146, 242, 260.
Bowring, Sir John, 321.
Bryce, James, Prof., 32.
Buchanan, President, 23, 135, 317, 323.
Buddhism, 23, 322.
Burgoyne, General John, 1.

Calendar, 100.
Cannibals, 14, 16.
Cannon, 74, 90, 94, 111, 143, 279.
Casembroot, Admiral, 69.
Cass, Hon. Lewis, 312, 314.
Cats, 26, 27, 72.
Cemeteries, 37, 43, 60.
Cha no yu, 110, 111, 220, 230.
Chamberlain, Prof. B. H., 30, 151, 198.

Charts, 82.
Cheese, 37.
Chicago, 27.
Children, 76, 196.
China, 15, 117, 236, 238, 310, 317.
Chinese, 90, 91, 96, 100, 109, 173, 174, 236, 238, 260.
Chop-sticks, 234.
Christianity, 61, 120, 223, 224.
Christmas, 14, 98-100, 120, 244.
Chronology, 117.
Clarke, Judge, 23.
Cleanliness, 41.
Clothes, 55, 98, 106, 183, 184, 209, 219, 224-232, 256.
Coal, 27, 267, 269.
Coinage, 113, 114, 128, 132.
College of the City of New York, 10.
Commissioners, 206.
Confucius, 260.
Consular courts, 124, 150, 160.
Consuls, 124, 138, 148, 266, 298.
Cotton, 78, 79, 148, 155, 156.
Council of State, 142, 164, 165, 211, 215, 228, 243, 287, 306, 314.
Cross, 224, 235, 264.
Crucifixion, 235, 236.
Cullum, Gen. Geo. W., 326.
Currency question, 105, 113, 114, 129, 132, 136, 138, 150, 160.
Curtius, Mr. H. Donker, 178, 264, 307, 312, 315.

Daimiōs, 206, 292-295, 296, 297.
Daley, Judge C. P., 326.
De Graeff, Governor, 144.
De Quincey, Miss, 23.
De Witt, Rev. Thomas, 20.
Decoration Day, 148.
Déshima, 125, 126, 137, 141, 181, 233, 264.
Déwa no Kami, 178.
Diana, Russian frigate, 60, 86, 90, 143.
Dierst, Rev. W. F., 149.
Diet, Imperial, 295.
Doctors, 195, 196, 233, 312.
Dogs, 255, 266.
Dougherty, Mr., 133, 147, 176.

348   INDEX.

Droppers, Prof. Garret, 76.
Dutch, 20, 30, 34, 68, 69, 74, 75, 121, 125-128, 136, 142, 144, 151, 161, 178, 181, 188, 196, 224, 233, 243, 255, 272, 301, 312, 315, 316.

Earthquakes, 34, 43, 73, 78, 214, 300.
Easter, 141, 142.
Echizen, 293, 294.
Elgin, Lord, 318, 321, 322.
Emperor, 336.
English, 87, 88.
English language, 2, 120, 148, 151.
Etiquette, 49, 50, 55, 56, 211, 212, 219, 230.
Eulenberg, Count, 322.
Extra-territoriality, 124. *See* Consular Courts.

Fabius, Captain, 69, 89, 125, 137.
Fankwei, 26, 152.
Fans, 185, 234.
Fauna. *See* Natural History.
Favored nation, 258, 315.
Feudal system, 50, 118-120, 292-295.
Fireworks, 74.
Flag of Japan, 33, 94, 194.
Flag of the United States, 22, 26, 58, 60, 94, 167, 182, 200.
Flowers, 73, 79, 149, 296, 297.
Food, 37, 55, 66, 67, 71, 106, 109, 212.
Foote, Rear Admiral A. H., 168-172.
Formosa, 16, 27, 71, 329.
Franklin, Doctor Benj., 29.
Fraser, General, 1.
French, 5, 87, 88, 321.
Fuji San, 2, 30, 67, 187, 197, 222.
Fujisawa, 193-196.
Fuji-Yama. *See* Fuji San.
Fukui, 261, 271.

Goats, 37.
Gold, 154, 155.
Golownin, 75.
Grant, General U. S., 326-328.
Gregg, Hon. David F., 135.
Gresham, Secretary W. Q., 236.

Habersham, Lieut. S. W., 81.
Hakodaté, 133, 134, 162, 169, 176, 305.
Hakoné, 189-191.
Hakuzan, 30.
Hall, Mr. Edward F., 135, 136, 138.
Hamersly, Mr. T. H., 326.
Hara-kiri, 82, 92, 235, 300, 313.
Harbors, 33, 250, 267, 270, 271, 280.
Harris family, 3, 4.
Harris, Townsend, ancestry, 3, 4; birth, 4; early life, 5; his mother, 6, 7; political opinions, 6; unmarried, 8; life in New York, 8-12, 91; Free Academy, 10; religious views, 11; trading voyages, 12, 13, 16; travel homewards, 17; personal habits, 23; his temperance, 23; treaty with Siam, 25, 26; exposes a sham, 26; emotions on seeing Japan, 28; his Sundays, 38, 40, 51, 93; hints at use of force, 130; birthday, 175; starts for Yedo, 182; asserts his dignity, 190; in Yedo, 201; treaty made, 312; leaves Yedo for Shimoda, 312; sickness, 313; return to Yedo, 313; threatens to go to Kiōto, 314; returns again to Shimoda, 316; trip to China, 322; appointed Minister Resident, 322; sticks to his post in Yedo, 322; assists Lord Elgin, 322; resigns his office, 324; return home, 325; in New York, 326-330.
Hayashi, Professor, 206, 210, 222, 311.
Hemp, 79.
Heusken, Mr. C. J., 20, 21, 30, 56, 65, 92, 98, 164, 169, 174, 183, 199, 204, 225, 262, 323.
Hildreth, 2, 224.
History of Japan, 115-122.
Hō-jō, 188, 191.
Holland, 20, 70.
Hondo, 61, 117, 267, 270.
Hong-Kong, 27, 169, 280.
Horses, 71, 91, 92, 98, 194, 195, 209, 216, 225, 241.
Hosmer, Captain, 135, 137, 138.
House, Mr. E. H., 329.
Hotta, Bitchiu no Kami, 112, 207, 214, 215, 217-222, 228, 231, 249, 298, 312, 314, 317.
Hydrography, 82, 242.

Idzu, 30, 36, 158, 192.
Ii, Kamon no Kami, 310, 317, 320, 321, 323.
India, 17, 23, 156, 187, 193, 194, 220, 311.
Infanticide, 76.
Interpreters, 20, 34, 35, 42, 221, 301.
Iwasé, Higo no Kami, 253, 320, 321.
Iyémochi, 317.
Iyésada, 316, 317.
Iyéyasŭ, 119, 190, 281, 292-295, 311, 316.

Japanese embassy to America, 323.
Japanese language, 151, 301.
Japanese moral traits, 105, 111, 115, 117.
Japanese physical traits, 108, 158, 159, 198.
Japanese servants, 61, 62, 67, 146, 220.
Japanese simplicity of life, 154, 204, 232, 234.
Japanese social traits, 180, 189, 198, 199, 204, 303.
Junks, 30, 95, 192.

INDEX. 349

Kaempfer, 65, 66, 188, 192, 193, 197, 269.
Kaga, 297, 300.
Kamakura, 118, 188.
Kami, 75, 206, 218, 293.
Kanagawa, 197, 206, 207, 322. See Treaty of.
Katsu Awa, 323.
Kawasaki, 180, 197–200.
Kii, 286, 293, 303, 317.
Kikuna, 182.
Kimberly, Lord, 345.
Kiōto, 19, 27, 118, 120, 269, 274, 275, 313, 314.
Kitashirakawa, Prince, 310.
Kiushiu, 27, 29.
Knox, Dr. Geo. Wm., 119, 260.
Korea, 28, 81, 84, 109, 116, 156, 179.
Kow-shing, 343.
Kudan, 205.
Kugé, 293, 294.
Kurino, Minister, 345.

Laws of Japan, 54, 75, 76.
Lease of grounds, 125.
Leeches, 195.
Legation in Yedo, 322-325.
Licentiousness, 109, 115.
Lighthouses, 27, 33, 82.
Li Hung Chang, 262.
Lincoln, President, 18, 324.
Lingas, 194.
Linschoten, 28.
Literature of Japan, 143, 146.
Luhdorf, Mr., 162.
Luxuries, 154.
Lying, 17, 63, 132, 133, 136, 156, 158, 257, 300.

Machinery, 79, 156.
Malay influence, 82, 108, 116.
Manchuria, 344.
Maps, 66, 235, 243.
Marcy, Hon. Wm. L., 17, 18, 33, 177.
Matthews, Professor Brander, 328, 329.
Mattoon, Mr., 171.
McDonald, Mr. Ronald, 2, 171.
Mediation of the United States, 299.
Medicines, 90, 91, 195, 233.
Medusa, Dutch frigate, 68, 69, 70, 126, 137.
Méiji, era of, 77, 339.
Messenger Bird, 135–139.
Mexico, 322.
Miako, 267, 269, 288.
Michelet, 2.
Mikado, 117, 121, 122, 270, 288, 292, 300, 313, 319.
Minamoto, 281.
Mint, 128, 132.
Mishima, 188, 189, 192.
Missionaries, 160.
Mississippi, U. S. S. S., 319, 322.

Mito, 293, 302, 311.
Money, 59, 65, 105, 113, 114, 143, 150, 263, 279.
Morals, 105.
Moriyama Yenosŭké, 59, 61-63, 128, 130, 140–142.
Morse, Prof. E., 109, 173, 178.
Mosquitoes, 58.
Mourning, 297.
Mutsu, Count, 345.

Nagasaki, 2, 124, 125, 150, 159, 188, 196, 224, 233, 271, 303, 312.
Nakamura, Déwa no Kami, 159, 180, 181.
Naniwa, 22.
Natives, 335.
Natural history, 24, 26, 27, 36, 37, 59, 60, 71, 72, 73, 79, 157.
Navy of Japan, 33, 69, 197, 237.
Neesima, Dr. Joseph, 193.
New Year's Day, 99, 100, 104, 106, 246, 284.
Niigata, 270, 271, 303.
Nishiki-yé, 176.
Nitobé, Dr. Inazo, 2, 32, 215, 262, 323.
Nobility, 292-295.
Norimono, 50, 108, 183, 184, 190, 191, 200, 209, 219.

Odawara, 191, 192.
Ogiso, 188.
Oiso, 193.
Okubo, Ichiō, 32.
Oliphant, Laurence, 151.
Opium, 90, 91.
Osaka, 22, 267, 270, 275, 276, 280, 282, 292.
Osborne, Captain S., 318.
Oshima, 72, 151, 152, 186.
Ota dō Kuan, 2.
Otori, Minister, 343.
Owari, 302.

Parkes, Sir Harry S., 25, 152, 318.
Penang, 14, 24, 195.
Perry, Commodore M. C., 15, 18, 19, 35, 40, 42, 92, 102, 111, 116, 120, 121, 133, 145, 192, 197, 206, 222, 254, 257, 279, 318, 323.
Phallic worship, 194.
Philadelphia, 336.
Phrenologist, 307.
Pierce, President, 17, 18, 19, 177, 178.
Ping-yang, 344.
Policemen, 198, 202, 203.
Pontaitine, Admiral, 86.
Population, 66, 76, 197.
Port Arthur, 344.
Portman, Mr., 158.
Ports, 267, 271, 275, 283.
Portsmouth, U. S. S. S., 167, 171, 172.
Portuguese, 144, 145.

350 INDEX.

Possiet, Commodore, 84–88.
Postage stamps, 341.
Powhatan, U. S. S. S., 319, 322, 323.
Presents, 25, 56, 175, 212, 235, 242, 256.
President's letter, 162, 172, 174, 207, 225, 230.
Pretorium, 118, 120, 121.
Printing, 176.
Prisons, 75, 76.
Proverbs, 55.
Pruyn, Hon. Robert, 324.
Punishments, 75, 76.

Rats, 60, 72.
Reed, Mr., 133, 147, 176.
Regents in Yedo, 140, 141.
Representative institutions, 295.
Residence of aliens, 150.
Résumé Statistique de l'Empire du Japan, 198.
Rice, Mr. E. E., 162, 163, 165, 305.
Richardson, Mr., 197.
Roads, 185, 189, 190, 194, 199.
Roberts, Mr. Edmund, 25.
Rodgers, Rear Admiral John, 81, 133, 134.
Roman history, 118.
Rō-nins, 261, 262, 286.
Russians, 60, 61, 84–96, 272, 284, 306, 321.

Saint Eustatius, 144.
Sakai, 275, 280, 283.
Saké, 91, 107, 110, 221.
Salutes, 144, 148, 163, 169, 170, 279, 290, 322, 323.
Samurai, 98, 260, 261, 294.
Sandy Hill, 4, 326.
San Francisco, 171.
San Jacinto, U. S. S. S., 21, 22, 24, 56, 58, 64, 146, 152, 167, 168, 170.
Saris, Captain, 316.
Satow, Mr. E. M., 30, 146.
Satsuma, 142, 197, 293.
Scenery, 72, 77, 156.
Sebastopol, 87, 88.
Séoul, 343.
Seward, Hon. Wm. H., 2, 18, 19, 324.
Seymour, Admiral, 169.
Shimada, Saburo, Mr., 319.
Shimoda, 19, 33, 42, 46, 53, 64, 68, 78, 86, 116, 185, 192, 205, 216, 257, 312, 319.
Shimonoséki, Mr., 141.
Shimonoséki battle, 68, 329.
Shimonoséki treaty.
Shinagawa, 200.
Shinano no Kami, 173, 204–207, 213–215, 225, 228, 245, 247, 253, 278, 320, 321.
Shintō, 37, 46, 47, 64, 194.
Ship-building, 33, 69, 143, 197.

Shōgun, 118–120, 140–142, 179, 281.
Siam, 18, 19, 25, 26, 85, 112, 121, 139, 171, 176, 177.
Small-pox, 196.
Soshi, 262.
Spaulding, Mr. J. W., 61.
Spies, 99, 139, 241.
Star Spangled Banner, 26.
Statistics, 95, 141, 156, 198.
Sumptuary laws, 154.
Sundays, 38, 40, 51, 93, 139, 180, 198, 199, 223, 240, 301.
Surveys, 81, 82.
Swords, 107, 155, 261, 326–328.
Symbolism, 50, 64, 106, 109, 110, 174, 184, 233, 297.

Tai-kun, 179, 229–232, 248, 293, 297, 318.
Tariff, 284, 285, 304, 305.
Tatnall, Commodore, 319, 320, 321.
Tea-making, 110, 111.
Temples, 38, 39, 46, 64, 185, 189, 322.
Things Japanese, 80.
Tigers, 27.
Times, New York, 177.
Tōkaidō, 188–199.
Toké, Tamba no Kami, 206, 210–212, 219, 246.
Tōkiō, 21, 78.
Toko-no-ma, 109, 211, 221.
Tokugawa, 281, 292, 294.
Tokutomi, 310.
Tonnage of Japan, 95, 284.
Torture, 236.
Transactions of the Asiatic Society of Japan, 67, 72, 76, 119.
Trays, 211, 212, 221, 231, 234, 235.
Treaties, 75, 85, 86, 94, 123–130, 159, 160, 315, 322, 323. *See* Siam.
Treaty of Kanagawa, 125, 126, 133, 134, 147, 158, 206, 258. *See* Perry.
Tsuda Sen, Mr., 307.
Tsuruga, 270.
Tycoon, 19, 27, 179, 211.
Typhoon, 67, 68, 71, 189, 196.

Union Club, 329.
United States, 32, 310.
University of Tōkiō, 205.
Uyédono, 206, 210.

Vaccination, 196.
Von Siebold, 27, 30, 235.

War with China, 33, 176.
Washington, 290.
Weasel, 72.
Wéi-Hai-wéi, 344.
Wetmore, Hon. Prosper M., 177, 326.
Whales, 2, 165.
Whitman, Mr. C. O., 195.
Williams, Dr. S. Wells, 36, 40, 258.

Wood, Surgeon W. M., 22, 26, 30, 48, 53.

Yalu River, 33.
Yamabushi, 74, 75.
Yamagata, Count, 310.

Yedo, 2, 66, 118, 201-206, 243, 249, 268, 274.
Yokohama, 197, 322, 324.
Yokosŭka, 33.
Yoritomo, 118, 179, 193, 281.
Yoshihito, 342.